"In his innovative work, Michał Dudek expands the normative binaries that sustain hierarchically normative ontologies in law by flattening such strata through dynamic, material, and communicative dimensionalities that reexamine the human and nonhuman, the social and nonsocial, the institutional and everyday. *On Flat Ontologies and Law* is a must-read for those who think deeply about law, life, and the realized in-between."

Sarah Marusek, *University of Hawaii, USA.*

"The intersection of law and flat ontologies is exerting considerable influence, challenging established hierarchies, and ushering in a new era in the legal landscape. Both timely and path-breaking, this convergence has the potential to reshape our understanding of law, offering new perspectives on inclusion and ethical considerations within the legal framework. By recognizing the status of all entities, whether human or non-human, this convergence fosters the emergence of new theories and adapted practices."

Anne Wagner, *Université de Lille, France.*

"This is a book not to be missed by anyone interested in the theory and philosophy of law. In addition to the more usual linguistic, psychological, social, and institutional dimensions of law, the author leads us to discover an often ignored but equally compelling facet: the material dimension of law."

Giuseppe Lorini, *Università degli Studi di Cagliari, Italy.*

I0888231

On Flat Ontologies and Law

This book examines the importance of flat ontologies for law and sociolegal theory. Associated with the emergence of new materialism in the humanities and social sciences, the elaboration of flat ontologies challenges the binarism that has maintained the separation of culture from nature, and the human from the nonhuman. Although most work in legal theory and sociolegal studies continues to adopt a non-flat, anthropocentric and immaterial take on law, the critique of this perspective is becoming more and more influential. Engaging the increasing legal interest in flat ontologies, this book offers an account of the main theoretical perspectives, and their importance for law. Covering the work of the five major theorists in the area – Gabriel Tarde, Bruno Latour, Manuel DeLanda, Karen Barad and Graham Harman – the book aims to encourage this interest, as well as to explicate the important problems of and differences between these perspectives. Flat ontologies, the book demonstrates, can offer a valuable new perspective for understanding and thinking about law.

This book will appeal mainly to scholars and students in legal theory and sociolegal studies; as well as others with interests in the posthumanist turn in philosophy and social theory.

Michał Dudek is Assistant Professor in the Department of Sociology of Law at the Faculty of Law and Administration, Jagiellonian University in Kraków, Poland.

Discourses of Law

series editors
Peter Goodrich, *Benjamin N. Cardozo School of Law, USA*
Michel Rosenfeld, *Benjamin N. Cardozo School of Law, USA*
Daniela Gandorfer, *University of Westminster Law School, UK*

The publisher gratefully acknowledges the support of the Jacob Burns Institute for Advanced Legal Studies of the Benjamin N. Cardozo School of Law to the series *Discourses of Law*.

for information about the series and details of previous and forthcoming titles, see https://www.routledge.com/Discourses-of-Law/book-series/SE1036

A GlassHouse Book

On Flat Ontologies and Law

Michał Dudek

Routledge
Taylor & Francis Group
a GlassHouse book

First published 2024
by Routledge
4 Park Square, Milton Park, Abingdon, Oxon OX14 4RN

and by Routledge
605 Third Avenue, New York, NY 10158

a GlassHouse book

Routledge is an imprint of the Taylor & Francis Group, an informa business

© 2024 Michał Dudek

The right of Michał Dudek to be identified as author of this work has been asserted in accordance with sections 77 and 78 of the Copyright, Designs and Patents Act 1988.

All rights reserved. No part of this book may be reprinted or reproduced or utilised in any form or by any electronic, mechanical, or other means, now known or hereafter invented, including photocopying and recording, or in any information storage or retrieval system, without permission in writing from the publishers.

Trademark notice: Product or corporate names may be trademarks or registered trademarks, and are used only for identification and explanation without intent to infringe.

The book was prepared within the research project "Flat Ontologies, Law and Its Ontology", sponsored by the National Science Centre, Poland (Registration number 2018/31/D/HS5/00294).

British Library Cataloguing-in-Publication Data
A catalogue record for this book is available from the British Library

Library of Congress Cataloging-in-Publication Data
Names: Dudek, Michał (Lawyer), author.
Title: On flat ontologies and law / Michał Dudek.
Description: Abingdon, Oxon [UK] ; New York, NY : Routledge, 2024. |
Series: Discourses of law | Includes bibliographical references and index.
Identifiers: LCCN 2023055833 (print) | LCCN 2023055834 (ebook) |
ISBN 9781032577791 (hardback) | ISBN 9781032577814 (paperback) |
ISBN 9781003440963 (ebook)
Subjects: LCSH: Law--Philosophy. | Ontology. | Sociological jurisprudence.
Classification: LCC K231 .D83 2024 (print) | LCC K231 (ebook) |
DDC 340/.1--dc23/eng/20231214
LC record available at https://lccn.loc.gov/2023055833
LC ebook record available at https://lccn.loc.gov/2023055834

ISBN: 978-1-032-57779-1 (hbk)
ISBN: 978-1-032-57781-4 (pbk)
ISBN: 978-1-003-44096-3 (ebk)

DOI: 10.4324/9781003440963

Typeset in Sabon
by Taylor & Francis Books

In memory of my beloved dad, Tomasz Dudek (1959–2022)

Contents

List of figures xv
Acknowledgements xvi

1 Introduction: Law, its Ontologies and the Mere Idea of Flat Ontology; or, How Flat Ontologies Differ from Ontologies of Law and Why Should We Care? 1

1.1 Adequacy Question and Value Question 1
1.2 What is Meant by "Law"? 2
1.2.1 LAW, *Law* or law? 2
1.2.2 Text and Meaning and Media for Them 3
1.2.3 Top-Down and Bottom-Up Geneses of Law 4
1.2.4 Social Communication About Law 5
1.2.5 Law's Materiality 5
1.3 Preliminaries on Flat Ontology 7
1.3.1 Basics of Genealogy 7
1.3.2 Problem of Too Narrow Conceptualisations 8
1.3.3 The Mere Idea of Flat Ontology – A Proposal and General Characteristics 9
1.3.4 Addressing Incorrect Impressions 13
1.3.5 Illustration and Test of Removal 15
1.4 On Ontologies of Law (in Relation to Flat Ontology) 17
1.4.1 Need for Review and Its Guiding Assumptions 17
1.4.2 Materiality Ignorance 18
1.4.3 Materiality Belittling 21
1.4.4 *Intermezzo* on Contemporary Analytical Social Ontology 22
1.4.5 Modest Materiality Equalisation 25
1.4.6 Some Self-Criticism 26

1.4.7 Early Reflections on Flat Ontology and Ontologies of Law 27
1.4.8 Flat Ontology-Inspired Ontologies of Law (and Other Legal Studies) 31
1.5 Reasons for the Investigations and Their General Course 33
1.5.1 Situating the Book 33
1.5.2 Representative Sample of Flat Ontologies 34
1.5.3 Adopted Approach 35

2 Gabriel Tarde's Monadology (of Law); or, Will Law Still Exist If Some Parts of It Are Removed? 44

2.1 Not … an Easily Classifiable Thinker 44
2.1.1 Also a Science-Fiction Author 44
2.1.2 Forgotten but Rediscovered 44
2.1.3 One Great Work or Many Great Works? 45
2.2 Stepping Into … Tardean Monadology 47
2.2.1 Scepticism 47
2.2.2 Anti-holism 47
2.2.3 The Big, the Small and Relational Character of Properties 49
2.2.4 Having Instead of Being 51
2.2.5 Avidity 52
2.2.6 Posthumanism 53
2.2.7 Monadological Understanding of Society 54
2.2.8 Tardean Monadology as Flat Ontology 55
2.3 Focusing on … Monads 55
2.3.1 Formal, Relative, Compositional and Linked 55
2.3.2 On Possession(s), Being Avid, Dominant and Leading Monad 56
2.3.3 The Big's Simplicity and Fragility and the Small's Complexity and Independence 57
2.4 Law and … Tarde's Monads 58
2.4.1 Law as Not an Emergent Entity 58
2.4.2 Law's Utter Fragility 60
2.4.3 Independence of Law's Small 61
2.4.4 Heterogeneity of Law's Composition 64
2.4.5 Law's Avidity 65

3 Bruno Latour's Actor-Network Theory (of Law); or, What About Law's Outside (Plasma)? 69

3.1 Not … a Winemaker 69

3.1.1 After Tarde 69

3.1.2 A Bird's-Eye View at Latour's Oeuvre 70

3.1.3 "Latour and Law? Just Not That Again!" 71

3.1.4 Actor-Network Theory or Theories? 72

3.1.5 On an Inquiry into Modes of Existence Project 74

3.2 Stepping into … Latourian Actor-Network Theory 77

3.2.1 To Exist by Actions, to Act and Become Stronger (and Weaker) Thanks to Allies 77

3.2.2 Against Domains, Hierarchies and Critique, For Descriptivism 78

3.2.3 Nonhumans as Actors, Delegates, Mediators and Intermediaries 80

3.2.4 Scattering of Action 82

3.2.5 Significance of Nonhumans for Humans 83

3.2.6 Issue of (Anti)Essentialism, Translation and the Irreduction Principle 84

3.2.7 What About (Anti)Emergentism? 86

3.2.8 (Claim to) Universality 87

3.2.9 Latourian Actor-Network Theory as Flat Ontology 89

3.3 Focusing on … Actor-Networks 90

3.3.1 Not Only Synonyms 90

3.3.2 Broad Sense of Action 91

3.3.3 Against Potentiality 92

3.3.4 (Scattering of Action and) Basic Features of Interactions 93

3.3.5 Reasons for the Inevitability of Translations 95

3.3.6 Basic Ways of Becoming Stronger 96

3.3.7 Mediators and Intermediaries 97

3.3.8 Delegates 98

3.3.9 Plasma 100

3.4 Law and … Latour's Actor-Networks 101

3.4.1 Is There Anything Beyond Law? 101

3.4.2 Is There Anything Beyond Law that Law Can Act Upon? 107

3.4.3 Law's Functioning (But Not by Itself) 108

3.4.4 Sources of Law's Strength (and Weakness) 109

3.4.5 Law as a Chain of Mediations and Delegations 111

4 Manuel DeLanda's Assemblage Theory (of Law); or, Can Law's Components Exist Outside Law? 117

4.1 Not … a Filmmaker (Anymore) 117
4.1.1 Snapshot of DeLanda's Work 117
4.1.2 Drawing from Many Sources (Not without Controversy) 119
4.1.3 Some Deviations from DeLanda (In What is to Follow) 119
4.1.4 Reservation Concerning Virtuality and the Diagram 120
4.2 Stepping into … DeLandaean Assemblage Theory 121
4.2.1 One Plane, Many Scales, No Essences and No Transcendence 121
4.2.2 Realism 122
4.2.3 Immanence, Historicity and Contingency 123
4.2.4 Emergence, Properties, Tendencies and Capacities 124
4.2.5 Against Micro- and Macroreductionism 127
4.3 Focusing on … Assemblages 128
4.3.1 Emergent Whole 128
4.3.2 Bottom-Up, Top-Down and Exteriority Relations 129
4.3.3 Materiality and Expressivity of Components 131
4.3.4 (De)Territorialisation and (De)Coding 132
4.3.5 DeLandaean Assemblage Theory as Flat Ontology 133
4.4 Law and … DeLanda's Assemblages 135
4.4.1 Law as an Emergent Whole 135
4.4.2 Material and Expressive Components of Law 138
4.4.3 Law's Components in Relations of Exteriority 140

5 Karen Barad's Agential Realism (of Law); or, Does Law Fit the Binary or Non-binary Model of Intra-Action? 149

5.1 Not … an "Ordinary" Physicist (Anymore) 149
5.1.1 Note on New Materialism(s) 149
5.1.2 Why Barad? 150
5.1.3 From Lattice Gauge Theory to … 151
5.1.4 Baggage of Physics, Ethico-Onto-Epistemology and Addressing the Unaddressed Issue (Just Another One) 152
5.2 Stepping Into … Baradian Agential Realism 153
5.2.1 Anti-individualism and Priority of Relations 153
5.2.2 Dynamism, Anti-essentialism and Against (Presupposed) Domains 153

5.2.3 Post-anthropocentrism (and a Short Remark on Baradian Agential Realism as Flat Ontology) 154
5.2.4 Anti-representationalism and Moving Past the Divide of Realism and Social Constructivism 155
5.2.5 Interpreting Bohr Extendingly 156
5.3 Focusing on … Intra-Actions 157
5.3.1 Neither Kantian Noumenon nor Phenomenon, but Close to Bohrian Phenomenon 157
5.3.2 Bohrian Model (In Baradian Interpretation) 159
5.3.3 Baradian Model 160
5.3.4 Problems with Binarism 162
5.3.5 Beyond the Binary Model 166
5.4 Law and … Barad's Intra-Actions 168
5.4.1 Law from Intra-Action with Something, Something from Intra-Action with Law 168
5.4.2 Dual Responsibility of Law and Transgressing the Input and Output of Law Distinction 169
5.4.3 Law Regulating Only That What is Already Legal 170
5.4.4 Rejecting the Classical Distinctions 171
5.4.5 Adequacy for Law Between the Binary and Non-Binary Intra-Action 172

6 Graham Harman's Object-Oriented Ontology (of Law); or, Is Law Exhausted by Under- and Overmining? 177

6.1 Not … a Sports Reporter (Anymore) 177
6.1.1 To Be in Constant Development (and the Downsides of That) 177
6.1.2 Classifying the Works of Harman 178
6.1.3 Second Wave of Object-Oriented Ontologies and Speculative Realism 180
6.2 Stepping Into … Harmanian Object-Oriented Ontology 181
6.2.1 Against Onto-Taxonomy, For Objectifying Everything (Humans Included) 181
6.2.2 Against (Overestimating) Changes, for (Appreciating) Stability 182
6.2.3 Essentialism 183
6.2.4 The Real and the Sensual 184
6.2.5 Pan(?)experientialism 185
6.2.6 Withdrawal 186
6.2.7 Unknowability of the Real 187

6.3 Focusing on … Objects 188
6.3.1 Towards the Current Model 188
6.3.2 Between Undermining and Overmining, and Complete, Exclusively Sensual and Exclusively Real Object 189
6.3.3 Harmanian Object-Oriented Ontology as Flat Ontology 194
6.3.4 Not Only Real and Sensual, and Objects, but Also … Qualities 195
6.3.5 Object-Object Relations and Emergence 198
6.4 Law and … Harman's Objects 200
6.4.1 Some Law's Components Are Real Objects, Some Are Not 200
6.4.2 Law, Real-Sensual, Object-Qualities Distinctions and Harmanian Emergence 202
6.4.3 Around Law and Domestic and Foreign Relations 205
6.4.4 A Few Final Thoughts 208

7 Conclusion: Flat Ontologies – With Some Adequacy Problems, Yet Valuable to Law; or, What Comes of It All? 212

7.1 The Adequacy Question 212
7.2 The Value Question 216
7.3 Doing Justice 222
7.4. What to Do Next? 224

Index 228

Figures

2.1 Tardean big-small dynamics (using Venn diagram). 59
3.1 Actor-network (with plasma). 101
3.2 Actor-network (without plasma). 104
4.1 Assemblage and its parts. 131
5.1 Bohrian and Baradian basic (binary) model. 160
5.2 One element in two (binary) intra-actions. 163
5.3 One element in multiple (binary) intra-actions. 164
5.4 One element in multiple (binary) intra-actions "mediating" between other elements. 165
5.5 Non-binary model. 167
6.1 Harmanian object (between under- and overmining). 192

Acknowledgements

This book was prepared within the research project "Flat Ontologies, Law and Its Ontology", sponsored by the National Science Centre, Poland (Registration number 2018/31/D/HS5/00294). Although I, as its author, am solely responsible for it (with all its possible substantive shortcomings), there are several people who, in this or other ways, have contributed to my work and whom I would like to say here once again "thank you very much for your help".

I benefited greatly from the community of my home Department of Sociology of Law at Jagiellonian University, Kraków, Poland, especially the seminar meetings, where I could present portions of the ongoing work on the book and gain some additional, often invaluable, insights. All those who participated in these meetings and with whom I worked and talked almost daily during the project helped me, but I would like to express my special gratitude to Krzysztof Pałecki and Mateusz Stępień (with whom I could always talk on specific, often quite technical, issues of the book and specific arguments in it, and the former has read the entire manuscript of the book) and to Janina Czapska (who, as the chair of my home department, created a supportive environment to realise the project).

Practically, all the following investigations and arguments in this book were also presented outside my department during various conferences and workshops. I thank all those who commented on parts of the research presented as different papers during these events: the 19th International Sociological Association World Congress of Sociology "Power, Violence and Justice: Reflections, Responses and Responsibilities", in the Session "The Relational-Processual Turn in Sociology: Theoretical Discussions and Debates", 15–21 July 2018, Toronto, Canada; the Conference "New/Old. Materialism in Literature, Art, Critique", 7–9 December 2018, Wrocław, Poland; the 9th Congress of Young Scholars of Legal Theory and Philosophy "Theory and Philosophy of Law in the Face of Contemporary Challenges", 4–6 September 2019, Toruń, Poland; the 17th Polish Sociological Congress "Me, Us, Them? Subjectivity, Identity, Belonging", in the Group "Public Sphere: Functions and Dysfunctions", 11–14 September 2019, Wrocław; the Socio-Legal Studies Association 2021 Conference, in the Socio-Legal Jurisprudence Stream, 30 March–1 April 2021, hosted by Cardiff University, Wales, United Kingdom; the Social Ontology 2021

Conference, 9–21 August 2021, hosted by University of California San Diego, United States; the Critical Legal Conference 2021 "Frankenlaw. Community, Division, Modernity", 2–4 September 2021, hosted by University of Dundee, Scotland, United Kingdom and University of Victoria, Canada; the Conference "Analytic Philosophy Meets Legal Theory", 30 September–3 October 2021, Kraków and the Conference "Re-Thinking Agency: Non-Anthropocentric Approaches", 3–5 February 2022, hosted by University of Warsaw, Poland.

During the realisation of the research project, which is finalised with this book, I had the pleasure of organising an online workshop "Artifacts, Powers, Intra-Actions: Flattening the Ontology of Law", 15 February 2021, where I not only presented some part of my own work and discussed it but also listened and talked about the work of others. I thank all those who took part in it, especially Giuseppe Lorini and Olimpia Giuliana Loddo.

At one of the earlier stages of work on the book, I was approached by Piotr Dziewałtowski-Gintowt, the then Chairman of the student Scientific Circle of the History of Doctrines, operating at my home Faculty, with the proposal to organise a meeting about my project. This idea came to fruition on 27 November 2019, in Kraków, and I would like to thank the organisers and all those who attended for their interest.

Separate thanks must go to Colin Perrin, Naomi Round Cahalin, Cathryn Henderson, Hamish Ironside and the Discourses of Law series editors, especially Peter Goodrich, who expressed a sincere and deeply thoughtful interest in my work and navigated the entire book publishing process very efficiently.

I also want to express my gratitude to anonymous reviewers for their insights and help in making the book better, and to Anne Wagner, Sarah Marusek and Giuseppe Lorini for their endorsements for this work.

Finally, I thank my beloved family for their unwavering, rock-solid support and love, especially my wonderful wife Joanna, our incredible daughter Julia and my beloved parents. Tragically, during the work on the project, my dad fell seriously ill and passed away. This book is in his memory.

Chapter 1

Introduction

Law, its Ontologies and the Mere Idea of Flat Ontology; or, How Flat Ontologies Differ from Ontologies of Law and Why Should We Care?

1.1 Adequacy Question and Value Question

This book aims to investigate what can be considered a representative sample of a highly intriguing contemporary (yet having a considerable genealogy that is still to be traced in detail) discourse in humanities and social sciences – the so-called flat ontologies – from the perspective of contemporary, mostly Western or Global Northern law. As is made clear below, flat ontologies are often quite explicitly proposed as all-encompassing ontological frameworks that are meant to account for anything there is. Their ambitions are, without exaggeration, truly grand. However, do they really meet their promise? This book aims to address this question, and law – in the suggested historically and geographically narrowed sense, which is justified below – is a specific litmus test for flat ontologies. Is law somehow problematic to these frameworks? Does it have some features that do not fit these ontologies or remain in tension with their principles? These questions can be reversed to the following form: Is the application of flat ontologies to law – an attempt to embrace it with their theoretical apparatus and underlying assumptions – problematic, and if yes, in what way exactly? Perhaps some ontological propositions of the investigated frameworks about what there is in the world and is fundamental for it are hardly realised by law, or their realisation is debatable, to say the least. In short, the main research issue that this book addresses can be called the adequacy question.

However, this is not the only problem discussed here. Namely, even if an ontological framework may prove to be inadequate to law for certain reason(s), it may still offer some interesting insights about it. The given theory may not be entirely a good fit for law, but it still provides important avenues for investigating law, which may even prove to not have any precedent. In short, this book also aspires to address the value question. What can be used – in a very broad, theoretical and empirical or practical sense – for law from flat ontologies, even when their adequacy may turn out to be controversial?

As already implied, the conducted analyses problematise the selected flat ontologies' adequacy to law, but they also bring to the fore what can be regarded as their value when dealing with law. As usually is with similar tasks,

DOI: 10.4324/9781003440963-1

the agenda for the book is the result of many underlying assumptions and further implications, which must be carefully presented for clarifying the whole enterprise proposed in this study. Below, in this Introduction, we will address the adopted sense of law, the mere idea of a flat ontology, provide a relevant classification of other ontologies of law for comparison, justify the selection of representative flat ontologies to be investigated and explain how this book is situated with other relevant studies and how it differs from them.

1.2 What is Meant by "Law"?

1.2.1 LAW, Law or law?

As suggested, some explanation is needed about the reasons behind assuming a more historically and geographically narrowed contemporary Western or Global Northern understanding of law for the sake of investigations proposed in this book. To do this, let us recall here Antony Allott's (1980: viii) quite interesting and useful distinction among LAW, *Law* and law.

LAW indicates the law as such, which was, is and will be present in specific forms of law. Allottian LAW is the abstract, yet essential, idea that is (supposed to be) realised within any actual case of law. The second concept – *Law* – designates existing legal orders. For example, the law of the Roman Empire or that of contemporary European countries is an instance of Allott's *Law*, not LAW. The third concept – law – refers to specific regulations of existing legal orders. The infamous *poena cullei* (e.g. Bauman 1996: 23) and something so mundane as current traffic light regulations in various state legal orders are both instances of law.

Given this background, when this book addresses flat ontologies from the perspective of contemporary Western or Global Northern law, it should be understood in terms of Allott's *Law* or *Laws* – actual legal orders of civil or common law traditions – as well as Allottian laws; ultimately, specific legal regulations are components of the entire legal orders. This book does not aim to engage LAW, law as such or law in general. This decision is based on the conviction that the prospect of addressing law outside of any geographical, historical, political or cultural context is dubious, at least from socio-legal perspective.

First, one can say that there was, is and most likely will be no actual LAW in Allott's sense. All that was, is or will be relevant in the discussed context is *Law* and law. Moreover, if we as legal scholars or all those interested in the phenomenon of law are in our everyday lives immersed in specific instances of legal orders and their regulations, for instance, of home countries or communities, experience them, and are often flooded with information about a particular law and its rules and not law in general, then the mere possibility of adequately thinking about law as such should be questioned. How can anyone be sure and convinced that their understanding of such law in general is correct and not entangled in the legal reality in which they are involved in most of their lives? Similarly, how can anyone be sure that what they consider Allottian LAW will still be valid and adequate in future legal orders that are yet to come?

These sentiments can be easily associated with Donna J. Haraway's (1988) – one of the most important figures for new materialism, a burgeoning field that is critical for flat ontologies – idea of situatedness of any knowledge practice. Even if I, the book's author, would like to and have actually tried to somehow free myself of the specific forms of law in which I live, think about, study and read or hear about the most, I would not succeed. My possible accounts of law in general, besides being something purely fictional as there was and is no such thing, would still be significantly marked by where and how I am situated.

To avoid as much as possible some ultimately individual, if not personal, projections on law in general that most likely would prove to be inadequate from the perspective of grasping law as such, this book is focused on the law that is the closest to me, for better or worse, but also many others – contemporary Western or Global Northern law. Having said that, let us now move on to some presentation of it, broad enough to embrace both the civil and common law traditions, which will allow us to clarify the common point of reference for the sake of what is to follow in the book.

1.2.2 Text and Meaning and Media for Them

Law in its chosen geographical and historical form for the following investigations is commonly associated with texts. Contemporary texts of law in the Western or Global Northern context are noncasuistic, perfunctory and often require special skills to be properly understood. Ultimately, law is not only text but also what can be inferred from this textual basis during interpretation. Meanings of contemporary legal texts are not as self-evident as many of us would probably wish for. To actually know what to do, the simple reading of a legal provision in some texts is often not enough. Usually, it needs some unpacking because contemporary texts of law can be said to have a peculiar feature of often having a complex meaning compressed in just a few words, as the entire legal interpretation-focused jurisprudence and legal dogmatics and their achievements constantly show.

However, talking about text also implies, besides meaning, some foundation for it, form, vessel, that is, communication media and tools like paper, print, computers, software, servers, working stable internet connections and power networks. Any rule must somehow be communicated to all those that should comply with it (e.g. Fuller 1969: 49–51). We largely moved from carving rules in stone or reading aloud some new edicts of a ruler in market square in front of a gathered group of people. Once these methods were functional and realised their purpose, but the growing human populations and the increasing complexity of reality and such ideas on social life, like equality, forced, or were in parallel with, significant changes in physical media for the texts of law (e.g. Boehme-Neßler 2011: 32–44). For a long time now, we have been using print to disseminate law more effectively in mass societies. The relatively recent (from a broad historical perspective) development of generally understood digital information technologies has supplemented this necessary aspect of law, but it also has significantly complicated it.

Ultimately, the printed on a piece of paper text of some regulation is, to a certain extent, more independent than the text of the same regulation accessed through various electronic devices and adequate software. The latter are entangled in something so seemingly trivial in contemporary everyday life, yet very complex and fragile, like the constant access to electric power and internet connection. Without them, electronically mediated access to the text of law becomes impossible. Thus, the much older analogue technology of printed paper documents proves to be paradoxically more resistant and stable than what is commonly considered a great civilisational leap.

1.2.3 Top-Down and Bottom-Up Geneses of Law

Although the relations and characteristics of the main physical media used for the texts of law are critical, we should also acknowledge the complex geneses of these texts (their contents). On the one hand, it is understandable to associate legal acts, regulations and a plethora of provisions within them with formal, direct authors of these texts that reside in some political, legislative bodies like the parliament and specific commissions within them – already an area of immense internal complexity.

On the other hand, as especially the sociology of law from its very inception, for instance, in the works of Eugen Ehrlich, reminds us, the roots of published and valid legal regulations reach much deeper than official lawmaking (e.g. Ehrlich 1922). Namely, law, as seen in various codes, can be regarded as a specific response to or confirmation of what has already been happening in a regulated society. In other words, when one would like to know who the real, though often involuntary, authors of valid law are, one should look in the mirror, at the face of their neighbours, people passing in the sidewalks and the generations of their parents and grandparents. For if law regulates behaviours, it is in a specific way subsequent to them; emerges out of intersubjective, social practices and that what can be said to underlie them like human emotions, aspirations or values.

However, people's everyday actions are not only the specific beginning of law and the object of its regulations. What people do can lead to the end of some law. For instance, according to the *desuetudo* principle, a previously valid law can lose its validity because it is no longer applied (e.g. Grabowski 2013: 302). Only superficially can one say that the nonapplication of some law is due to the way in which legal application officials, especially judges, work. The fact that some judges or public administration officials do not apply in their proceedings some valid rules can be just a consequence of social practices of ordinary people, which have changed so much that the rule in question became irrelevant, even obsolete, and this is why law application institutions stopped issuing decisions on its basis.

1.2.4 Social Communication About Law

The significance of everyday social practices reaches beyond the suggested sense of genesis, supporting, but also specifically ending the law. Namely, because of, especially contemporarily, very dense networks of social, intersubjective relations, people have some orientation in what is legally required of them (e.g. Studnicki 1968: 30). Of course, the mentioned texts of law are quite easily available, but very few law's addressees actually use differently reproduced (in printed book form or through electronic display on the screen of a computer, tablet or smartphone) legal acts, not to mention the official journals of law. In particular, ordinary people in their relations and communication with each other simply pass on the contents of law, but their expressions of these can be very different, for better or worse. Without playing this relaying role, one can wonder what legal orders in massive contemporary societies would look like, because it is doubtful that the variously reproduced texts of legal acts, for instance, in digital legal information databases, including commercial ones, and official publications of law in governmental journals can themselves be sufficient to uphold law and its satisfying functioning.

Passing on the contents of law by ordinary people in everyday life activities can have positive effects, in the case of not only the low readership of official texts of law or difficulties they pose in their understanding but also some malfunction of infrastructure that supports digital journal of laws. Just imagine a blackout – like the one described by Jane Bennett (2010: 20–38), another scholar often associated with new materialism – in a country where, due to technological advancements, the only official form of publication of law is through a dedicated government website. Such a major power network malfunction would make it impossible to get to the official texts of law; thus, any form of compensation for this and other imperfections of them should be valued. However, as already suggested, people talking to each other about law can also significantly misinform themselves about it. The official law can be quite different from what they think it is and what they speak or write about it.

1.2.5 Law's Materiality

If this merely passing glimpse at law, in its assumed sense, may appear as projecting a quite complex image of it, then the things are even more complicated. Note that, so far, we have not even suggested the issue of buildings for legal institutions (e.g. Mulcahy 2011). All these merely mentioned parliament members, judges and public administration officials must have some physical, tangible infrastructure where they can realise their responsibilities – buildings, subordinated to the intended functions of institutions they are supposed to host, and their lobby, corridors connecting offices, voting halls, courtrooms, all with lesser (in a spatial, not functional sense) equipment, such as computers, printers, desks and chairs. Of course, history knows instances of lawmaking or law application taking place in an open field, quite literally, but in our narrowed sense of law (to contemporary Western or Global Northern realities), such a practice is either impossible to return to (because of the law in force and given its questionable appropriateness to current conditions) or, at best, significantly exceptional (e.g. Mulcahy 2011: 7). Buildings and the entire material infrastructure (often adorned with relevant symbols, scales in courthouses being just one of them) required for contemporary legal institutions are only one of the many examples of what can often be regarded as inessential objects for law, which actually are critical and far from merely supplementary.

Ultimately, if we bring up judges and courtrooms, we should also acknowledge that judges, as well as many other broadly understood legal officials, have distinct dress codes for their respective roles in law (e.g. Watt 2013: 79–121). Moreover, these outfits are either necessary to properly fulfil the functions of a given kind of official, or having them on in certain events can significantly change the way they can be legally classified. For instance, there are countries, of both civil and common law traditions, where to validly act as a judge in the courtroom during proceedings, the judge must wear a dedicated robe or consider that potential attacks or other aggressive, offensive behaviours against the officers of specific legal institutions may be differently evaluated depending on whether the officer in question was uniformed during the incident. Again, then, something that may be quite easily dismissed at first glance as merely superficial in our legal orders proves to be much profound.

As another illustration of such a duality, we can consider something that connects clearly with what we began our brief, if not perfunctory, presentation of what we should have in mind throughout this book when talking about law. As mentioned earlier, law is most definitely of texts, put into different media, communicating various meanings, with crucial emphasis on instructing on how to act in different situations and contexts. The success of these instructions depends on various factors, both internal to law's addressees (e.g. their sense of responsibility and duty) and external (e.g. predicted legal consequence for rule transgression and scope of control by relevant institutions). However, given that a significant majority of what is legally regulated is intersubjectively observable as it simply involves concrete actions of corporeal human beings in time and space, one can try to somehow alter the physical possibilities so that it becomes easier or more difficult to, respectively, comply or not comply with law (depending on the exact character of such technologically enforced rule; e.g. Lorini et al. 2021, 2023; Lorini and Moroni 2022). For instance, speed limits can be enforced (and specifically communicated at the same time) by traffic signs or speed bumps. The highly controversial prohibition of sleeping in public can be controlled by police officers or can be in an even more stable way enforced by specially constructed public benches, which are simply unfit to sleep on them. Similarly, to a certain extent, copyrights can be reminded by simple textual messages displayed on the screen before the movie starts or can be imprinted in the mere medium for that movie (especially downloaded file) in the form of digital rights management protections (e.g. Lessig 2006: 116–117). These and other inventions that can come to mind may in very different ways change how law functions and is perceived in society; on this ground, they should also be considered.

Although the above brief remarks are nothing more than merely sliding across the surface of complexities of law in the contemporary Western or Global Northern context, they should fulfil their intended function – to sketch with what flat ontologies are confronted in this book. Their generality is meant to make it possible to accommodate both civil and common law realities. In various details, especially concerning the role played by judges and their decisions in the entire legal order, they differ significantly. Nevertheless, it is not impossible to adopt a perspective that grasps both or at least their contours.

1.3 Preliminaries on Flat Ontology

1.3.1 Basics of Genealogy

Once one of the issues fundamental for this work – assumed understanding of law that is to be confronted with flat ontologies – is presented in more detail, we can now move on to the mere idea of a flat ontology. This idea can and is variously realised and expanded in specific flat ontologies, whose selection for the book is justified later. For the moment, let us focus on the mere idea of a flat ontology. This concept was first used explicitly in Roy Bhaskar's *A Realist Theory of Science* (2008), one of the foundational works for critical realism. Bhaskar's understanding of a flat ontology differs significantly from the current, most widespread understanding, which is also crucial for this book. According to Bhaskar, a flat ontology is basically an anthropocentric ontology, the one that ultimately subordinates reality to human scientific perception. It is an ontology that should be avoided, as it projects a shallow, superficial image of the world. In Bhaskar's words:

> In this way [of flat ontology] the world, which ought to be viewed as a multi-dimensional structure independent of man, came to be squashed into a flat surface whose characteristics, such as being constituted by atomistic facts, were determined by the needs of a particular concept of knowledge.
>
> (Bhaskar 2008: 35, see also 57, 253)

In contrast, contemporarily, a flat ontology commonly means something as far from human-centredness as possible, an ontology that avoids any prioritisation of anything over anything else (whether human, nonhuman, inanimate, animate, natural or artificial). Instead of projecting various hierarchies among beings (for instance, of importance or worthiness of a serious treatment), it equalises, puts beings that are commonly associated with specific domains (e.g. inorganic, organic, human, nonhuman, social and natural) on a nonhierarchical plane, hence flatness. This sense, guiding the entire book, was explicitly inaugurated by Manuel DeLanda – whose assemblage theory (AST) is analysed from the perspective of law in this book – more specifically, in his important take on Gilles Deleuze's philosophy *Intensive Science and Virtual Philosophy* (2002). In accordance with this work, a flat ontology is "made exclusively of unique, singular individuals, differing in spatiotemporal scale but not in ontological status" (DeLanda 2002: 47). In other words, a flat ontology here does not deny that there are bigger and smaller entities (in accordance with a specific scale or point of reference) but insists not to associate with such differences any differences in the ontological significance of specific beings.

One can safely say that since DeLanda's change of meaning of the phrase (compared to the Bhaskarian sense), "flat ontology" became increasingly popular. Many thinkers, often of quite different academic disciplinary affiliations, who developed their own ontological frameworks started to utilise the notion with respect to their own work. The work of past thinkers began to be analysed in terms of whether they can be regarded as flat ontologists (e.g. Jones 2014; Tampio 2015: 56). Moreover, the concept proved to be highly inspirational and influential not only among philosophers *sensu stricto* but also among a wide variety of humanities and cultural studies scholars, anthropologists, geographers and, finally, social scientists (e.g. Fox and Alldred 2017; Schatzki 2019: 69–72).

1.3.2 Problem of Too Narrow Conceptualisations

Usually, when a specific notion gains traction and is used by various scholars, its sense starts to fluctuate. Especially interesting, though also problematic, is narrowing the sense of a flat ontology, in effect of which the frameworks that can be justifiably regarded as flat ontologies are excluded from the concept. Consider, for instance, the work of the geographer James Ash (2020: 345, 350) or social scientists Nick J. Fox and Pam Alldred (2018: 318, 325–326) – two visible popularisers and developers of the notion of a flat ontology in sociology (Fox and Alldred 2017). By stressing, in their understanding of a flat ontology, the practically constant dynamism of beings (that things are never really done, finished or stable, but are still in the process of becoming), relationality (the interconnectedness of entities) and anti-essentialism, they exclude Graham Harman's object-oriented ontology (OOO) – a framework analysed later in this book – from the idea of a flat ontology. This is quite paradoxical because Harman himself is for the large part of his work (with some caveats that are addressed in the chapter on his framework) sympathetic to this idea and considers his own ontology as its instance. However, he strongly opposes emphasising the mentioned dynamism and relationality and is a defender of essentialism. That would be enough to exclude him from flat ontologies, if sticking to the approach of Ash, Fox and Alldred, the approach of narrowing the idea of flat ontology.

Surprisingly, one of the more well-known systematic developers of a flat ontology, Levi R. Bryant, can also be suspected of the similar narrowed and exclusionary understanding of the commented concept. In his important *The Democracy of Objects*, he states that

> flat ontology argues that all entities are on equal ontological footing and that no entity, whether artificial or natural, symbolic or physical, possesses greater ontological dignity than other objects. While indeed some objects might influence the collectives to which they belong to a greater extent than others, it doesn't follow from this that these objects are more real than others. Existence, being, is a binary such that something either is or is not.
> (Bryant 2011: 246)

While our investigations on some of the representative flat ontologies in the book problematise the equalisation of the symbolic and physical, Bryant mentions, for now the most crucial is that his formula rejects the idea of correlation among the strength, power, degree of influence of one being on another and degree of its reality. However, in accordance with such an understanding of a flat ontology, Bruno Latour's actor-network theory (ANT) – another framework considered in this book as perhaps the most paradigmatic, representative flat ontology – would be, paradoxically and in opposition to most of the opinions in the literature, excluded from the concept. Namely, if to be means to act or to influence others, as Latour (e.g. Latour 1996: 373; 2004: 75, 237; but see also Latour 1988: 158, §1.1.5, 227, §4.5.9; Latour 2005: 137) famously argues, then one can say that in his ontology, the degree of reality of some entity is dependent on the degree to which it exerts its influence on other beings – the more something changes others, the more it exists. This specific approach is rejected in the Bryantian formula of a flat ontology.

Of course, no one is suggesting here that Bryant's distinction between the strength of beings and the mere existence considered in a binary way is wrong in the context of his original position. The only intention here is to provide another illustration of the problem with narrow understandings of flat ontology and their consequences of excluding frameworks that most definitely can be considered flat ontologies, despite the narrowing conceptualisations. Ultimately, it would be quite unfortunate to decide to analyse flat ontologies in terms of their adequacy to law and value for investigations about law, but understand flat ontology in a way that would exclude Latour or others.

1.3.3 The Mere Idea of Flat Ontology – A Proposal and General Characteristics

Against this background, before we even start considering specific representative flat ontologies with law on our minds, we should first specify the adopted understanding of the mere idea of a flat ontology, which avoids the suggested problems of narrow approaches, is inclusive and does not exclude frameworks that still deserve the name of flat ontologies and are treated as such by their own authors and many others. The suitably capacious understanding of the mere idea of a flat ontology can be as follows. A flat ontology is an ontology that consists of two strictly connected "moves": to stop prioritising what is usually described as human and to stop ignoring or belittling what is usually described as nonhuman or extrahuman, in ontological investigations in general (the reality in its entirety) or of specific entities (e.g. the ozone hole or a bureaucratic institution). That what is usually elevated (human) and that what is most commonly degraded or ignored to the point of not even being mentioned (nonhuman) are supposed to meet on one plane.

There are, then, two most important implications from this brief formula: pluralism and nonhierarchy. The former advises not to reject in advance various entities as, for instance, (allegedly) unimportant or trivial, while the latter advises not to assume any *a priori* hierarchies of entities, "ladders of beings" (e.g. Lovejoy 1964). Both implications are applicable to ontological investigations in general and of specific subjects of inquiry. These two implications are especially important at the beginning of any ontological inquiry in accordance with the idea of a flat ontology. Ultimately, the analyses of a specific entity can lead to some exclusions or hierarchies. For instance, some things may prove unimportant to the constitution and maintenance of the chosen subject of inquiry, and among the important ones there may be some more crucial than others. However, before one even begins thinking about such a hypothesis regarding an investigated object, pluralistic and nonhierarchical commitments of flat ontology force any investigator at the beginning of their work to consider numerous highly heterogeneous entities and to be cautious about any possible assumptions regarding the inequality relations between them. In other words, despite the high abstractness of a flat ontology, its actual use in the analyses must be detailed and pay serious attention to even the most seemingly trivial issues (compared to the main subject of inquiry).

The general, if not perfunctory, character of what was just proposed about the mere idea of a flat ontology is intended to avoid the issue of too narrow conceptualisations. However, most importantly here, this idea can be variously realised by specific flat ontologies, as seen in the following five chapters. The concrete flat ontologies can and do complement the foundational assumptions and ambitions of the mere idea of a flat ontology through various more detailed propositions (along with assumed by them the basic ontological units we will start acknowledging later). What a specific flat ontology proposes, the other can explicitly reject. For instance, while both DeLanda's AST and Gabriel Tarde's monadology (MON) – the oldest framework addressed in this book – fall under the idea of a flat ontology, they still differ significantly; in particular, Tarde is anti-holistic, anti-emergentist, while DeLanda is a vocal proponent of emergentism. The former denies the actual existence of bigger entities which have properties that are not found among their components. Instead of adopting a position of irreducibility of bigger (emergent) beings to their smaller parts, Tarde argues in favour of specific reductionism, some may say that even an extreme one. In turn, DeLanda is strictly against such reductions to smaller and smaller components, as an advocate of emergent entities with features specific to them only, which are something more than the mere sum of their parts.

Despite these and other differences among specific flat ontologies – which will become clear with each chapter of the book and be briefly summarised as part of the Conclusion – they all share, with the mere idea of flat ontology, a grand, universal ambition to be all-embracing ontological frameworks. We will verify whether this, dare we say, quite cheeky attitude of flat ontologies is justified as being actually realised with respect to law, but right now, we should try to better understand this grand ambition. A flat ontology is an attempt to find a way of thinking about what exists, which would be universally or as broadly as possible adequate to what exists. It is the search for such regularities, features or dynamics that can be found in entities that are "traditionally" ascribed to what are often considered different domains of reality, among which there are usually seen some clear hierarchies and inequalities. Namely, flatness in the mere idea of a flat ontology and its specific instances is often about avoiding or at least being sceptical of the idea that reality consists of different ontological layers, considered as real domains, not only results of some analytical differentiations, and that some layers are supposed to be more fundamental than others, which can be regarded as merely possible but not a necessary derivative of some foundation. One of the more well-known instances of a nonflat ontology would be Nicolai Hartmann's (1953: 46) layered ontology with subsequent nonorganic, organic, psychic and spiritual levels. Interestingly, despite some strong voices against separating reality in such a way (for instance, by György Lukács 1984: 447–450; who, somewhat paradoxically, himself proposed a specific layered ontology – Lukács 1984: 8), Hartmann still significantly influenced ontology of law in the twentieth century (e.g. Bröstl 2016: 625; De Sousa e Brito et al. 2016: 507, 508).

However, before we look at this field of inquiry in the indicated time period to better situate the entire enterprise of juxtaposing flat ontologies with law, there is at least one more thing to stress concerning the universal ambition characteristic of flat ontology. By arguing in favour of a specific universal trait or process among all there is, flatness, equalisation among the human and nonhuman is achieved or at least thought to be achieved. Each flat ontology can be said to have its own way of ontological flattening, which will become clearer later in the book when we will focus on the chosen flat ontologies. For now, let us just acknowledge that, for instance, Karen Barad's agential realism (AGR) – the representative flat ontology chosen for the focused analysis in the book – argues in favour of the thesis that everything that exists is due to its relations with others, which are also constituted or even emerge out of relations and are not present prior to these relations. In other words, the reconstructable Baradian motto "relata do not preexist relations" (Barad 2007: 140, 334), having roots in their interpretation of Niels Bohr's writings, is considered a general ontological "law"; thus, all things that exist are subjected to it and are equal to each other in its light.

However, these and other ways of flattening are not the only features of flat ontologies that show their universal ambitions. Perhaps the most intriguing aspect of these frameworks – instantiations of the mere idea of a flat ontology – is that their adopted basic ontological units are not domain-specific. They are meant to refer to entities that are usually regarded, for instance, social as well as those out of the conventionally understood nonsocial domain. The features of such a unit assumed in a given flat ontology are thought to be formal, general enough to be found in everything. In turn, units often adopted in other ontologies are, in a way, dedicated to what is often assumed to be specific parts of reality. Just consider the concepts of social and institutional facts, widely used in the contemporary, more analytically oriented ontologies of law, which can be most easily associated with social ontology in the spirit of John R. Searle (especially Searle 1995, 2010). Not only their mere names ("social" and "institutional") seem to already narrow them to some form of an exclusively human, social domain. The sense of these concepts is also very human-centred as it addresses the ascription of meanings to different phenomena and events, the practice of people agreeing on some way of understanding or treating something in their community. Obviously then, such domain-specific basic ontological units are simply not meant to address anything outside the domain they are clearly dedicated to. In turn, the idea of a flat ontology can be realised by adopting domain-nonspecific units that are meant to fit not only human communal life practices with strong emphasis on their linguistic character but also diseases, pieces of technology, large-scale economic phenomena and all the rest (as mentioned earlier, we will see whether this is the case in the example of law).

More important here is to explain why I used in the last sentence the somewhat uncertain phrase "can be realised" instead of simply "is realised". This is because there are investigations of various thinkers that can be quite easily associated with the basic, definitional sensitivities of the idea of a flat ontology, but they do not specify their basic ontological units with the same degree of attention as other comparable frameworks. For instance, Haraway shares the general anti-anthropocentric, heterogeneous and equalising ontological commitments so typical of a flat ontology, but it is debateable whether she proposes and consistently follows throughout her oeuvre an assumed basic unit in a comparable manner as, for instance, flat ontologists that are analysed in this book (but see her use of the concept of relationship, Haraway 2003: 77). Before we say something more about them, the reasons why their sample is chosen for the book and how exactly they are approached here, we should add basic information on the idea of a flat ontology and give some insight into how actually to think in accordance with such an idea, how to conduct a flat ontological analysis.

1.3.4 Addressing Incorrect Impressions

Like any idea of a significant degree of generality and abstractness, the idea of a flat ontology is also susceptible to various misguided impressions. So far, we have noticed that, despite the possible initial impression and perhaps somewhat paradoxically, the general and abstract flat ontology forces us to focus on concrete details. It is not an impractical idea that would, at most, remain in the minds and papers of a few theoreticians. Ultimately, the pluralism and non-hierarchy provoke us to take a good look at all different entities that appear in the context of the main, chosen subject of inquiry, regardless of their size (small, even miniscule and easy to overlook may prove to be crucial) or provenance (even investigating something exclusively human and social, it may turn out that even nonorganic, both natural and artificial, is involved, and its omission in the analyses would be, at least, questionable). In short, a flat ontology is superficially an exclusively armchair and pipe type of theory, while it actually stimulates to leave the smoke-filled and dim-lit office and investigate whatever the object of interest is much more practically and tangibly (e.g. Fox and Alldred 2018: 323). Perhaps this is a reason why so many social scientists are interested in flat ontologies and why this first book-length confrontation of flat ontologies with law is proposed by the sociologist of law.

For the same reason, the accusations that flat ontologies are apolitical and insignificant from the perspective of social injustices and fighting against them are simply incorrect. The attention to detail implied by the mere idea of a flat ontology, even when tackling what is often regarded as a big or macro phenomenon, such as social domination or oppression, can prove to be very useful. Ultimately, these big problems that one may be fighting against are most likely entangled with or co-constituted by the small and fragile. In consequence, what usually (without lenses of flat ontology) comes across as strong and practically invincible starts to be seen as defeatable. As John Law – another, besides the already mentioned Latour, well-known representative of ANT – said in the vein of Michel Foucault (1978: 94) – "the masters of the universe may also have feet of clay" (Law 1992: 379).

Some voices have also criticised the idea of a flat ontology on the account that it does not allow any differentiation than a simple binary "is-is not" (e.g. Brassier 2015: 66–67; Mussell 2017: 87; see also Schaffer 2009: 354). Indeed, all that exists is supposed to be put on a single plane, but it does not result in the impossibility of any more detailed characterisation of entities. Specific flat ontologies – realisations of the mere idea of a flat ontology – most definitely allow differentiations in terms of, for instance, components of a given entity, specific properties and relations with others. Moreover, as already mentioned, in accordance with the discussed idea, flattening is something to do at the very beginning of a specific inquiry. Hierarchies and inequalities among entities someway relevant to the chosen object of analysis are not forbidden. They are allowed in a flat ontology but cannot be assumed or presupposed in an *a priori* fashion (e.g. Latour 1993: 107–108; Harman 2016b: 4; 2018: 54–55). Having said that though, taking the opportunity, one should also be aware of such scholars who seem to fall under the flat ontology rubric but are in a specific way more radical, such as Andrew Pickering (2008: 4), who is dismissive of hierarchies and treats them as nothing more than a description and not as anything real (which could be proven during an analysis).

The idea of a flat ontology and its specific representatives clearly advocate the end of anthropocentrism, which is especially easy to commit in humanities and social sciences and they can most definitely be associated with the sentiments of the even broader intellectual (and not only) phenomenon of posthumanism (e.g. Wolfe 2010; Braidotti 2013; Ferrando 2019). Having said that, it is, unfortunately, easy to see at first glance in flat ontologies a radical bypassing or belittling of the human. However, in accordance with the idea of a flat ontology, the human is not and should not be ignored or degraded. It is and should be considered, along with what is nonhuman. This is, in the end, the definitional feature of a flat ontology – to stop prioritising the human and degrading the nonhuman so that both sides meet on one plane. Perhaps the reason for the commented wrong impression about a flat ontology is a deeply felt fear that, as soon as we start thinking of the human as just another element of the ontological landscape, its value will also be equated with that of the rest. As probably most strongly stressed by Barad, a flat ontology is also of axiological relevance, but it does not entail a vulgar positive correlation between the ontological and axiological statuses of beings, as most likely assumed in the mentioned criticism.

Given that the investigations inspired by the idea of a flat ontology concerning an entity that is often regarded as strictly human and social frequently show significance for that entity of various other elements – for instance, material, organic, nonorganic and those that cannot be associated with human communicational, meaning-centred practices – this idea can be accused of advocating some form of determinism (e.g. Bryant 2011: 288). For instance, if an apparently exclusively linguistic practice proves to be, after its analysis, utterly dependent on some tangible technologies, even crude ones, like paper, cables and bricks, the idea of technological determinism may come to one's mind. However, this is just another wrong impression, which should be refuted at the very beginning of our analyses of flat ontologies. As already mentioned, the formal, domain-nonspecific character of the basic units for the ontological inquiry assumed in various flat ontologies shows that these frameworks are, in general (with some reservation concerning Harmanian OOO), as far as possible from explaining different phenomena with causes of just one type. Moreover, their critical stance towards separating reality into different domains or layers underlies the fact that, if employed in actual research, the idea of a flat ontology results in diagnoses that are multi-factor to a very large degree, which itself may also be detrimental, as we will discuss later. At this point, it should also be added that the multi-factor look at various phenomena provoked by the idea of a flat ontology practically forces researchers to study them in a truly inter- or transdisciplinary manner. Even when studying something that is most commonly associated with a specific domain and scientific discipline, the sensitivities of a flat ontology will stimulate the transgression of the usual boundaries. Perhaps most interestingly, the social will prove to be not exclusively social and the natural will not be exclusively natural.

1.3.5 Illustration and Test of Removal

For the sake of all those of us who may still have difficulties in coming up with their own illustration of what a flat ontology practically entails, let us think for a while about an object that is most commonly seen in terms of something strictly human, in the sense of human linguistic meanings, ideas and semantics – a poem. From the perspective of a flat ontology, one should be cautious of analysing it only in categories of human mental processes, creativity, sensitivity and some competences of the author (not only those more specialised, concerning the approaches of structuring a poem, but also more general language competence). Perhaps the commonsensical approach of grasping entities such as a poem through these human elements, largely confined to the linguistically mediated imagination, would most likely be criticised as unjustified reductionism from the position of a flat ontology – reducing something that is much more complex to only a part of its real composition.

In turn, other, nonflat ontological positions that are also posed with the challenge to address the chosen object of a poem would disagree. For instance, from their position, grasping the poem in terms of a practically bare human product – that is, without any appeal to, for instance, various material technologies – would not be an unjustified reduction but as precise and adequate as possible. In the opinion of nonflat ontologists, a poem is not reduced to some ideal, ideational, immaterial semantics but is simply just that or, to be more precise, an instance of that.

The hypothetical, perhaps somewhat tongue-in-cheek, response to that from the flat ontology camp could be the following: "Fine, so a poem is something for which the published paper tomes or literary journals with specific poem or websites that contain it (and are maintained by a plethora of even more diverse beings, such as various software, computer hardware, human moderators and administrators, and, last but not least, power plants) are irrelevant. So, let's get rid of them and we'll see just how poem is doing". Such a response comes from the need to stress that, without any more durable physical media for semantic content, that content itself would either not exist (for even the author may forget their work if it is not recorded) or, at best, exist in a very private manner (for instance, in the mind of its author, who effectively memorised it), which incapacitates its potential social, cultural existence and significance.

This brief example does not only try to present the definitional commitment to treating both the typically human and nonhuman on an equal footing (the apparently exclusively semantic, linguistic work of human ingenuity is made to meet entities that are often way beyond the human, even up to the point of being able to exist past humans), pluralism, nonhierarchy (even when addressing something seemingly well-defined, of clear boundaries, such as a poem, one ends up with a wide array of heterogeneous beings where it is difficult to state what is more important and what is less) and the dismissal of a layered or domain ontology (the profound, even sublime, sphere of works of culture proves to be practically inconceivable without the tangible, often harsh reality involving paper pulp, ink, press machinery and kilometres/miles of cables). The poem case illustrates one of the tools for practically performing a flat ontology. Interestingly, this tool has not yet been brought to the fore in the relevant literature. In fact, there are still relatively little clear expositions of how exactly to perform ontological flattening (with the notable exception of Latour 2005: 174, where he talks of "a series of *clamps* to hold the landscape firmly flat"). This is just another reason to propose here the idea of test of removal, already hinted between the lines in our problem of poem.

The test of removal entails asking the following question: What would happen to an object of our analysis, whatever it is, if it would be stripped off everything that, in accordance with more usual thinking or more mainstream ontologies, is treated as something of lesser importance for that object? In other words, if some argue of a specific entity as, for instance, purely social, intersubjective and human semantic construct, and some broadly understood material infrastructure is said to often uphold it but neither be its part nor be existentially necessary (but merely some stabilising mechanism that may or may not be, while the construct in question persists), then one should simply try to verify it. This can be achieved by at least trying to imagine what most likely will happen to our chosen object if we start removing all those that are regarded as ultimately inessential (though if present, they fulfil some functions) for that object.

The test of removal is then a more specific, graspable tool for the idea of a flat ontology, which, when employed, will quite easily equalise the human and nonhuman, work for the sake of pluralism and nonhierarchy and disrupt reality distinctions in line with some of its usually assumed domains. Of course, it cannot be ruled out that, while employing the test of removal, some hypotheses will come to mind on differing degrees of broadly understood importance for our main object of interest among the several entities that are unearthed in the test. Such an outcome is possible due to the caveat mentioned earlier, that a flat ontology is not entirely against any hierarchies but most definitely against presupposed ones, which were not proven or justified during the actual analysis. Here, we can just say that the specificities of the chosen object of inquiry from which one starts and of the entities acknowledged during the test of removal most likely influence whether we will still end up with some hierarchy. Nevertheless, flat ontology and the test of removal most definitely produce different, often much more expanded, accounts of chosen beings as compared to other approaches in ontology.

1.4 On Ontologies of Law (in Relation to Flat Ontology)

1.4.1 Need for Review and Its Guiding Assumptions

Having said something more on the idea of a flat ontology, we should return, for a moment, to the problem of law, more specifically addressing the following question: Why even bother trying to think about law using some flat ontologies when the ontology of law as a field of inquiry is practically as aged as any reflection on law? In consequence, is there anything new, interesting and wise to say in this respect with flat ontologies? In other words, our analyses of flat ontologies from the perspective of law must be preceded by an overview of the ontologies of law. To make the specificity of flat ontologies clearer, some contrast is required that will also make it easier to situate this entire book in relevant discussions. Only after such an overview and some initial reflections following it will we be in a good position to address the final preliminaries before the proper analyses of the chosen flat ontologies.

The following review of various approaches to the ontology of law is determined by a few guiding assumptions adopted for it. Given that, from most propositions concerning law, one can infer some underlying ideas on the ontology of law, the review simply must adopt a narrower approach. It should only focus on investigations that explicitly take up the issue of ontology of law or are commonly regarded as significant for that matter. Moreover, despite the historically and geographically narrow approach to law, presented earlier, the review below takes a more general perspective. Some, even only necessarily brief, engagement with ontologies of law, and not only with ontologies of law in exclusively contemporary Western or Global Northern sense, seems, on the one hand, more academically honest, and on the other hand, much more adequate in the discussed context. Ultimately, if we want to gain some background against which to locate the entire agenda of this book and have an initial answer on why law is approached from the perspective of flat ontologies, the more we acknowledge from discussions on the ontology of law, the better. In terms of the time period covered by the review – just as the chosen flat ontologies analysed in the book belong to the period ranging from the turn of the nineteenth and twentieth centuries to the first half of the third decade of the twentieth-first century, as revealed below – the ontologies of law review spans the same timeframe. Next, because flat ontologies often emphasise (nonhuman) materiality (not only because materiality is often argued to be co-constitutive of other types of entities, including those that are usually regarded as purely ideational or semantic, but also by arguing that material entities are not utterly passive in the face of humans but are in fact active and even endowed with a specific kind of agency), the review is made in accordance with the following question. Is materiality – from papers, printers and ink, through computers, electric power networks and optical fibre internet connections, and through speed bumps, police batons and prison cells and buildings – considered in a given ontology of law, and if yes, in what way exactly?

Although this guiding criterion for the proposed review makes it different from others comparable in the literature (e.g. Pattaro 1991: 146; Załuski 2009: 130–137; Andina 2016: 57; Roversi 2018b), it shares with similar research endeavours a practically unavoidable flaw: its incompleteness or selectiveness. Even when the review timeframe is strongly narrowed, the immense richness of investigations about the ontology of law in the researched period makes it impossible for the review to be satisfactory for everyone. Ultimately, one can always say that something has been omitted or treated without the necessary subtlety. Thus, the review below should not be approached as entirely comprehensive from the perspective of actual discussions on ontology of law. Nevertheless, it is still proposed here in order to address the initial hypothesis that, in most deliberations on the ontology of law in the researched period, the materiality is neglected, and already on this ground, they differ significantly from what is suggested by the mere idea of a flat ontology. If this is the case, then the task posed in this book to investigate the representative sample of flat ontologies from the perspective of law is justified, not redundant. Flat ontologies propose something new in comparison to most ontologies of law. We will already start seeing it by recalling ourselves some voices in discussions on the ontology of law and filtering them through the issue of materiality, which appears to not have been attempted before in the literature.

When it comes to the materiality in various ontologies of law, we can make the following categorisation of these ontologies, which is illustrated with some examples below. There are ontologies which explicitly or implicitly ignore materiality and exclude any traces of material things from law or, to be more precise, their accounts of it. Let us call such an approach in the ontology of law, as a specific field, materiality ignorance. Within the investigated period, there are also ontologies of law that do not ignore materiality but, to a certain extent, take it into account while, in the end, still belittling it, and do not treat it as a comparably or equally important part or aspect of law compared to others considered in a specific ontology of law. This option can be simply called materiality belittling. The penultimate tendency is rather in the minority in the broad and varied ontological investigations about law but is still noticeable. Namely, there are some efforts in the studied timeframe that aim to equalise materiality with other elements that are most usually stressed and prioritised in the majority of ontologies of law. These efforts end up with modest equalisation, usually in the sense of merely stressing the indispensability of physical media for texts of law and not suggesting the relevance of other instances of materiality. Finally, besides the just-suggested category of modest equalisation of materiality, there is the final one. Relatively recently, ontologies of law that are clearly inspired by flat ontologies and consequently engage in much more outright materiality equalisation have been proposed.

1.4.2 Materiality Ignorance

Perhaps the clearest and specifically radical instance of materiality ignorance can be seen in Niklas Luhmann's systems-theoretical take on law (remembering his highly specific take on ontology, e.g. Luhmann 2013: 185). In the end, he presents his standpoint quite clearly in one of the most mature expositions of his approach to law: “neither paper nor ink, neither people nor other organisms, neither courthouses and their rooms nor telephones or computers are part of the [legal] system” (Luhmann 2004: 73–74). It is consistent with, the fundamental for his theory, focus on the communicational, the semantics to such an extent that even people are excluded from the systems (though there are still attempts to “materialise” Luhmann’s theory, e.g. Philippopoulos-Mihalopoulos 2013). It is mentioned here not without a reason. At first glance, one can easily get the impression that materiality ignorance must have the form of some strictly anthropocentric, if not humanistic, ontology (the examples of which are to follow below). In turn, Luhmann shows that one can largely ignore materiality (though one should remember that he ultimately devotes much space to the analysis of the significance of writing, e.g. Luhmann 2004: 234–243) and, at the same time, consider the various social systems, law being just one of them, beyond humans. His example provokes to say that within the materiality ignorance approach, one can try to identify extrapersonal ontologies of law, which argue that law is something outside or beyond human beings.

In terms of some other potential (and, as such, open to much more detailed discussions) instances of such extrapersonality, various religious natural law theories can come to mind. Namely, locating law in some highest divine entity (or entities) can be said to both ignoring (nonhuman) materiality and excluding humans. However, one can immediately respond to that by stressing that religious natural law theories often make a crucial distinction between law of the divine specific to a given religion and the law created by humans (with varying degrees of compatibility to the first kind of law). Given that, to determine whether some religious natural law theory engages in materiality ignorance and extrapersonality more directly relevant to our discussion here, one should investigate its propositions not on the highest law but on worldly law. Indeed, given the mere number of specific religions with their respective theories of law and the immense richness of each of them, any engagement with them in such a brief review would most likely result in nothing more than an exclusionary selection. We would be able to deal with only one or two traditions and neglect all the rest. This is most definitely an instance of unavoidable incompleteness that we have already openly announced earlier. However, this does not mean that the issue of natural law theories will not return. We will refer in a moment to their different, nonreligious current, which locates law not in the highest divine being but in us ourselves, particularly in human reason.

Back on the track, note that materiality ignorance in ontologies of law does not necessarily have to be combined with a rather controversial stance of law’s extrapersonality. Namely, one can identify what can be named intrapersonal ontologies of law that ignore materiality beyond human beings and locate law within the specific contents of human minds. What is rather commonly known as Leon Petrażycki’s psychological or psychologistic theory of law may be regarded as their prime example due to his famous localisation of law as a special, dual, imperative-attributive kind of emotions felt by individuals (e.g. Petrażycki 1955: 49, 62; obviously, with a caveat on his distinction between positive and intuitive law, and what they assume, 57, or his brief remark on merely recording function of documents in the context of legislation, 156). Perhaps the legal solipsism position developed by Edoardo Fittipaldi (2012: 10) – "the hypothesis according to which legal realities exist exclusively in the psyche of each individual" – is one of the best examples of the continuing influence and importance of such a way of thinking. The general idea that law is something out of a very broadly understood human mentality is not limited to highly specific Petrażyckian visions. Ultimately, one can see in nonreligious natural law theories that prioritise in their accounts of law the largely humanistic, secular reason (with perhaps contemporarily the most well-known example of John Finnis 2011), practically the very same standpoint – that law is so much within humans that any nonhuman tangibility of law is, at least, omitted in respective accounts.

Within the very broad category of ontologies of law that ignore and even exclude materiality from law, there are also interpersonal ontologies that emphasise locating law neither beyond (like extrapersonal) nor in human beings (like intrapersonal ontologies) but among people in the social practices of communal life. Under interpersonal ontology of law appear to fall such diverse approaches to law as Ehrlich's classical, to a certain extent, pioneering vision of sociology of law (e.g. Ehrlich 1922), where law is simply what emerges out of everyday human social interactions and a significant part of contemporary legal positivism with its clear interest in the community of legal officials (e.g. Hart 2012: 116). Closely connected to the analytical positivist philosophy of law, the research current of artifact theorisation of law is also worth mentioning directly, as its representatives often explicitly state that law is basically a human, semantic construct that comes from some interpersonal agreements in a given population but is still said to be immaterial (e.g. Burazin 2018: 113–114; Ehrenberg 2016: 170; Himma 2019: 125, 137; 2020: 81; Marmor 2018: 59; 2023: 94; Roversi 2018a: 98; Tuzet 2018: 217).

Anticipating here already some of the reflections below, especially those flowing from Latourian ANT, intra- and interpersonal types of materiality ignorance can be criticised from the positions of a flat ontology on the following ground. Products of the human mind, heart and soul and interactions with fellow people, are very limited without materiality. Even something as contemporarily trivial as print is indispensable to go from an utterly private, intrapersonal legal emotion or reasoning on the proper way of behaviour to something more communal and social that may influence others. Moreover, the mere process of reaching an agreement in a population on their law, without such basic materiality, would be extremely limited. To imagine this, just try to answer the following question: With how many people can one maintain relations, without any, even most basic, communication technologies? Bare human beings, considered without any material entities, can, in fact, do very little.

Believing that they can do something so grand as entire contemporary mass societies and law within them without materiality is, at best, a significant overestimation of human possibilities.

1.4.3 Materiality Belittling

When it comes to the second category of ontologies of law within the researched period, materiality belittling, a large part of the so-called institutional legal theory, whose main figures can be seen in Neil MacCormick and Ota Weinberger (e.g. MacCormick and Weinberger 1992; however, one should acknowledge institutional theory, which is, to a certain extent, post-MacCormickian and Weinbergerian, like Eerik Lagerspetz 1995, Dick W. P. Ruiter 2001 or Massimo La Torre 2010, and even earlier Italian or French institutionalists, most notably Santi Romano 2017 and Maurice Hauriou [Broderick 1970]), can be regarded as a clear instance of actually mentioning materiality, but only in a very perfunctory way, which acknowledges only a small part of what it does. Ultimately, institutional legal theory, under the strong influence of Searle's social ontology, takes from it the foundational distinction of brute and social/institutional facts. It renders material entities as mere screens for imposing human meanings (similarly, Elder-Vass 2017a: 91). Even though it is perfectly consistent with the clear linguistic focus of most of such theorising, note here that it also does not admit that materiality, among other functions, allows for bigger and more stable, broadly understood social structures and specifically acts, has an agency in its own right that often effectively imposes itself on the will and activities of humans. We will return to this suggested issue of the various roles played by materiality later, when briefly concluding this review.

What is more important here is to notice that the practice of mentioning materiality in various ontologies of law while only stressing its merely instrumental and inert character in relation to the entities or phenomena assumed to be of much greater significance for law is quite popular also beyond the institutional theorisation, but often shares its Searlean sensitivities. For instance, one of the most vocal proponents of the already mentioned artifact theory of law, Luka Burazin, proposes that "legal systems should best be conceived as abstract artifacts, i.e., created immaterial objects existentially dependent on a variety of other entities" (Burazin 2022: 15; which, on a sidenote, can be seen as a significant change in his position, especially when we consider one of the previous expositions of his theory, where he stressed the assumed ontological immateriality of legal systems by saying that "a legal system would not cease to exist if, for example, all the original normative texts of a system were destroyed"; Burazin 2018: 113–114). In accordance with such a statement, materiality (understood very narrowly as above all documents with normative texts) is nothing more than a condition for law, but law itself is immaterial. That is why this position can be deemed representative of ontologies of law that notice materiality but still belittle it.

Thus, while materiality ignorance's presumably main fault is its counter-factuality and projecting a vision where human beings can independently, stripped of any material things, achieve what is practically unachievable without materiality, the fault of materiality belittling is different. From the perspective of flat ontology sensitivities, it is good that ontologies that fall under this category in any way mention materiality and admit some function of it for their main object of inquiry; however, they notice way too little. There is much more to materiality in general and for the sake of law than they are ready to admit.

1.4.4 **Intermezzo on *Contemporary Analytical Social Ontology***

Before moving to the third category – modest materiality equalisation – this is perhaps the right moment to briefly address some issues concerning the contemporary, largely analytically oriented field of social ontology, which was brought up by mentioning Searle. He still seems to be one of the most influential figures in it and among a significant part of those who work on the ontology of law (consider, especially, Beever 2021, as well as Pietrzykowski 2009). This field, due to the works of Searle himself and other scholars whose approaches are comparable to his, has become a highly popular area of research in recent years.

Among other factors, this may be explained by the impression of originality created around it, which is convincing for some. However, some of the most important representatives of the field are rightly criticised for totally disregarding psychology, sociology, social theory and relevant philosophical works, even classical ones, such as the already mentioned Lukács's *Zur Ontologie des gesellschaftlichen Seins*. For instance, "Searle does not engage with foundational thinkers in the realm of social ontology claiming instead the position of the 'first author' in the field" (Krier and Worrell 2017: 3). Indeed, not only does he completely omit *The Social Construction of Reality: A Treatise in the Sociology of Knowledge* by Peter L. Berger and Thomas Luckmann (1991) – an omission almost famous among social scientists – and an even earlier classic, Talcott Parsons (e.g. Parsons 1951), but one may also wonder at the way Searle treats Émile Durkheim (e.g. Durkheim 2013) and Max Weber (e.g. Weber 1947) in the main expositions of his own theory (Searle 1995: xii; 2010: 62, 105, 154). A similar thing can be said of another very significant figure in what contemporarily came to be named social ontology – Raimo Tuomela, who, for instance, in one of his earlier works *A Theory of Social Action* (Tuomela 1984: 57, 133, 493) is extremely brief in his engagement with Weber and Parsons (e.g. Parsons 1949). It is rather striking considering the contribution of these two crucial scholars to thinking about social action.

Most likely, such cases provoke statements on the main figures in the contemporary field of social ontology and their own suggestions or clear expressions about their originality, like the following: "[s]uch claims of originality are [...] a result of 'collective intentionality': these authors have agreed to ignore, avoid, and distantly disparage already foundational works" (Krier and Worrell

2017: 3; see also Becker 2011: 274–275). One can add to this the following question expressing some bewilderment in the face of many works in contemporary social ontology: How can one attempt to propose what are supposed to be philosophical foundations for social sciences practically without seriously engaging them or perhaps not knowing them well? However, to be more thorough and fair, one must also stress that not all authors who, to a certain extent, inspired the development of the commented field of research deserve such criticism. In the end, in *On Social Facts*, Margaret Gilbert (1989) approaches both Durkheim and Weber with much attention.

Having said that, of course, some important problems with what can be considered foundational figures and works for the contemporary field of social ontology may not be crucial for that field in the future, depending on how it will be developed. Looking at its current popularity – leaving the topic of how well it is justified – it surely will be developed. In the process, the practically paradigmatic model status of Searlean social ontology, in relevant literature (e.g. Burman 2023: 19–82), and its characteristic approach to materiality can be replaced by another framework.

Sticking to the materiality criterion, we can already see some social ontologies that emphasise in their accounts of various entities (objectively speaking also nonhuman, material) intentional human beings somehow reaching an agreement between them and then acting in coordination. This emphasis is to such an extent that materiality is dismissed even in accounts of given entities that, objectively speaking, are also nonhuman, which without materiality would even risk losing their identity. Not to be groundless, consider the following statement from Tuomela:

> an organization may also own or otherwise involve various material elements and tools, such as buildings, that it needs for fulfilling its functions, but it does not seem plausible to say that it is partly constituted by this kind of hardware.
>
> (Tuomela 2013: 15, footnote 9)

In other words, Dave Elder-Vass's – one of the few contemporary social ontologists who sees the need to take materiality much more into account – following commentary on the debates in which he himself partakes is most definitely correct, also with respect to much of the discussions on ontology of law:

> these debates have tended to ignore the non-human material world. Being charitable, we might say that we have abstracted from the influences of ordinary objects, but that would be misleading. Usually the work of social ontologists does not show any evidence that they have even considered whether abstracting from ordinary objects would be justifiable, and this is equally true of the advocates of many different and competing positions. Individualists focus on the causal contributions of human individuals to

> social events, while advocates of more structural positions have generally linked causation to groups of human individuals constituted into social forms of one kind or another – perhaps societies, families, or organisations, for example. Social ontology is largely enacted as a discourse about human beings and the question of whether higher forms might be produced by their interaction. Even the materiality of human beings themselves is often relegated to the background. The focus is placed instead on communication, language, and intentionality as if the material substrata of such phenomena were of no real significance to social interaction.
>
> (Elder-Vass 2017a: 90)

However, besides some part of contemporary, mostly analytically oriented social ontologies that can be said to be engaging materiality ignorance, and rather conservative and significantly belittling materiality approaches similar to Searle, whose "interest in the material object is merely that it provides a means of authenticating a meaning ascribed by humans and their linguistic practices" (Elder-Vass 2017a: 91), there are also participants of those debates that want to recognise materiality more fully. As mentioned, Elder-Vass, at least since his declaration "it is becoming increasingly clear to me that many social entities with causal powers are composed of not *only* groups of people but *also* nonhuman material objects" (Elder-Vass 2016: 113; see also his earlier work, e.g. Elder-Vass 2010: 157), has been more explicitly analysing the significance of materiality (Elder-Vass 2017a, 2017b).

Obviously though, considering the whole plethora of materiality's aspects and roles does not mean adopting a standpoint of a flat ontology. In the end, its idea assumes not only the pluralism of the entities considered but also their nonhierarchy (at least at the very beginning of inquiries about a chosen object). Having said that, even social ontologies that actually try to do justice to materiality may ultimately still be based on the idea of some form of human superiority. One may wonder whether this is not the case with one of the more influential voices in contemporary social ontology – Tony Lawson. When he talks about multicomponentality (Lawson 2019: 56) and social entities including both humans and material things (Lawson 2019: 63), he suggests a general flat ontology's sensitivity. However, his theory's central idea of social positioning – the creation of some positions within the social structure and occupying them, by both humans and nonhumans, who acquire as a result some specific statuses, also of broadly understood normative relevance (Lawson 2019: 12) – proves to be still strongly grounded in prioritising human interpersonal interactions, because "social reality is seen to depend fundamentally on the generalised acceptance" (Lawson 2019: 16). However, contemporary social ontologists do not necessarily have to fall back into more explicitly anthropocentric positions. It is proven by Sally Haslanger, who argues, among other things, that "at least some social phenomena are best understood as systems, or parts of systems, that involve more than individuals and their attitudes" and that "there is an interdependence between the material, the cultural, and the psychological in social systems, and this interdependence is crucial for many forms of social explanation" (Haslanger 2022: 514).

All this illustrates that there is much going on in the contemporary analytically oriented social ontology. One cannot exclude the possibility that, due to ongoing debates, materiality belittling will become increasingly limited (e.g. Burman 2023: 2, 75, 79, 86) and such a turnout will also influence those ontologists of law who like to inspire themselves with current social ontology.

1.4.5 Modest Materiality Equalisation

After this specific detour, we may think for a moment about the third option recognisable in the researched period – modest materiality equalisation. Over a century ago, Czesław Znamierowski, who to a large extent anticipated in his writings a field of social ontology in the spirit of Searle (as Lorini and Żełaniec 2013 convincingly show), considered the being of legal acts and proposed to understand them as a specific arrangement of heterogeneous elements, which is an indivisible whole, "a psychophysical complex" (Znamierowski 1921: 21). In particular, as its parts, Znamierowski considered the original physical document of an act, its various copies and subjective, mental processes of considering the contents of a legal act as valid. In other words, materiality, here considered narrowly as written or printed documents, grows in this position to be equal to mental and semantic elements, usually prioritised in the ontologies of law. To a certain extent, a similar approach can be seen in one of the clearest interventions in the ontology of law by Aleksander Peczenik (1984: 109), where he states that "the law is a complex (tuple) of legal norms (themselves being complexes of inscriptions or utterances and their meaning), some acts and mental processes of various persons involved in legislation, interpretation, etc., some other norms, and finally, each interpreter's weak evaluative endorsement". Materiality equalisation is present here in regarding inscriptions as indispensable parts of legal norms and in the effect of law in general.

These two examples are rather modest when it comes to equalising the significance of materiality for law with that of the other constituents or aspects of law. Ultimately, both Znamierowski and Peczenik speak here only of physical documents, whereas materiality embraces much more. Then, from the broadly understood perspective of a flat ontology, on the one hand, such modest materiality equalisation is good, as it, to a certain extent, pluralises what is understood as law in a mostly nonhierarchical way. On the other hand, it can be regarded as insufficiently pluralising because there are many other entities that can be regarded as indispensable for law, but they are not acknowledged in the commented accounts.

Despite such similarity, there is a significant difference between Znamierowski and Peczenik that is relevant here. Namely, Znamierowski did not only anticipate in some of his earlier writings social ontology in the Searlean type but also suggested regulatory activities that are not dependent on semantics and meaning or usually understood communication but involve intervening in the physical environment, which makes some behavioural choices practically impossible (Znamierowski 1934: 73–77; see also Łopatka 1998). From this perspective, it can be said that Znamierowski also anticipated, way before a somewhat similar remark in the second edition of Karl Olivecrona's *Law as Fact* (Olivecrona 1971: 129), what (among others) Latour is so famous for – showing convincingly how relevant are the ways in which the nonhumans act on us, humans (especially, Latour 1992).

1.4.6 Some Self-Criticism

The fourth and final category in the proposed review refers to ontologies of law that are clearly inspired by specific flat ontologies and, consequently, engage in much more outright, immodest materiality equalisation, which is only a part of their pluralisation and nonhierarchicality, along with their various other features. Ultimately, note that a flat ontology's characteristic features are not limited to the proposed approach to materiality. Given that such flat ontology-inspired ontologies of law are the most recent interventions in the debates on the fundamental questions concerning law, one cannot say that they are especially numerous. Under the last category of our review fall works of Margaret Davies and Andreas Philippopoulos-Mihalopoulos (especially Davies 2017 and Philippopoulos-Mihalopoulos 2015). However, some engagement with a flat ontology also appears in the work of David Delaney (especially, Delaney 2010: 14–15), not to mention that Latour himself – one of the flat ontologists as such – engaged law on more than one occasion (e.g. Latour 1988: 204, §3.4.3; 2010; 2013: 357–379; 2015). Given that these thinkers' analyses are directly related to the agenda set in this book, let us say something more about their contribution later, after some concluding comments on the review proposed thus far.

First is some self-criticism. As mentioned earlier, this review does not address explicitly, by name, several standpoints and authors important to the reflection on the ontology of law in the researched period. Moreover, when given some more time and space for investigations about them, it would most likely become clear that ascribing them confidently to a specific category concerning the treatment of materiality can be difficult. Hans Kelsen can come immediately to mind. Though his purificationist ambition to focus only on law and "to eliminate from the object of this description everything that is not strictly law" (Kelsen 1967: 1) could already justify putting him among other materiality ignorers, his concept of the spatial sphere of validity of norm (Kelsen 1967: 12) can somewhat complicate it.

Let us consider another example of the already mentioned Swedish legal realist Olivecrona and his following argument about legal rules:

> We talk of them as if they were always there as real entities. But this is not exact. It is impossible to ascribe a permanent existence to a rule of law or

> to any other rule. A rule exists only as the content of a notion in a human being. No notion of this kind is permanently present in the mind of anyone. The imperative appears in the mind only intermittently. Of course the position is not changed by the fact that the imperative words are put down in writing. The written text — in itself only figures on paper — has the function of calling up certain notions in the mind of the reader. That is all.
>
> (Olivecrona 1939: 47–48)

The last two sentences here suggest some form of materiality belittling, but all that precedes it sounds like a strongly intrapersonal ontology of law, comparable, to some commentators (e.g. Fittipaldi 2012: 12, footnote 9), with Petrażyckian vision.

Finally, when it comes to some recent examples, consider Robert S. Summers, who says the following:

> form and formal features hardly make up the whole of the law. Much in the effective functioning of law is not formal at all: rule content consisting of social policy or moral principle, various trained personnel, material resources, communicative devices, social acceptance, coercive capacity, and more.
>
> (Summers 1999: 238)

When he frequently refers to material resources (Summers 1999: 242, 243, 245, 246, 247), some may be tempted to consider him as engaging in materiality equalisation. However, Summers's emphasis on what he terms "form" strongly undermines such an impression. This emphasis is seen, for instance, in his words:

> formality is one of law's most important characteristics. Indeed, it may be that form is law's most foundational characteristic, for without form there can be no law at all, even when such non-formal ingredients of law as trained personnel, required material resources, and knowledge of effective legal technique happen to be readily available in abundance.
>
> (Summers 1999: 226)

Also undermining this impression is Summers speaking explicitly of the mentioned material resources only in terms of their complementariness (see later, fuller exposition of his theory, Summers 2006: 5, 14, 98, 127, 290). Despite acknowledging the role of materiality in law, though in rather vague terms – just consider the plethora of referents for "material resources" – he ultimately follows a hierarchical way of thinking and clearly prioritises the mental and ideational.

1.4.7 Early Reflections on Flat Ontology and Ontologies of Law

Despite the obvious problem of addressing explicitly, by name, only a small part of relevant voices in the ontology of law and some tensions that one can experience when attempting classification in line with materiality ignorance, belittling and its modest equalisation, the conducted review appears to realise its function. It provides a background against which the analyses of specific representatives of the mere idea of a flat ontology prove worthy of some effort. Here, we can bring to the fore the following, still early, remarks on the relation between the ontologies of law overviewed thus far and what flows from the mere idea of a flat ontology.

In reference to one of the most crucial debates in jurisprudence in my home country, Poland, on the ontological dimensionality of law (see, unfortunately not that numerous, English publications on it, e.g. Wróblewski 1986; Opałek 1999), we may imagine the scale between the extreme positions arguing in favour of strict ontological homogeneity or one-dimensionality of law and standpoints defending ontological heterogeneity or multidimensionality (Sarkowicz in Sarkowicz and Stelmach 1996: 23–28). One can imagine the former through, for instance, ontologies that would understand law to be an exclusively linguistic entity. In turn, the latter consider law not as something that is out of a specific domain of broadly understood reality but as an entity that transgresses a few domains. As mentioned earlier, the mere idea of a flat ontology invites us to abandon thinking about reality in terms of various domains. Nevertheless, the basic intuition out of classical Polish discussions on the ontology of law can be useful for our purposes here. Namely, a flat ontology suggests an extremely heterogeneous ontology of law, perhaps the actual one end of the imagined scale. In comparison, the ontologies of law in the researched period appear to be either homogeneous, confining law to a specific kind of being, which can be seen in various forms among ontologies that ignore materiality, or somehow heterogeneous, assuming a complex, multicomponent character of law. From the perspective of a flat ontology, the former ontologies of law can be regarded as strictly, even radically reductionist, taking the objective complexity of law and arguing that it is something homogeneous, out of a specific domain. In turn, even if the authors of the latter would consider their frameworks as already sufficiently showing the highly complicated character of law, from the perspective of a flat ontology, it would most likely still be too little, too selective and too conservative.

Speaking, between the lines, of radicality. At first glance, the mere idea of a flat ontology can be seen by some as insolent and, in fact, radical, with its utter pluralism and nonhierarchy and all that follows them. However, given the image of debates on the ontology of law in the researched period, we may propose a different narrative. According to it, a flat ontology promises a moderation, a middle ground between the specific extreme of extrapersonal ontologies that both deanthropocentrise and dematerialise law, the strong tendency to account for law in practically exclusively anthropocentric categories and the highly selective treatment of materiality (which often focuses more on paper and ink than on wires and concrete), frequently rendered as merely passive in the presence of humans and their thoughts, words and actions.

To recognise this moderation, let us summarise here the faults with respect to the materiality committed by reviewed ontologies or, to be more precise, their first three categories. The main fault of materiality ignorance is the counterfactuality and overestimation of the human possibilities to act beyond any material entities. The ontologies of law that fall under this category propose such a slimmed-down vision of what law is that they can even be regarded as paradoxical and self-defeating with respect to some of their other propositions. Ultimately, if someone dematerialises law and, at the same time, considers what that law does or should be doing in the material world of humans and not only humans, then the issue emerges on how to reconcile these two sentiments. One can either resign from the instrumental approach to law or stick to an exclusively immaterial law and argue, for instance, that law as such is mental or ideational, but it can influence through some other entities, like writings on a piece of paper. However, although one can assure that such entities are not necessary for law, they actually are. Similarly, if law – especially contemporary, developed in a massive and complex society – is seen by some in the communal life of ordinary people or professionals, in their agreements and conventions, then materiality should be acknowledged and stressed, given its importance to these phenomena. For humans themselves, bare, without materiality, cannot do much, also with respect to interactions with each other and creating and upholding some broadly understood stable order among them, including legal orders. Sticking, then, to materiality ignorance among those who work on the ontology of law provokes the very same critique Latour raises against materiality-ignorant sociologists:

> If sociologists had the privilege to watch more carefully baboons repairing their constantly decaying "social structure", they would have witnessed what incredible cost has been paid when the job is to maintain, for instance, social dominance with no thing at all, just social skills. [...] It's the power exerted through entities that don't sleep and associations that don't break down that allow power to last longer and expand further—and, to achieve such a feat, many more materials than social compacts have to be devised. This does not mean that the sociology of the social is useless, only that it might be excellent for studying baboons but not for studying humans.
>
> (Latour 2005: 70)

Materiality belittlers' fault is different, as they do not ignore what is in practice unignorable but see way too little in materiality. Being matrices for human meanings is just one role played by nonhumans, also with respect to law. Contemporary Western or Global Northern law would simply not exist without nonhumans. Materiality plays an invaluable part in law's creation, scope, maintenance and functioning. To acknowledge this, let us take up the test of removal and think of, for instance, the work of parliamentary commissions without computers, the breadth of contemporary law and its systemicity without printing and possibilities given by digital databases, law enforcement services stripped of their material equipment like surveillance cameras, dedicated cars and batons or court proceedings without courthouse. However, it would be significantly misguided to think that materiality is merely passive and servile. Just as we humans in our everyday lives often must adjust to the surrounding things and what they enable us or force us to do, law is similarly at the mercy of nonhumans. This is because computers and databases may malfunction, some rodents may bite through some crucial cables in a police car, or a courtroom may be in such poor condition aesthetically that the presiding judge's authority is also somewhat belittled. Even the strictly semantic components of law, the meanings of provisions in legal acts appear to fluctuate depending on their tangible referents. For instance, the punishment of imprisonment predicted in penal law may appear more or less serious and deterring due to what prisons and cells in a given country's penitentiary system look like. Indeed, humans ascribe meanings to nonhumans, but the exact way nonhumans are seems to influence back the meanings.

Finally, modest materiality equalisation's fault is conservatism in seeing as indispensable for law only a very small portion of nonhuman materiality. What was mentioned above, with respect to materiality belittling, and even earlier, for instance, when providing a general image of law adopted for investigations in this book, proves that there is much more to materiality than Znamierowski and Peczenik's mere inscriptions and papers, and it can also be equalised with other assumed components of law.

In comparison, a flat ontology and its representatives can avoid these faults. It also avoids anthropocentrism, which is so prevalent in accounting for law, especially through references to human interpersonal actions and communication, and thinking about reality in terms of different domains. While various reviewed ontologies of law are often clearly based on binary distinctions, like social-natural or is–ought, a flat ontology argues in favour of disrupting this dualistic way of thinking, as it can easily fall back into assuming (not proving) hierarchies. However, to be sure, such an antidualistic stance is quite easy to propose and uphold due to a very specific issue, which can also be deemed the most significant difference compared to the reviewed ontologies of law. Namely, a flat ontology programmatically considers that what exists on a specifically high level of generality, that what is stereotypically seen as, for instance, social and nonsocial, can be easily embraced with the same conceptual apparatus. This is because flat ontologies, as they are subjected to focused scrutiny below, often operate with universal, domain-neutral concepts, such as actor-network, assemblage or object. In comparison, what can be deemed as ontologies of law, which widely utilise concepts such as already mentioned social or institutional facts are already dedicated to some domain of reality (which implies other domains presumably requiring different concepts) and practically presuppose the main characteristics of entities to be investigated – that they are exclusively or predominantly human and social and, thus, their other aspects are rendered either inexistent or unimportant and merely a background.

1.4.8 Flat Ontology-Inspired Ontologies of Law (and Other Legal Studies)

Having brought to the fore rather the clearest and the most immediate divergences between a flat ontology and recurring features of how the ontology of law is often approached, we can, at last, move on to the still least numerous kind of ontologies of law, which clearly share some sentiments with the mere idea of a flat ontology, draw from its concrete representatives and are much more keen to engage in immodest materiality equalisation. Thus, they can be regarded as, at least, interesting propositions. However, they all share, with a bigger or smaller intensity, that what can be deemed as a problem in the legal treatment of flat ontologies, a problem that this book aims to address.

First, let us consider Davies's unlimiting of the law project (Davies 2017). It does tremendous work to broaden the perspectives about law, but it treats flat ontologies in a purely instrumental fashion. Davies takes from them various threads, ideas and conceptual tools for the sake of her own narrative and analysis or treats them as merely a background for them. However, as we will return to this issue in a moment, it is advisable to consider these ontologies not only as springboards for one's own project but also try to do them justice by treating them as subjects worthy of inquiry.

Moreover, building one's own proposal with some other theoretical resources may project a vision that they are very similar to each other. However, as already suggested, concrete flat ontologies, while in general adhering to pluralism and nonhierarchy, are very often different from each other. Referring to a few of them even on the single page may provoke their reading, which significantly blurs what is highly specific to them and how they can prove to be incompatible with each other in some crucial, even defining aspect.

Let us now return to Davies. Her most recent work on "ecolaw" (Davies 2022) can be seen as a somewhat different, even more radical, vitalistic project than that from the mentioned *Law Unlimited*. Namely, in the latest book, Davies takes something that most usually is associated with humans or some kinds of animals – normativity – and expands it to everything else, including nonhuman, nonanimal dead matter. In a way, then, the flat ontologies investigated in this book can be rendered as far from radical, even more than we considered above, because they simply argue that some rather very basic, primary features or regularities, such as possessing others, in the very broad sense, are common – can be found in everything. Davies's proposal to endow everything with normativity is, in comparison, very different.

When it comes to another example of the ontology of law inspired by flat ontologies, consider Philippopoulos-Mihalopoulos's highly original and eclectic (even more than Davies) spatialisation of law (Philippopoulos-Mihalopoulos 2015). He does not only engage in the same issues as Davies – treats various flat ontologies merely instrumentally for the sake of his own framework and does not pay enough attention to crucial differences between them. He is also explicitly sceptical about the idea of a flat ontology, which makes our projects even more different from each other. Just consider the juxtaposition of his notion of continuum with what he names flat ontology in, for instance, the main exposition of his theory (Philippopoulos-Mihalopoulos 2015: 3, 5, 11). He treats a flat ontology as something that would quite literally and radically equalise everything that exists. However, such a reading is in strict contradiction to what concrete flat ontologists propose. Ultimately, as mentioned earlier, a flat ontology is not about forbidding literally any difference but about forbidding the assumption or presupposition of any difference or hierarchy at the very beginning of inquiry about something. Consider, as an illustration of this point, the well-known argument of Latour that there can be hierarchies and relatively stable domination structures, but they are the product of numerous processes and should be accounted for – should be explained, not used as explanations (e.g. Latour 1996: 372), or Sergio Tonkonoff's reading of Tarde, which stresses the move from heterarchy to hierarchy (Tonkonoff 2017: 38, 75).

Back to the main thread, speaking of Philippopoulos-Mihalopoulos and legal geography, it is the field of legal inquiry that can actually be regarded as the first to draw inspiration from flat ontologies. Another one already mentioned, Delaney's nomospheric project (Delaney 2010: 14–15), comparable in its scope to that of Philippopoulos-Mihalopoulos, is one of the first instances of using Barad's AGR in a legal context, but in a rather brief if not perfunctory manner, while it deserves much more focused analyses from legal scholars.

While some of the latter scholars have engaged in general projects concerning the ontology of law using flat ontologies, as seen above, there are also scholars who have used them for somewhat different type of legal inquiries. There is a growing number of studies devoted to the careful analysis of some more concrete subjects, even way narrower than law as such or law in the contemporary Western or Global Northern context, which draw from flat ontologies. Given that these works are dedicated to some highly specific cases, events or phenomena, they ultimately devote much more attention to the chosen subject of inquiry and, in effect, treat theoretical resources instrumentally or as a background, without delving deep in their nuances and differences. Consider, for example, and restricting oneself here only to monographical works, Jannice Käll's posthumanisation of digital property (Käll 2023), Jana Norman's posthuman approach to legal subjectivity (Norman 2022), or that of Emily Jones (2023) look at international law's engagement in cutting-edge military technologies and pressing environmental issues through the lenses of posthumanism, which, interestingly, can be seen as following earlier studies on international law's relations to a myriad of material entities (Hohmann and Joyce 2018). These and many other comparable studies (e.g. Assiter 2021), also in the shorter chapter or article forms (e.g. Graham et al. 2017; Hohmann 2021; Käll 2022), are highly valuable contributions to their respective subject matters. However, they still do not appear to treat flat ontologies, their claim to universality and, thus, the question of their adequacy and value to law seriously enough to regard them as worthy of dedicated and detailed analyses, and not only as some resource that ultimately is treated quite superficially. This book fulfils this noticeable gap, proving itself to be quite distinct from both flat ontology-inspired contributions to the ontology of law and more specific studies focused on much narrower issues that draw from various flat ontologies.

1.5 Reasons for the Investigations and Their General Course

1.5.1 Situating the Book

In light of what was just said, we reach here the proper moment to explicate some reasons guiding this entire enterprise and provide some information on how and why we will proceed in the chapters to follow.

While the above remarks on Davies could have been treated as outright criticism, the truth is much more nuanced. Davies's call to end with more or less narrow conceptualisations of law and instead trying to draw a wider, even braver, more expanded view on "what is law?" is most definitely needed. However, there are at least two possibilities when it comes to that call. Either one can try to build, from scratch or with the use of various conceptual tools and inspirations, one's own original wide ontology of law, which would address all its assumed parts, or one can first try to verify whether there are some already made ontologies, which would simply be appropriate for such legal application. This book is grounded in a strong conviction that it is much more reasonable and, in a way, academically honest and fair to adopt the latter first. Accordingly, it seems necessary to verify the adequacy and value of some noticeable voices in humanities, philosophy and social sciences arguing in favour of a very wide approach in ontology, also in the ontology concerned with seemingly exclusively human-made, social entities. Flat ontologies are an example. In short, this book is a proposal of specific back-to-basics. Instead of mixing different threads from various flat ontologies and using them instrumentally only to move forward one's narrative, it tries to test them using law. Ultimately, this is the thing that should be done – flat ontologies have explicitly very general, universal ambitions, so it should be verified whether they meet their promise. Are they adequate to law? Even if they prove to be problematic in this respect, are they still somehow valuable for engagement with law?

While there are general, theoretical books about law that selectively utilise different threads from various flat ontologies (sometimes even those that are in opposition to each other) as springboards for the approaches they present, until now there has been no book that carefully investigates representative flat ontologies, as subjects worthy of dedicated research and not only of instrumental treatment, from the legal viewpoint. Moreover, works dealing with somewhat more concrete issues or empirical cases and drawing for their sake from flat ontologies do not treat them with much-needed care, attention and, dare we say, patience. Ultimately, while analysing, for instance, the regulatory environment concerning silkworms, one can quite easily end up being highly preoccupied with the details of this or any other comparably concrete issue and its intricacies. As a result, one will rather use some theoretical resources than wonder in a very focused manner about their usability for law in the first place. Against this background, as mentioned earlier, this book does the latter – something not done before – and fulfils the noticeable gap in the literature. It juxtaposes law with selected flat ontologies, with a strong focus on their theoretical details, whether they seem to fit law and what they offer for theoretical and practical engagement in law.

1.5.2 Representative Sample of Flat Ontologies

While we established some basic points of reference for investigations – we approximated the sense of law for their sake, provided an original overview of ontologies of law and proposed the reconstruction of mere idea of flat ontology – we did not justify the sample of concrete flat ontologies to analyse. We only suggested, during the above, that we will deal with Tardean MON, Latourian ANT, DeLandaean AST, Baradian AGR and Harmanian OOO. However, the question is why analyse these and not some others.

First, all chosen flat ontologies are explicit about their assumed most basic units of analysis or assumed components of reality, which makes them initially very clear and convenient for our agenda. For Tarde, it is monad; for Latour, actor-network; for DeLanda, assemblage; for Barad, intra-action; and for Harman, object. Moreover, all chosen flat ontologies constitute coherent discourse, in the sense that, more or less, all of them engage with each other. Tarde's MON is not only regarded as a specific ancestor of Latour's ANT (Latour 2002: 117). Both are also commented on from the perspective of Harman's OOO (Harman 2009, 2012). Moreover, Harman comments on DeLanda's AST (e.g. Harman 2010: 170–198) and Barad's AGR (e.g. Harman 2016a) but also works with DeLanda (DeLanda and Harman 2017).

In consequence, this book appears as the first attempt at a careful analysis of this flat ontology discourse, on the example of its closely connected representatives, from the perspective of law. With respect to the novelty of this book, one can respond that there is Kyle McGee's (2014) study, but it is devoted entirely to Latour (and does not consider Latour's relevant post-2014 work on law; Latour 2015), while this book analyses not only ANT but also other flat ontologies from the legal perspective. Even when dealing with Latourian ANT, we will still manage to bring to the fore issues that appear to be underanalysed in the relevant debates.

Reaching the end of the reasons for the proposed selection, we can say the following. Naturally, law, due to its complex social existence and functions, may come across as a specific kind of being to analyse using rather highly abstract ontologies claiming to be universal in their applications. Fortunately, all flat ontologies chosen are explicitly thought of as useable in the context of social entities and phenomena. Even OOO has been applied in *par excellence* social contexts both by Harman himself (Harman 2016b; 2018: 105–146) and other scholars (e.g. Pierides and Woodman 2012; Lemke 2021: 21–39; Franco et al. 2022). Finally, along with personal ambitions and actual achievements of Tarde, Latour, DeLanda, Barad and Harman, the ways of thinking represented by them became a significant, widely commented subject of interest among a wide variety of scholars, including social scientists. This also justifies choosing them.

I.5.3 Adopted Approach

With fuller knowledge of what and why we will deal with below, let us also address the issue of how we will do it. Quite important in this respect is the intended readership. The book can be said to be written with emphasis on a specific type of reader in mind – people with interest and competence in general inquiries about law, who may not be already acquainted with flat ontologies.

Having said that, it does not mean that readers who already know, to a lesser or greater extent, the analysed frameworks will not find anything new. First, the book contains what can be said to be authorial interpretations and reconstructions of chosen flat ontologies, which may be significantly different from that of some of the readers with some prior orientation in relevant frameworks. In addition, even though the discourse referring to flat ontologies is not new, one can still say that various manners of reading, interpreting and using flat ontologies are only emerging as there are many uncertainties as soon as one delves deeper into these frameworks. Second, even those who are somehow familiar with the discussed flat ontologies, even broadly understood legal scholars and people with interest in law, will see the novelty in what follows, because there has been no comparable confrontation of various flat ontologies, focused on their basic figures for ontological inquiries, with law, which in turn allows to juxtapose these frameworks with each other, bring to fore their specifics and find what is problematic in them and what is still inspiring and useful, perhaps not only for law.

Such a general assumption about readership has further consequences. Given that this book is, to a certain extent, an exercise in thinking about law along with flat ontologies in a very focused manner, for those who may have their first contact with them through this work, flat ontologies must first be properly reconstructed and introduced. Each of the following five chapters – devoted to one of the chosen flat ontologies – is composed of four comparable sections. The first one provides some necessary basic context for a given flat ontology and scholar responsible for it; in particular, it puts it into a broader perspective of relevant intellectual currents and inspirations and justifies the selection of the source material utilised in the analyses. The second section reconstructs and discusses some fundamental sentiments, sensitivities and commitments underlying the given framework, introducing it. The penultimate section focuses on the details of the main unit for ontological inquiries assumed in the analysed flat ontology. All these steps are necessary for the sake of intended readers and to enable them as much as possible to think with flat ontologies when approaching law. Moreover, dedicating a separate chapter for each flat ontology fits well our ambition of doing justice to each framework and not mixing these frameworks with one another. In short, we try to be as far as possible from the so-called ecumenical approach to these frameworks (Mitchell 2014: xx, 180–181, footnote 21) and from treating their lexicon too lightly (Usher 2019: 14). After such indispensable work, the final section in each of the following five chapters discusses law from the perspective of the selected flat ontology. As one can easily guess, the Conclusion of the book gathers and summarises all the results concerning the adequacy question and value question. It also addresses some potential paths for furthering what this book is so focused on – intersecting flat ontologies with general inquiries about law.

Returning to the crux of investigations to follow, given the relatively narrow yet of fundamental significance research questions posed in this book, often the technical details we engage in, the general reasons guiding this work and its intended readership, when dealing with each of the chosen flat ontologies, there are several things we are not doing. While we provide a glimpse into the inspirations and sources for the analysed flat ontologies, we do not assess, for instance, how much the latter are faithful to the former. Moreover, given that the work of each chosen flat ontologists reaches way beyond ontology, we do not provide a comprehensive overview of their respective oeuvres. Such a move is unnecessary given the agenda set for this work. It, in connection with the intended readers, also has the following consequence. When dealing with flat ontologies themselves, mostly in the second and third sections of the five chapters to follow, the analyses follow largely authorial, original interpretations of the source material in the form of relevant writings of the selected thinkers. As such, they are a result of the not uncommon sentiment expressed by, for instance, Ian Hacking (Madsen et al. 2013: 44), that when engaging the thought of an influential thinker, one should exclusively focus on their work and not their various commentators. While an exclusive focus on the source material would be rather understandable in the case of this book, it ultimately is not that puristic. Namely, below, we do not avoid making some references to relevant secondary literature. Nevertheless, given the reasons driving this book, we will rather keep such engagement to a minimum. However, what we actually try to avoid at all costs below is imposing on the reconstructions and discussions of source materials that precede their explicit confrontations with law, concepts and notions clearly foreign to them. In other words, this work can be said to be quite different from, for instance, David Toews's recent engagement with Tarde (Toews 2022: 75), where Tardean ideas seem to be significantly filtered through Toews's favoured vocabulary, like Donald Rumsfeld's known unknowns and unknown unknowns (see also Krogerus and Tschäppeler 2023: 84–87), or the Harmanian take on Latourian ontology, which appears to be largely subordinated to Harman's own theoretical project (e.g. Harman 2009). Of course, this does not imply that we are prejudging the quality of these and other similar works in relation to the present work. They are just different from this book, as there have been, to date, no comparable efforts of critical and highly detailed confrontation of law with the main flat ontologies.

Finally, before we proceed, in line with all talk of "confrontation" here, one can easily have the impression that the general aim here is to structure a somewhat different way of thinking about the world and its implications for thinking about law. In reference to the title of the Series in which this book is published, one can say that this book is about confronting some important yet general intellectual discourse with law and jurisprudential discourse. However, another interpretation is also in place or even more apt. The discourse of so grand, universal ambitions as that of flat ontologies is already a discourse about law, as law is just another thing in the world that these frameworks attempt to grasp. Interestingly, most authors considered in the following chapters do not engage law explicitly. Nevertheless, since they practically make the claim to be universal, they also, willingly or not, engage law. From such an angle, the book is not about confronting some discourse with a specific object and discourse about it but about a kind of discourse of law that needs to be done some justice to, brought to the fore and have some attention and focus devoted to in order to assess what it says about law, to what extent it is acceptable and convincing and what its problems and controversies are.

References

Allott, Antony. 1980. *The Limits of Law*. London: Butterworths.

Andina, Tiziana. 2016. *An Ontology for Social Reality*. Trans.: Sarah De Sanctis. London: Palgrave Macmillan.

Ash, James. 2020. Flat Ontology and Geography. *Dialogues in Human Geography* 10 (3): 345–361.

Assiter, Alison. 2021. *A New Theory of Human Rights: New Materialism and Zoroastrianism*. Lanham: Rowman & Littlefield.

Barad, Karen. 2007. *Meeting the Universe Halfway: Quantum Physics and the Entanglement of Matter and Meaning*. Durham: Duke University Press.

Bauman, Richard A. 1996. *Crime and Punishment in Ancient Rome*. London: Routledge.

Becker, Howard S. 2011. [Reviews of John R. Searle, *Making the Social World: The Structure of Human Civilization*; Paul A. Boghossian, *Fear of Knowledge: Against Relativism and Constructivism*]. *Science, Technology, & Human Values* 36 (2): 273–279.

Bennett, Jane. 2010. *Vibrant Matter: A Political Ecology of Things*. Durham: Duke University Press.

Beever, Allan. 2021. *Law's Reality: A Philosophy of Law*. Cheltenham: Edward Elgar.

Berger, Peter L., and Thomas Luckmann. 1991. *The Social Construction of Reality: A Treatise in the Sociology of Knowledge*. London: Penguin Books.

Bhaskar, Roy. 2008. *A Realist Theory of Science*. Abingdon: Routledge.

Boehme-Neßler, Volker. 2011. *Pictorial Law: Modern Law and the Power of Pictures*. Trans.: Martina Birkhoff and Lindsay Gasser. Heidelberg: Springer.

Braidotti, Rosi. 2013. *The Posthuman*. Cambridge: Polity Press.

Brassier, Ray. 2015. Deleveling: Against "Flat Ontologies". In *Onder invloed: Wijsgerig festiwal Drift, 2014* [*Under Influence: Philosophical Festival Drift, 2014*], Channa van Dijk, Eva van der Graaf, Michiel den Haan, Rosa de Jong, Christiaan Roodenburg, Dyane Til and Deva Waal (eds), 64–80. Amsterdam: Omnia.

Broderick, Albert (ed.). 1970. *The French Institutionalists: Maurice Hauriou, Georges Renard, Joseph T. Delos*. Trans.: Mary Welling. Cambridge, MA: Harvard University Press.

Bröstl, Alexander. 2016. 20th-Century Legal Philosophy in Czechoslovakia, the Czech Republic, and the Slovak Republic. In *Legal Philosophy in the Twentieth Century: The Civil Law World. Tome 1: Language Areas*, Enrico Pattaro and Corrado Roversi (eds), 613–634. Dordrecht: Springer.

Bryant, Levi R. 2011. *The Democracy of Objects*. Ann Arbor: Open Humanities Press.

Burazin, Luka. 2018. Legal Systems as Abstract Institutional Artifacts. In *Law as an Artifact*, Luka Burazin, Kenneth Einar Himma and Corrado Roversi (eds), 112–135. Oxford: Oxford University Press.

Burazin, Luka. 2022. Legal Systems as Abstract Artifacts. In *The Artifactual Nature of Law*, Luka Burazin, Kenneth Einar Himma, Corrado Roversi and Paweł Banaś (eds), 1–15. Cheltenham: Edward Elgar Publishing.

Burman, Åsa. 2023. *Nonideal Social Ontology: The Power View*. New York: Oxford University Press.

Davies, Margaret. 2017. *Law Unlimited: Materialism, Pluralism, and Legal Theory*. Abingdon: Routledge.

Davies, Margaret. 2022. *EcoLaw: Legality, Life, and the Normativity of Nature*. Abingdon: Routledge.

DeLanda, Manuel. 2002. *Intensive Science and Virtual Philosophy*. London: Continuum.

DeLanda, Manuel, and Graham Harman. 2017. *The Rise of Realism*. Cambridge: Polity Press.

Delaney, David. 2010. *The Spatial, the Legal and the Pragmatics of World-Making: Nomospheric Investigations*. Abingdon: Routledge.

De Sousa e Brito, José, José Manuel Aroso Linhares, Luís Meneses do Vale, Ana Margarida Simões Gaudêncio and Alessandro Serpe. 2016. 20th-Century Legal Philosophy in Portugal. In *Legal Philosophy in the Twentieth Century: The Civil Law World. Tome 1: Language Areas*, Enrico Pattaro and Corrado Roversi (eds), 503–530. Dordrecht: Springer.

Durkheim, Émile. 2013. *The Rules of Sociological Method and Selected Texts on Sociology and its Method*. Second Edition. Ed.: Steven Lukes. Trans.: W. D. Halls. Basingstoke: Palgrave Macmillan.

Ehrenberg, Kenneth M. 2016. *The Functions of Law*. Oxford: Oxford University Press.

Ehrlich, Eugen. 1922. The Sociology of Law. Trans.: Nathan Isaacs. *Harvard Law Review* 36 (2): 130–145.

Elder-Vass, Dave. 2010. *The Causal Power of Social Structures: Emergence, Structure and Agency*. Cambridge: Cambridge University Press.

Elder-Vass, Dave. 2016. *The Profit and Gift in the Digital Economy*. Cambridge: Cambridge University Press.

Elder-Vass, Dave. 2017a. Material Parts in Social Structures. *Journal of Social Ontology* 3 (1): 89–105.

Elder-Vass, Dave. 2017b. Materialising Social Ontology. *Cambridge Journal of Economics* 41 (5): 1437–1451.

Ferrando, Francesca. 2019. *Philosophical Posthumanism*. London: Bloomsbury.
Finnis, John. 2011. *Natural Law and Natural Rights*. Second Edition. Oxford: Oxford University Press.
Fittipaldi, Edoardo. 2012. *Everyday Legal Ontology: A Psychological and Linguistic Investigation within the Framework of Leon Petrażycki's Theory of Law*. Milan: Edizioni Universitarie di Lettere Economia Diritto.
Foucault, Michel. 1978. *The History of Sexuality: Volume 1: An Introduction*. Trans.: Robert Hurley. New York: Pantheon Books.
Fox, Nick J., and Pam Alldred. 2017. *Sociology and the New Materialism: Theory, Research, Action*. London: Sage Publications.
Fox, Nick J., and Pam Alldred. 2018. Social Structures, Power and Resistance in Monist Sociology: (New) Materialist Insights. *Journal of Sociology* 54 (3): 315–330.
Franco, Paolo, Robin Canniford and Marcus Phipps. 2022. Object-Oriented Marketing Theory. *Marketing Theory* 22 (3): 401–420.
Fuller, Lon L. 1969. *The Morality of Law*. Revised Edition. New Haven: Yale University Press.
Gilbert, Margaret. 1989. *On Social Facts*. Princeton: Princeton University Press.
Grabowski, Andrzej. 2013. *Juristic Concept of the Validity of Statutory Law: A Critique of Contemporary Legal Nonpositivism*. Trans.: Małgorzata Kiełtyka. Berlin: Springer.
Graham, Nicole, Margaret Davies and Lee Godden. 2017. Broadening Law's Context: Materiality in Socio-Legal Research. *Griffith Law Review* 26 (4): 480–510.
Haraway, Donna. 1988. Situated Knowledges: The Science Question in Feminism and the Privilege of Partial Perspective. *Feminist Studies* 14 (3): 575–599.
Haraway, Donna. 2003. Cyborgs to Companion Species: Reconfiguring Kinship in Technoscience. In *Chasing Technoscience: Matrix for Materiality*, Don Ihde and Evan Selinger (eds), 58–82. Bloomington: Indiana University Press.
Harman, Graham. 2009. *Prince of Networks: Bruno Latour and Metaphysics*. Melbourne: re.press.
Harman, Graham. 2010. *Towards Speculative Realism: Essays and Lectures*. Winchester: Zero Books.
Harman, Graham. 2012. On the Supposed Societies of Chemicals, Atoms, and Stars in Gabriel Tarde. In *Savage Objects*, Godofredo Pereira (ed.), 33–43. Lisbon: INCM.
Harman, Graham. 2016a. Agential and Speculative Realism: Remarks on Barad's Ontology. *Rhizomes: Cultural Studies in Emerging Knowledge* 30.
Harman, Graham. 2016b. *Immaterialism: Objects and Social Theory*. Cambridge: Polity Press.
Harman, Graham. 2018. *Object-Oriented Ontology: A New Theory of Everything*. London: Penguin Books.
Hart, H. L. A. 2012. *The Concept of Law*. Third Edition. Oxford: Oxford University Press.
Hartmann, Nicolai. 1953. *New Ways of Ontology*. Trans.: Reinhard C. Kuhn. Chicago: Henry Regnery Company.
Haslanger, Sally. 2022. Failures of Methodological Individualism: The Materiality of Social Systems. *Journal of Social Philosophy* 53 (4): 512–534.
Himma, Kenneth E. 2019. *Morality and the Nature of Law*. Oxford: Oxford University Press.
Himma, Kenneth E. 2020. *Coercion and the Nature of Law*. Oxford: Oxford University Press.

Hohmann, Jessie. 2021. Diffuse Subjects and Dispersed Power: New Materialist Insights and Cautionary Lessons for International Law. *Leiden Journal of International Law* 34 (3): 585–606.

Hohmann, Jessie, and Daniel Joyce (eds). 2018. *International Law's Objects*. Oxford: Oxford University Press.

Jones, Brandon. 2014. Alfred North Whitehead's Flat Ontology: Casting the Bifurcation of Nature as the Other Hard Problem of Consciousness. *Journal of Consciousness Studies* 21 (5–6): 174–195.

Jones, Emily. 2023. *Feminist Theory and International Law: Posthumanist Perspectives*. Abingdon: Routledge.

Käll, Jannice. 2022. Critical Posthumanism, Justice, and Law. In *Palgrave Handbook of Critical Posthumanism*, Stefan Herbrechter, Ivan Callus, Manuela Rossini, Marija Grech, Megen de Bruin-Molé and Christopher John Müller (eds), 629–649. Cham: Palgrave Macmillan.

Käll, Jannice. 2023. *Posthuman Property and Law: Commodification and Control through Information, Smart Spaces and Artificial Intelligence*. Abingdon: Routledge.

Kelsen, Hans. 1967. *Pure Theory of Law*. Trans: Max Knight. Berkeley: University of California Press.

Krier, Daniel, and Mark P. Worrell. 2017. The Social Ontology of Capitalism: An Introduction. In *The Social Ontology of Capitalism*, Daniel Krier and Mark P. Worrell (eds), 1–11. New York: Palgrave Macmillan.

Krogerus, Mikael, and Roman Tschäppeler. 2023. *The Decision Book: Fifty Models for Strategic Thinking*. New, fully revised edition. Trans.: Jenny Piening. London: Profile Books.

Lagerspetz, Eerik. 1995. *The Opposite Mirrors: An Essay on the Conventionalist Theory of Institutions*. Dordrecht: Springer.

La Torre, Massimo. 2010. *Law as Institution*. Dordrecht: Springer.

Latour, Bruno. 1988. *The Pasteurization of France*. Trans.: Alan Sheridan and John Law. Cambridge: Harvard University Press.

Latour, Bruno. 1992. Where Are the Missing Masses? The Sociology of a Few Mundane Artifacts. In *Shaping Technology/Building Society: Studies in Sociotechnical Change*, Wiebe E. Bijker and John Law (eds), 225–258. Cambridge, MA: The MIT Press.

Latour, Bruno. 1993. *We Have Never Been Modern*. Trans: Catherine Porter. Cambridge: Harvard University Press.

Latour, Bruno. 1996. On Actor-Network Theory: A Few Clarifications. *Soziale Welt* 47 (4): 369–381.

Latour, Bruno. 2002. Gabriel Tarde and the End of the Social. In *The Social in Question: New Bearings in History and the Social Sciences*, Patrick Joyce (ed.), 117–132. London: Routledge.

Latour, Bruno. 2004. *Politics of Nature: How to Bring the Sciences into Democracy*. Trans: Catherine Porter. Cambridge: Harvard University Press.

Latour, Bruno. 2005. *Reassembling the Social: An Introduction to Actor-Network Theory*. Oxford: Oxford University Press.

Latour, Bruno. 2010. *The Making of Law: An Ethnography of the Conseil d'État*. Trans.: Marina Brilman and Alain Pottage. Rev.: Author. Cambridge: Polity Press.

Latour, Bruno. 2013. *An Inquiry into Modes of Existence: An Anthropology of the Moderns*. Trans.: Catherine Porter. Cambridge: Harvard University Press.

Latour, Bruno. 2015. The Strange Entanglement of Jurimorphs. In *Latour and the Passage of Law*, Kyle McGee (ed.), 331–353. Edinburgh: Edinburgh University Press.

Law, John. 1992. Notes on the Theory of the Actor-Network: Ordering, Strategy, and Heterogeneity. *Systems Practice* 5 (4): 379–393.

Lawson, Tony. 2019. *The Nature of Social Reality: Issues in Social Ontology*. Abingdon: Routledge.

Lemke, Thomas. 2021. *The Government of Things: Foucault and the New Materialisms*. New York: New York University Press.

Lessig, Lawrence. 2006. *Code: Version 2.0*. New York: Basic Books.

Lorini, Giuseppe, and Stefano Moroni. 2022. Non-Propositional Regulation. *Philosophical Investigations* 45 (4): 512–527.

Lorini, Giuseppe, Stefano Moroni and Olimpia Giuliana Loddo. 2021. Deontic Artifacts. Investigating the Normativity of Objects. *Philosophical Explorations* 24 (2): 185–203.

Lorini, Giuseppe, Stefano Moroni and Olimpia Giuliana Loddo. 2023. Regulatory Artifacts: Prescribing, Constituting, Steering. *International Journal for the Semiotics of Law* 36 (1): 211–225.

Lorini, Giuseppe, and Wojciech Żełaniec. 2013. And Yet there was Some: Czesław Znamierowski's Social Ontology. In *The Nature of Social Reality*, Claudia Stancati, Alfredo Givigliano, Emanuele Fadda and Giuseppe Cosenza (eds), 182–197. Newcastle upon Tyne: Cambridge Scholars Publishing.

Lovejoy, Arthur O. 1964. *The Great Chain of Being: A Study of the History of an Idea*. Cambridge: Harvard University Press.

Luhmann, Niklas. 2004. *Law as a Social System*. Trans.: Klaus A. Ziegert. Ed.: Fatima Kastner, Richard Nobles, David Schiff and Rosamund Ziegert. Oxford: Oxford University Press.

Luhmann, Niklas. 2013. *Theory of Society, Volume 2*. Trans.: Rhodes Barrett. Stanford: Stanford University Press.

Lukács, Georg (György). 1984. *Prolegomena: Zur Ontologie des gesellschaftlichen Seins. 1. Halbband* [*Prolegomenon: On the Ontology of Social Being. First Volume*]. Ed.: Frank Benseler. Darmstadt: Hermann Luchterhand Verlag.

Łopatka, Adam. 1998. Rules of Conduct Established by Physical Creations. In *Sources of Law and Legislation: Proceedings of the 17th World Congress of the International Association for Philosophy of Law and Social Philosophy (IVR), Bologna, June 16–21, 1995, vol. 3*, Elspeth Attwooll and Paolo Comanducci (eds), 71–73. Stuttgart: Franz Steiner Verlag.

MacCormick, Neil, and Ota Weinberger. 1992. *An Institutional Theory of Law: New Approaches to Legal Positivism*. Trans.: Ruth Adler and Neil MacCormick. Dordrecht: D. Reidel.

Madsen, Ole Jacob, Johannes Servan and Simen Andersen Øyen. 2013. "I Am a Philosopher of the Particular Case": An Interview with the 2009 Holberg Prizewinner Ian Hacking. *History of the Human Sciences* 26 (3): 32–51.

Marmor, Andrei. 2018. Law, Fiction, and Reality. In *Law as an Artifact*, Luka Burazin, Kenneth Einar Himma and Corrado Roversi (eds), 44–60. Oxford: Oxford University Press.

Marmor, Andrei. 2023. *Foundations of Institutional Reality*. New York: Oxford University Press.

McGee, Kyle. 2014. *Bruno Latour: The Normativity of Networks*. Abingdon: Routledge.

Mitchell, J. Allan. 2014. *Becoming Human: The Matter of the Medieval Child*. Minneapolis: University of Minnesota Press.

Mulcahy, Linda. 2011. *Legal Architecture: Justice, Due Process and the Place of Law*. Abingdon: Routledge.

Mussell, Simon. 2017. *Critical Theory and Feeling: The Affective Politics of the Early Frankfurt School*. Manchester: Manchester University Press.

Norman, Jana. 2022. *Posthuman Legal Subjectivity: Reimagining the Human in the Anthropocene*. Abingdon: Routledge.

Olivecrona, Karl. 1939. *Law as Fact*. Copenhagen: Ejnar Munksgaard.

Olivecrona, Karl. 1971. *Law as Fact*. Second Edition. London: Stevens & Sons.

Opałek, Kazimierz. 1999. The Complexity of Law and of the Methods of Its Study. In Kazimierz Opałek, *Selected Papers in Legal Philosophy*. Ed.: Jan Woleński, 49–62. Dordrecht: Springer.

Parsons, Talcott. 1949. *The Structure of Social Action: A Study in Social Theory with Special Reference to a Group of Recent European Writers*. New York: The Free Press.

Parsons, Talcott. 1951. *The Social System*. Glencoe: The Free Press.

Pattaro, Enrico. 1991. A Final Word. In *Controversies about Law's Ontology*, Paul Amselek and Neil MacCormick (eds), 142–152. Edinburgh: Edinburgh University Press.

Peczenik, Aleksander. 1984. Legal Data. An Essay about the Ontology of Law. In *Theory of Legal Science: Proceedings of the Conference on Legal Theory and Philosophy of Science, Lund, Sweden, December 11–14, 1983*, Aleksander Peczenik, Lars Lindahl and Bert van Roermund (eds), 97–120. Dordrecht: D. Reidel Publishing.

Petrażycki, Leon. 1955. *Law and Morality*. Trans: Hugh W. Babb. Cambridge: Harvard University Press.

Philippopoulos-Mihalopoulos, Andreas. 2013. Critical Autopoiesis and the Materiality of Law. *International Journal for the Semiotics of Law* 27 (2): 389–418.

Philippopoulos-Mihalopoulos, Andreas. 2015. *Spatial Justice: Body, Lawscape, Atmosphere*. Abingdon: Routledge.

Pickering, Andrew. 2008. New Ontologies. In *The Mangle in Practice. Science, Society and Becoming*, Andrew Pickering and Keith Guzik (eds), 1–14. Durham: Duke University Press.

Pierides, Dean, and Dan Woodman. 2012. Object-Oriented Sociology and Organizing in the Face of Emergency: Bruno Latour, Graham Harman and the Material Turn. *The British Journal of Sociology* 63 (4): 662–679.

Pietrzykowski, Tomasz. 2009. John R. Searle i ontologia prawa [John R. Searle and Ontology of Law]. *Studia Prawnicze* [*The Legal Studies*] 1–2 (179–180): 7–41.

Romano, Santi. 2017. *The Legal Order*. Ed. and trans.: Mariano Croce. Abingdon: Routledge.

Roversi, Corrado. 2018a. On the Artifactual—and Natural—Character of Legal Institutions. In *Law as an Artifact*, Luka Burazin, Kenneth Einar Himma and Corrado Roversi (eds), 89–111. Oxford: Oxford University Press.

Roversi, Corrado. 2018b. Ontology of Law. In *Encyclopedia of the Philosophy of Law and Social Philosophy*, Mortimer Sellers and Stephan Kirste (eds). Dordrecht: Springer. https://doi.org/10.1007/978-94-007-6730-0_59-1.

Ruiter, Dick W. P. 2001. *Legal Institutions*. Dordrecht: Springer.

Sarkowicz, Ryszard, and Jerzy Stelmach. 1996. *Teoria prawa* [*Theory of Law*]. Kraków: Wydawnictwo Uniwersytetu Jagiellońskiego.

Schaffer, Jonathan. 2009. On What Grounds What. In *Metametaphysics: New Essays on the Foundations of Ontology*, David Chalmers, David Manley and Ryan Wasserman (eds), 347–383. Oxford: Clarendon Press.

Schatzki, Theodore R. 2019. *Social Change in a Material World*. Abingdon: Routledge.

Searle, John R. 1995. *The Construction of Social Reality*. New York: The Free Press.

Searle, John R. 2010. *Making the Social World: The Structure of Human Civilization*. Oxford: Oxford University Press.

Studnicki, Franciszek. 1968. Some Applications of Communication Theory to Law. *Archivum Iuridicum Cracoviense* 1: 25–33.

Summers, Robert S. 1999. My Philosophy of Law. In *The Law in Philosophical Perspectives*, Luc J. Wintgens (ed.), 225–251. Dordrecht: Springer.

Summers, Robert S. 2006. *Form and Function in a Legal System: A General Study*. Cambridge: Cambridge University Press.

Tampio, Nicholas. 2015. *Deleuze's Political Vision*. Lanham: Rowman & Littlefield.

Toews, David. 2022. *Gabriel Tarde: The Future of the Artificial*. Abingdon: Routledge.

Tonkonoff, Sergio. 2017. *From Tarde to Deleuze and Foucault: The Infinitesimal Revolution*. Cham: Palgrave Macmillan.

Tuomela, Raimo. 1984. *A Theory of Social Action*. Dordrecht: D. Reidel.

Tuomela, Raimo. 2013. Who Is Afraid of Group Agents and Group Minds?. In *The Background of Social Reality: Selected Contributions from the Inaugural Meeting of ENSO*, Michael Schmitz, Beatrice Kobow and Hans Bernhard Schmid (eds), 13–35. Dordrecht: Springer.

Tuzet, Giovanni. 2018. A Strange Kind of Artifact. In *Law as an Artifact*, Luka Burazin, Kenneth Einar Himma and Corrado Roversi (eds), 217–238. Oxford: Oxford University Press.

Usher, Phillip John. 2019. *Exterranean: Extraction in the Humanist Anthropocene*. New York: Fordham University Press.

Watt, Gary. 2013. *Dress, Law and Naked Truth: A Cultural Study of Fashion and Form*. London: Bloomsbury.

Weber, Max. 1947. *The Theory of Social and Economic Organization*. Trans.: A. M. Henderson and Talcott Parsons. Ed.: Talcott Parsons. Glencoe: The Free Press.

Wolfe, Cary. 2010. *What Is Posthumanism?*. Minneapolis: University of Minnesota Press.

Wróblewski, Jerzy. 1986. Problems of Ontological Complexity of Law. *Theoria: An International Journal for Theory, History and Foundations of Science. SEGUNDA EPOCA* 1 (3): 641–654.

Załuski, Wojciech. 2009. *Evolutionary Theory and Legal Philosophy*. Cheltenham: Edward Elgar.

Znamierowski, Czesław. 1921. O przedmiocie i fakcie społecznym [On the Social Object and the Social Fact]. *Przegląd Filozoficzny* [*Philosophical Review*] 24 (1–2): 1–33.

Znamierowski, Czesław. 1934. *Podstawowe pojęcia teorji prawa. Część pierwsza. Układ prawny i norma prawna* [*Basic Concepts of Legal Theory. Part One. Legal System and Legal Norm*]. Second Edition. Poznań: Górski i Tetzlaw.

Chapter 2

Gabriel Tarde's Monadology (of Law); or, Will Law Still Exist If Some Parts of It Are Removed?

2.1 Not … an Easily Classifiable Thinker

2.1.1 Also a Science-Fiction Author

Let us begin with a thinker who, though not usually brought up in discussions on flat ontology, can most definitely be regarded as proposing one – Gabriel Tarde. Before focusing on his proposal, we should first acknowledge how much of a difficult-to-qualify person he was.

Tarde, lawyer by education, despite leaving a considerable intellectual legacy, cannot be imagined as a stereotypical academic practically buried in books and focused exclusively on his research. For a significant part of his life, he worked as an investigating judge – legal practice was no stranger to him. Moreover, his highly imaginative thinking apparently could not find sufficient output only in such intellectual work, because Tarde also wrote poems and even an entire science-fiction novel, translated as *Underground Man* (Tarde 1905).

This diversity is perhaps most clearly seen in his academic works. His practical work for the justice system and public administration can be connected with his interest and output in criminology and the philosophy of punishment (Tarde 1912). In addition to this line of his research, which can be regarded as addressing somewhat narrower subjects, are his works devoted to economic matters (Tarde 1902) and social theory (e.g. Tarde 1899, 1903). Most likely, the latter, built around such categories as imitation, opposition and invention, is what was most consistently developed by Tarde and with what he is most associated nowadays.

2.1.2 Forgotten but Rediscovered

One must also remember that for a large part of the entire twentieth century, Tarde was scarcely referred to in the academic discourse. Of course, Deleuze refers to Tarde on more than one occasion (Alliez 2009), and Foucault's vision of power illustrates very well some important ideas of Tarde (though without referring to him clearly, see Tonkonoff 2017: 117). However, sociology, the area

DOI: 10.4324/9781003440963-2

of inquiry which seems to have taken most of his attention, in the twentieth century has largely forgotten about Tarde's proposals. It is commonly argued that Durkheim's – an intellectual competitor of Tarde – focus on the social phenomena believed to be *sui generis* and not reducible to the level of individuals, crucial for sociology in the spirit of Parsons and Luhmann, repressed Tarde's emphasis on the individual and rejection of emergent, holistic entities over and above humans.

Nevertheless, the repressed returns and Tarde returned as well. Tarde resurfaced largely due to Éric Alliez – a former student of Deleuze – who edited a series of reissues of Tarde's books at the turn of the millennium. Interestingly, it was opened not with the chronologically oldest work but with a much later and shorter (but rich in ideas) essay, *Monadology and Sociology* (Tarde 1999, 2012), which is the focus of this chapter. In this work, Tarde engages not in criminological, penal-philosophical, socio-theoretical, economic or anthropological problematics but reveals his just another face. Tarde also proves to be thinking way beyond any usually understood disciplinary boundaries or assumed domains of reality and attempting his own metaphysics of the clear ambition to address everything there is, both human and nonhuman, without restricting the pluralism of entities and without presupposing hierarchies among them. Below, we will develop the argument that Tarde easily falls under the mere idea of a flat ontology as proposed in the Introduction and that his MON can be seen as originally developing this idea to the point of being different from other specific flat ontologies in many important respects.

2.1.3 One Great Work or Many Great Works?

However, at this point, we should explain why exactly the focus here is on one relatively short work of Tarde and not on some larger part of the entire corpus, or even the latter as such? Henri Bergson, a successor of Tarde in chairing Philosophy at Collège de France, said, in quite beautiful words, on the occasion of unveiling the monument in Tarde's hometown, Sarlat, to honour Tarde that there is a systematicity in his work. From the Bergsonian perspective, although Tarde was not a premeditated systematic thinker, he was so well attuned to the world that his varied interventions ultimately organised themselves into a system (Bergson 1909a: 94–95). In the face of this, we should be invoking much more out of Tarde's oeuvre than merely *Monadology and Sociology.*

However, even Bergson does not seem to be able to grasp the entirety of the work of his predecessor. His following generalising account of Tarde, made on different occasion, with a clear focus on human affairs and relations is in clear tension with strongly posthumanist Tardean MON:

> What dominates all his [Tarde's] philosophy is a certain very original point of view on causality. Causality *par excellence* is, in his eyes, that which operates in human societies, where an individual invents and where other

> individuals imitate him. It cannot be reduced to any of the types of causality described by physicists and metaphysicians. Imitation in fact manifests neither a mechanical impulse nor even, strictly speaking, a moral attraction. It is a certain action *sui generis* which is exercised from mind to mind.
> (Bergson 1909b: 6)

Moreover, Tarde (1901: 661) himself suggests that his entire work does not compose a unity, when he speaks explicitly about an "absolute barrier" between his monadological general theorisations and his social theory. Additionally, many early works devoted to Tarde's thought appear to omit, one must already admit, his quite peculiar ontology (e.g. Tosti 1897: 509–510; Lange 1904; Davis 1906; Mirek 1930; but see Bertrand 1904). In turn, contemporary commentators of Tarde often engage it directly but still admit that there is some difference between Tarde the ontologist and Tarde as a thinker on more classically understood social issues (e.g. Lorenc 2012: 92, footnote 30; Marrero-Guillamón 2015: 251; but see Terrier 2011: 94; see also Gibson 2020).

Not to be groundless, consider Tardean definitions of society. In crucial for his social theory *The Laws of Imitation* (Tarde 1903: 74, 87), he defines society in rather strictly anthropocentric categories, focusing on the notion of imitation, while his MON expands the concept of society to everything else, including nonhumans, by arguing that society is basically the mutual possession of everything else (Tarde 2012: 51). Moreover, even when looking at details within a single work of Tarde, one can notice some tensions. Just consider that Tarde's MON proposes what can be named a possessive criterion for existence, according to which to exist equals to have, while there is also in the very same essay a differential criterion for existence – to exist equals to differ (Tarde 2012: 52 and 40, respectively). However, let us leave aside here the issue of whether the former criterion – crucial in *Monadology and Sociology* – can be equalised with the latter.

What is more important here is to show that there are grounds to problematise continuity and far-reaching systematicity in Tarde's oeuvre. In contrast, given its scope and various potential approaches to reading it, one can also come up with some arguments in favour of the idea of the system still being present in Tarde's work. For instance, Tarde uses his specifically understood concepts of belief and desire in both his social theory (e.g. Tarde 1899, 1903) and MON (e.g. Tarde 2012: 16). Such overarching elements can then be understood as incentives to attempt a thorough reconstruction of the highly original thought of Tarde into a single framework. Obviously, given the reservation made in the Introduction that this book does not engage in a completely comprehensive reconstruction of the work of selected thinkers, we will narrow our interest to what in Tarde's work can be regarded as a highly specific instance of a flat ontology, rather strictly singular in his oeuvre.

2.2 Stepping Into ... Tardean Monadology

2.2.1 Scepticism

Let us begin with bringing to the fore some crucial assumptions or sentiments guiding *Monadology and Sociology*, a short but dense work that aspires to specifically address everything there is, both what can be regarded as human and social and nonhuman. First, one should notice a specific form of epistemic or cognitive scepticism or even the pessimism of Tarde when he argues that "the fundamental nature of things is strictly inaccessible, and we are obliged to construct hypotheses in order to penetrate it" (Tarde 2012: 34). Such a standpoint also provokes a kind of intellectual courage often bordering with extravagancy or, to be more precise, what at first glance may be seen as such. It is a feature that, to a certain extent, is common among flat ontologies, not only in the theses proposed by Tarde, as will become clear later.

Before moving forward though, let us notice that the openly admitted hypothetical character of Tarde's project can provoke just another critique of the mere idea of a flat ontology. Namely, it is much more epistemological than ontological if it is presented in terms of how one should think about reality. However, in response to such potential critique, one can say that even if Tarde, or in fact any other flat ontologist, proposed their frameworks with expressions of full certainty that they are accounting for the reality and not merely producing hypotheses about it, then they are still human beings, who are somehow situated in the world and just communicating their thoughts to whomever may be paying attention to them. Such an approach to this critique may then be regarded as just another argument in favour of abandoning the distinction between epistemology and ontology, as proposed clearly by some flat ontologists, especially Barad. Tarde himself does not appear to make such a proposal explicitly, so we may proceed to another, much more substantive, idea of his MON.

2.2.2 Anti-holism

Perhaps his most spectacular argument, which will also prove to be highly important for the issue of his MON's adequacy to law, is his (Tarde 2012: 6) outright rejection of any holistic beings, entities that have different properties in comparison to their parts, arising out of relations between their parts and becoming in the process, to a certain extent, independent of them. For example, let us notice that there is some practice of thinking about nations as *sui generis* entities, which in a specific way are over the individual people, which can be said to be representatives of a given nation (Tarde 2012: 7–8). Ultimately, one can say that nations as somewhat separate units persist despite the usual generational change or some more violent phenomena like wars or occupation and colonialism. However, despite the popularity of such a standpoint, Tarde opposes it, especially its rendition by his competitor during the formative years for academic sociology – Durkheim.

His idea of sociology and all later structural functionalist social sciences are founded upon a completely different sentiment than Tarde's – that there are such big entities which influence individuals and should be actual subjects of sociological inquiries. Just recall the Durkheimian sense of the social fact as a real force, external to individuals, that coerces them to certain activities (Durkheim 2013). Cultural values are a good example. Although it is rather difficult to argue that they do not have origins in humans themselves, they still achieve some independence and act back on individuals. Thus, while for Durkheim, the big – in a sense of holistic, nonreducible entities – and the small – the individuals – denote existing beings, though located on different planes (thus, his sociology is far from flat ontology sensitivity, at least in this very specific issue of levels of reality), Tarde treats this distinction differently, as already visible in his approach to explaining various phenomena.

Namely, Tarde (2012: 9–11) and his MON propose to explain all those entities that can be regarded as the big by reference to the smaller (in scale) elements. For instance, given the Tardean rejection of holism, he (Tarde 2012: 47) argues not to treat the big of nation or society as something over the smaller, in this case, individuals, as something that would also have specifics not found at the individual level. Instead, he proposes that the big is actually explainable by the small. If the big is not a holistic entity that somehow emerges out of its smaller parts but can be regarded as their mere averaging, then such an explanation scheme – the big by the small – is understandable. However, for Durkheim, it is something akin to anathema. The well-known Durkheimian juxtaposition of primitive and modern societies reveals that, in accordance with his vision of sociology, one should explain the small, like individuals, and their activities with the big, like holistic social entities. Referring to the small in search of an explanation would be seen by him as performing psychology and, as such, would be detrimental and even self-defeating for sociology and securing place for it in academia. Thus, while Durkheim (2013: 10) sees life "in the whole and not in the parts", Tarde (2012: 37, 47) invites us to stop giving the big a similar special, superior status and focus instead on the small, often very small, which, according to him, may exhaustively explain what appears to be big. Namely, for Tarde to explain something that can appear as big and towering over all the rest, one should go downward to small and even smaller elements that may be said to be combined with themselves in such a way that the big, from which one starts, becomes noticeable (but, once again, is not a holistic, nonreducible to its parts, entity).

This is also the very moment when Tardean monads come to the fore, or at least their rather formal sense of something relatively smaller composing something relatively bigger (Lorenc 2012: 81; Toews 2013: 396; Marrero-Guillamón 2015: 244, 246, 250; but see also Harman 2012: 35–36). Notice that here, we are avoiding the concepts of the simple and partless. Tardean monad differs from Gottfried Wilhelm Leibniz's (2014) because even what is significantly smaller than a bigger entity that is co-composed by it is still regarded by Tarde to be made from even smaller beings. Moreover, Tarde frequently refers to infinitesimality. In other words, this move downward towards smaller and smaller can have no end, as everything may prove to be composite, and the actual simple and partless, in the sense of Leibnizian monad, is either never reached or may simply not exist at all. There is much more to Tarde's monads though than their formal and relative character in the suggested sense, and we will address their other features once we finish giving insights into the rich assumptions of his MON.

Right now, it should be clear that while Tarde assumes compositionality of entities, he is clearly anti-holist. He does not think that out of some relations between various entities, something new can emerge that will be, to a certain extent, autonomous with respect to these specific antecedents. In complete opposition to Durkheim's sensitivity, for Tarde, everything there is, including the big and easily noticeable, comes from the infinitely small and can be accounted for with reference to it. Tarde's MON forces then to look very carefully at small details, for they can explain what is larger than them. Durkheim's sociologism is, in turn, supra-individualistic – the emphasis is placed on the big that is to explain the small. Even when one would think that given this difference, Tarde and Durkheim are their own opposites, the divergence between them and actually between Tarde and most thinkers relevant for social sciences becomes more glaring in the face of Tardean further thoughts on the entities that can be regarded big and small.

2.2.3 The Big, the Small and Relational Character of Properties

Tarde (2012: 37) argues that the big is, in fact, simpler and less complex than the small, and that the big is utterly dependent on the small. Notice that it is coherent with his anti-holism – rejection of the existence of entities emerging out of interactions between some smaller components, having features not found among these components and being, to a certain extent, autonomous of them and able to act on them. In consequence, anything that could be regarded as the big in some inquiry is rendered as a mere average out of relatively smaller elements; thus, practically, any change among them is regarded as having a significant, existential, impact on the big. In other words, for Tarde (2012: 47), the small is more important than the big, for if the former somehow changes its participation in the composition of the latter, or even stops such participation, the big can even cease to exist, while the small persists. To understand this point better and to address the assumed simple character of the big and complex of the small, consider some of Tarde's own examples.

First, let us refer once again to the case of nation. From Tardean perspective, the nation – as the big, as what can be regarded as somewhat separate and towering over its individual representatives – is, in fact, merely a specific factoring out what is in the small – individual people who identify themselves in terms of nation. While the characteristics of the individual nation representative may constitute a considerable list of various features – such as biological, psychological or socio-economic-educational, each significantly complex – the nation requires less space. This is because, for Tarde, the big is always a simplification of the smaller, nothing emerging out of it in the same vein as that of holism; thus, the small can, in fact, do without the big. Ultimately, it is completely conceivable that individual people can persist while their nation vanishes, but the opposite would be false. The nation dies with the deaths of its representatives.

A similar way of thinking is suggested by Tarde (2012: 41) himself to language. He practically juxtaposes the ethnic language – with its dictionary and various rules – with the actuality of the linguistic everyday practice of its users. The latter – with its imperfections, awkwardness, context-dependent denotations and connotations, changing rhythms and tone – is ultimately more complex than the purified and well-structured former. This indicates that the language will wither without its uses, but one can still speak and even be perfectly understood without language. Obviously, also in this example, Tarde can be read at least ambivalently. Either he irritates perhaps some of our more deeply internalised thinking habits, or he is just as commonsensical and reasonable as possible. Such ambivalence – a rather perfectly understandable reaction when confronted with Tardean MON, especially for the first time – will be only deepened when we will move to address perhaps the most outright speculative propositions of the commented framework.

However, before that, we should bring to fore the following, which was already suggested above (Tarde 2012: 47). Entities that can be seen as composing what is usually considered the big are never the elements of that big only. The small is not subordinated to the big it composes. It stays autonomous and does not lose itself in the composition it partakes in. It lends only a part or aspect of itself to a specific big, specific composition it co-creates with others. However, it can simultaneously be in many other compositions or, to be more precise, in different sets of relationships with different entities.

Moreover, Tarde assumes that, in dependence on with what exactly a specific entity is in relations – very peculiarly understood, as will become clear below – it gains its characteristics, but they also may change. To understand this point, let us look from a slightly different perspective at the individual and nation pair. If we, as individual human beings, would somehow be only in relations with our fellow nationals, then we certainly would be even significantly different from our current selves. Ultimately, along with being "in" nation, we are also "in" various other entities, or, being more accurate to Tardean anti-holism and its implications, we simply maintain relations with others, often of a completely different character than that suggested by nation. For instance, we are representatives of specific educational backgrounds, worldviews or creeds and professions. The relations with respective others, implied by these concepts and others that denote with whom or what one can maintain some interactions, have an influence on us. Of course, we use here an explicitly human-centred example, but for Tarde, the same applies to everything there is.

2.2.4 Having Instead of Being

Speaking of "is" or being, this is the moment to dive in the already announced, perhaps the most speculative part of Tarde's MON, which also explains some of the more perplexing threads above. Namely, Tarde's (2012: 52) point of departure is not a fundamental question about being. For Tarde, the focus on being is ultimately detrimental, as it projects a vision of reality, where the most crucial is the entity said to be, to exist. In other words, for Tarde's sensitivity, if one argues about the existence of some X, then they are not saying anything on, practically not even implying, some other entity or entities beyond that X. Instead of sticking to the usual being-centredness, in his MON, Tarde proposes to focus on having or possessing. Indeed, saying that some X has something else – whatever it may be, for instance, bigger, smaller, unitary or multiple – already fills the reality more. Ultimately, there is X – the possessor – and that what it possesses.

For Tarde, having or possessing plays a fundamental role in accounting for reality and its various inhabitants because any entity's features come from what that entity has. In other words, the relations from which entities gain their characteristics, as mentioned above, are possessive relations. Consider your current outfit. Depending on how we are dressed now, we appear, for instance, more dignified, serious or professional, more easy-going and laid-back or somewhat attractive. Of course, such Tardean possessivism is at high risk of being wrongly understood, because having or possessing, at the very first glance, can suggest humans, even their legal institutions, such as property, or, at most, some more developed animals. Such an interpretation would then be in strict opposition to a clearly posthumanist and, in fact, universal character and ambition of Tardean MON, which we will present later. For now, let us notice that just as we can be said to having our current clothes on us, which endow us with or bring to the fore some features, the following can be argued. Our clothes also have us, for our bodies fill them, make them move, stretch and bend, and during these and other activities, they gain a different set of properties than when just lying in our wardrobes.

In more general terms, Tarde is not just proposing to account for the properties of various entities through what they are having. He also stresses that what is had by some entity is also an entity that has others. It can be its possessor – which is the case of reciprocal possession, said by Tarde to be "superior" to unilateral possession (Tarde 2012: 56) – or it can have different entities. In fact, for Tarde, everything there is possesses (often its own possessors) and is possessed. One can then say that the relatively smaller elements that seem to constitute the big (but of not holistic or emergent properties) are just in the web of various possessive relations between themselves, some of which can appear to be more unilateral and others more reciprocal, but all are responsible for the features of all involved. For instance, one can belong to some sports club – be had by other members, as well as have them themselves. Each member lends some part of themselves to others associated, but also gains something from them, from remaining in these relations. A sports club – the big – would for Tarde only appear as something holistic with respect to its human members and other components – the small – but it would actually be regarded as something utterly dependent on them and reducible to them.

Once again, then, the small is rendered incomparably more important to the big than in reverse. Ultimately, one can decide to leave the club, which for Tarde would practically mean changing one's state of possessions – one would stop having others and stop being had by them (club human and nonhuman members, like balls or a hall to play in). Given the assumption that features of everything there is come from possessions, one would most definitely change one's properties through such a decision to resign, but one would still exist, due to one's other possessions (outside the club). Namely, as mentioned earlier, for Tarde, all that can be regarded as composing something relatively bigger than oneself is not existentially dependent on that big. It remains some autonomy, just like one can join but also resign from a sports club.

However, the entire commented possessivism in Tarde's MON clearly suggests that one's existence, features and thriving are tightly connected with having (which often is reciprocal – while one entity has some other, that latter has also the former). Moreover, in *Monadology and Sociology,* there is a suggestion of specific take on death, consistent with what we just said and imagined. If being is in a way substituted by Tarde by having, then losing all possessions would amount to the end of existence. Additionally, because possessions are often reciprocal – what we have, also possesses us (whatever we are) – death, in fact, can be named as "absolute independence", as suggested by Tarde (2012: 66). In order then to live – in the very broad sense of the word, because, in the end, Tarde's MON is meant not only to conventionally living beings but also to chemicals and stars – one just must be with others, possess (even if that entails also being possessed). For completely alone, not only would one achieve nothing (due to practically zeroed properties) but also cease to exist.

2.2.5 *Avidity*

The Tardean idea of properties depending on one's possessive relations (Tarde 2012: 53) invites us to consider his framework as strongly anti-essentialist. It is largely true, with one caveat, required in light of Tarde's (2012: 59–60) concept of avidity. Possessing others is not only a measure of one's existence and the way to gain one's properties. It is a fundamental trait or tendency identifiable in all, so it can be regarded as a modest, vestigial essentialism. Namely, Tarde assumes that everything there is, no matter if it can be considered, for instance, human, nonhuman, organic, inorganic, tangible or ideational, has a common feature of wanting to influence all the rest, beyond itself, in a way that is characteristic to itself. However, given that everything is also similarly expansive and possessive, these ambitions of various entities to become truly dominant are never realised. Their contact, or even clashes, make them specifically worn down. In other words, the fact there is, for example, no one utterly dominant political doctrine or ideology or that there is a world as we know it, with various entities, is due to the absence of one ruler of them all. Ultimately, there is no single anything that could be regarded as appropriating, specifically "swallowing" the rest. As Tarde (2012: 55) himself puts it, "[e]very being wants, not to make itself appropriate *for* external beings, but to appropriate *them* for itself".

This assumed feature of avidity is also important to clarify another feature of Tardean monads and, at the same time, the difference from Leibniz. Namely, while Leibnizian monads were isolated from each other (Leibniz 2014: 15), Tarde's monads – a concept abstractly and formally denoting various entities of different scales – are far from such characteristics. Moreover, for the reasons already revealed, Tarde argues that one cannot be isolationist and, at the same time, persist. For him, everything there is constantly engages in various interactions, clashes with others and, in this process, the avidity of all that is involved is averaged. When we introduced earlier the general idea of possessivism, one could get the wrong impression that for Tarde, that which is had by something else just surrenders to it. When supplemented with the avidity idea, we can clearly see that he imagines the world of entities that in order to live and function must possess others, but to do that, they also must defeat their resistance, as those others themselves have a preference to possess, not be possessed.

Think once again of some intellectual frameworks or doctrines from any academic discipline of your preference. Each such doctrine would like to rise to prominence in its respective discipline. However, to do that, it would have to defeat its competitors. These, when somehow attacked or undermined, defend themselves, but one cannot forget that they also want to become dominant; thus, attacking others for the sake of subjugating them is not strange to them. Consequently, instead of a single winner and a mass of defeated, the memory of which ultimately fades, we experience a plethora of ideas on the market. Similarly, instead of the reality in which there is one thing, there is a pluralism of beings.

2.2.6 Posthumanism

Avidity, the urge to appropriate others and resist their appropriation, is strongly involved in some other crucial points in Tarde's MON that need to be brought to the fore, nearing the end of not an easy task of reconstructing the basic, yet numerous assumptions of his original short metaphysical essay. Seeing avidity in everything most definitely suggests panpsychism, although Tarde (2012: 15) himself prefers psychomorphism. Moreover, when one considers passages like "the whole external universe is composed of souls distinct from my own but fundamentally similar", or on being "blinded by the prejudice of always considering ourselves superior to everything" and, finally, on "the prejudice of anthropocentrism" (Tarde 2012: 15, 22, 24), the already made suggestions on the posthumanist character of the Tardean framework should now be completely clear and justified. Tarde is opposed to human-centredness (at least in the commented *Monadology and Sociology*) and argues that what at first glance can be associated practically with humans only is, in fact, universal, for everything wants to have and not be had.

In this light, it is truly surprising that such modern-sounding outright anti-anthropocentric sentiments of Tarde are very often omitted in important works on posthumanism (both monographs, e.g. Wolfe 2010; Braidotti 2013; Ferrando 2019, and some collections, e.g. Thomsen and Wamberg 2020; Herbrechter et al. 2022), despite Latour's (2002) – a crucial figure for posthumanism – largely successful popularisation of Tarde. This wonderment becomes even greater in the face of just another way Tarde contradicts the deeply held anthropocentrism. To notice this, let us return to the issue of the Tardean definition of society.

2.2.7 Monadological Understanding of Society

In *Monadology and Sociology*, in what may come across as clear divergence from his works on social theory, Tarde defines society not as something grand, massive, clearly visible and full of human beings. In contrast, for him "*everything is a society*, [...] every phenomenon is a social fact" (Tarde 2012: 28), because society is nothing exclusively human or of some more developed nonhuman animals, but it is "each individual's reciprocal possession, in many highly varied forms, of every other" (Tarde 2012: 51). Such an unusual standpoint is perfectly consistent with what has already been mentioned about Tarde. If he ultimately assumes the specific compositionality of beings, acquiring mere existence and properties through what one has (a set of possessive relations), then any entity is a gathering (with no holistic properties, which could not be found among the members of such gathering but being merely their averaging). Even something miniscule in some scale and thus possible to consider truly the simple and partless, upon the specific investigation mode proposed by Tarde of infinitesimal downward move, is to reveal its swarming character.

Seeing sociality, so originally understood, in everything leads to the following consequence – being at least sceptical of thinking in terms of various domains or layers of reality that would have some features or regularities that are unique to them and, thus, require different conceptual apparatus to address them (Tarde 2012: 29). This scepticism is coherent with Tarde's (2012: 58–59) clearly expressed dislike towards the idea of some laws (not in the legal sense) towering over some phenomena, which, due to these laws, are practically forced to follow some scenario. Instead of projecting a similar vision of the level of reality where some actual phenomena take place and some other plane of laws that guide them, Tarde appears to be a supporter of a completely different approach – to search for the causes of the observed phenomena immanently, among the phenomena themselves, and not assume some transcendent reservoir of explanations. This is quite consistent not only with his anti-holism but also with his specific downward reduction, paying attention to the small and even smaller to account for the big.

2.2.8 *Tardean Monadology as Flat Ontology*

Despite the rather concise form of *Monadology and Sociology*, it is, in fact, full of crucial assumptions, not always expressed as clearly as one would wish for. This is why it took us this much time to reconstruct them in an understandable manner. Before bringing to the fore some important traits of Tardean MON's basic unit for ontological inquiry – monad – some of which we already anticipated above, and then discussing it from the perspective of law, let us say the following.

Although Tarde's MON is rarely associated with a flat ontology explicitly, the above should convince us that it falls under that name. It has truly universal ambitions. It accounts for the pluralism of entities, out of different commonly understood domains or layers of reality, and scales, being wary of any ontological prejudices that would at the very outset prioritise something over others or assume hierarchies. Moreover, as we will see in a moment, it does not preclude any possible hierarchies due to its suggestion of a monad that may be regarded as leading or dominant among others that in conjunction can be said to constitute some entity (Tarde 2012: 18, 58, 62).

Nevertheless, here, more important is to see once again that Tardean MON's ontological flattening is very specific, for Tarde equalises in a very peculiar way – arguing in favour of universal possessivism and avidity. No one and nothing are exempt from the existential necessity and urge to possess and avoid being possessed. From this highly specific perspective, everything can be said to be the same, but the result of constant contacts and even clashes between avid, possessive entities is far from an undifferentiation.

Finally, we can notice Tarde's desire to escape thinking in terms of domains or layers. Tarde constantly speaks in terms of the big and the small but notice that these are merely relative categories used for the exposition of his framework, not to argue that there are two categories of being. On the one hand, Tarde's anti-holism is against thinking about big and supposedly irreducible entities towering over what, to a certain extent, gave rise to them. On the other hand, his focus on infinitesimality is meant to disrupt potential faith in small entities, for they, as we said earlier, are also out of a myriad of others. There are, then, just entities – averaging of other entities, which are averaging of other entities, and so on, *ad infinitum*.

2.3 Focusing on … Monads

2.3.1 *Formal, Relative, Compositional and Linked*

Tardean MON's assumptions already cover most of what monad is according to Tarde. However, to be as clear as possible, let us bring to the fore all crucial features of Tarde's understanding of that concept, having itself a considerable history in philosophy.

First, we can stress once again that Tardean monad differs significantly from Leibnizian vision. For Tarde, monad is not an absolute simple element, which cannot be analysed through its parts because it just does not have them. In *Monadology and Sociology*, monad gains a rather formal and relative meaning as an entity that can be regarded as smaller, from the perspective of the object that is subjected to some analysis in the first place. Moreover, monad, as something smaller relevant for something bigger, can itself be analysed through its components, even smaller entities. In other words, Tarde's monads are not partless. Divergences from Leibniz do not end here. Namely, just as Leibniz's monad is closed or windowless, Tarde's (2012: 57) monads are open and constantly engage in abundant relations with other entities, which, as said, can also be considered monads depending on our main object of inquiry.

Theo Lorenc's (2012: 81) – an English translator and a contemporary commentator of the discussed treatise by Tarde – comment seems a good illustration of the remarks on monad's formal, relative, not partless and not isolated characteristics: "if one's interest is in human societies or animal species, the element [monad] will be the individual human or animal; if in an organism, the cell; if in material entities, the atom". Note that individual human or animal in respective societies, cells in some organism and atoms in some material beings are themselves "deconstructable" into even smaller entities; Tarde argues that such downward move is infinitesimal. Moreover, they are constantly related to other entities, at least of the same kind, like human to human, animal to animal, cell to cell and atom to atom.

2.3.2 On Possession(s), Being Avid, Dominant and Leading Monad

The fact that what can be considered monads interact with each other is interpreted by Tarde in a highly specific manner. First, just as we discussed it above, for him, "to exist" should be replaced by "to have". Any being's existence entails possessing something else. In other words, in accordance with Tarde's framework, when one accounts for the existence of a specific entity, one simultaneously accounts for something else, which is had by that entity. However, it should be stressed once again that, for Tarde (2012: 56), although unilateral possession (for instance, X has Y, but Y does not have X) is still possible, reciprocal possession is considered more important. Let us also acknowledge here that Tarde (2012: 55–56) mentions possessions between individual elements and between an element and the entire group of other elements, but still the distinction of unilateral and reciprocal possession appears to be much more engaging for him. Moreover, given that possession is not a binary but gradual phenomenon, thus allowing us to regard as having even a relation between the nonorganic, material artifact and its human user – just recall our previous discussion on our clothes possessing us, their wearers – it is safe to say that reciprocal possession is more common than unilateral possession. Through their possessions, entities – which may be regarded as monads from the perspective of something else – gain or acquire their properties, which, in turn, influence what entities can actually do.

One can see then in this approach some far-reaching anti-essentialism – things in the world prove not to have some features that are theirs only, irrespective of the current state of broadly understood relations with other entities. However, Tardean anti-essentialism appears, in the end, not to be absolute because of the assumption of avidity. Everything has the urge to have, to possess others and not be had by them. Because such avidity is common, the appetites of entities engaging with each other are most commonly averaged. In effect, there is no single utterly dominant monad, but the actual plurality of entities, which, despite their continuing possessiveness, cannot be completely satisfied, as they constantly meet with others with similar urge.

One can say, then, that the Tardean monadological view of reality assumes a significant competitiveness in it but with no absolute winners, which could completely wipe out all rivals. However, note here that as long there is no single dominant monad in the entirety of the world – if it were, there would be no world as we and other entities know it – there can be some leading elements within some relatively larger entities. Namely, Tarde's focus on infinitesimality means that everything is specifically made from something else, something relatively smaller (various monads), but even those smaller elements can prove to be of a compositional character when investigated in more detail. This common trait of compositionality, one might add heterogeneous, fits well the rather unorthodox understanding of the concept of society. Everything is said to be a specific society of elements that have each other and are had by each other, but it is possible that some among them are more effective in imposing on others, and that the entity-society they make is not just the result of some more even balance.

2.3.3 The Big's Simplicity and Fragility and the Small's Complexity and Independence

Such groupings of reciprocally possessing entities (the small) can be said to constitute some other entity (the big), but, as already said, there are some crucial reservations concerning this constitution. Tarde rejects the idea of some holistic entities emerging out of interactions between some lower-level objects, having properties not found among them and being, to a certain extent, independent of and towering over them. In short, for Tarde, there are no wholes that would be more than the mere sum of their parts, to refer to the popular phrase concerning emergent entities. However, one would also specifically err, if one would understand Tardean MON as arguing in favour of the thesis that what can be seen as the big is literally the sum of its smaller elements. In fact, for Tarde, that what can be considered as big is actually smaller, less complex than the sum of its parts (see also Latour 2002: 121). Any relatively bigger entity than its smaller elements (monads), besides most likely taking part in some even bigger object and thus being its monad, is nothing else but a specific simplification or averaging of all things that can be said to compose it. Just recall the nation and language examples above. Nation can be said to be made from its representatives, but it can still be regarded as less complex than any individual national with its thoughts, competences, plans or, last but not least, intestinal flora. Similarly, ethnic language, with its grammar and vocabulary, can be seen as only averaging of a myriad of utterances, which, due to their own subtle situational characteristics, can be said to be more complicated. This highly specific understanding of the big in relation to the small has the following implications.

The big, the one that is merely a simplification or averaging of that which gives rise to it, is very fragile. Practically, with each change or move of its smaller parts, the big is also significantly changed, even up to the point of losing its previous identity. In contrast, the smaller elements – monads – are independent of the big and, as such, they can detach themselves from it with no similarly serious consequences for themselves. Nationals can exist even if there is no nation anymore, and one can still speak and be understood even if there is no language with all its meticulously written rules.

Luckily, one can see in *Monadology and Sociology* a slight suggestion of an additional tool to understand this quite perplexing point better when Tarde's talk about points becoming "an indefinitely enlarged sphere[s] of action" and on "interpenetrating spheres" (Tarde 2012: 26–27) suggests Venn diagrams. Accordingly, one can imagine that each of the overlapping circles in it represents a single small element (monad), which, of course, upon investigation, would prove to be compositional as well. In the middle of the diagram is a shape created through overlapping of all involved circles, which can be seen to represent Tardean big – nothing more than simplification or averaging of components, which are not entirely subordinated to the one specific big but can take part in many more. Just as when one of the overlapping circles in the Venn diagram is removed from it and, in effect, the central area loses its previous shape, one can similarly imagine the relation between the small (monads) and the big (which can be one of the monads for something even bigger). Entities that co-constitute another entity (but not in the holistic, emergent sense) can function beyond it, but the thing co-constituted by them can be even changed beyond recognition with each of their moves (Figure 2.1). Tardean MON stresses, then, the dynamism of what there is, even up to the point of provoking to acknowledge some utter fragility of things.

2.4 Law and … Tarde's Monads

2.4.1 Law as Not an Emergent Entity

Having recapitulated the Tardean sense of the monad, largely out of the previous reconstruction of main assumptions in his MON, we can finally address the issue of its adequacy and value for law. It seems difficult to get rid of the sense of clear ambivalence when it comes to the issue of Tarde's MON and

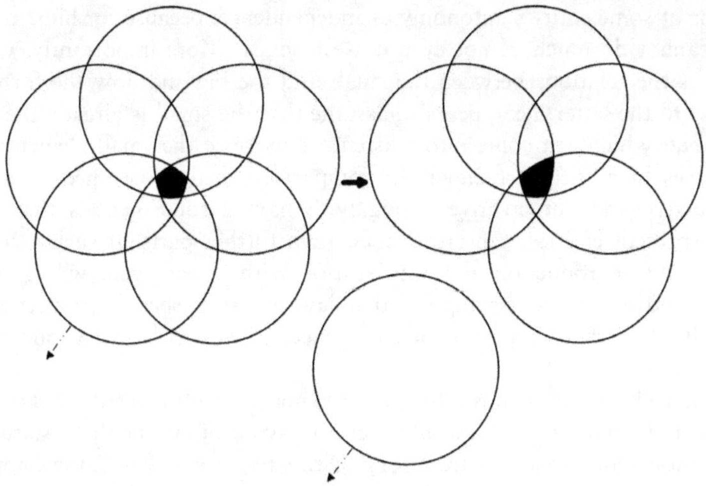

Figure 2.1 Tardean big-small dynamics (using Venn diagram).

law. Tarde suggests many points that seem to fit law. However, many of them seem to be related to some leading commitments of Tardean MON, which can be regarded as the most controversial here, and, as a result, these fitting points can also be questioned. Let us begin by addressing these commitments.

Notice once again that Tardean MON is in strict opposition to the idea of holistic, emergent beings, which are, to a certain extent, autonomous, independent of that what gives rise to them but still can impose themselves on them, influence them and have properties not found among them. Accordingly, from Tarde's perspective, there simply would not be law as an emergent entity, because emergence as such is rejected. Consequently, law would be denied features that can easily be associated with the idea that it is an emergent entity, somewhat different from and independent of its parts. In particular, consider, for instance, the broadly understood traits of law's autoreproduction and autocreation – that law (re)makes itself using its very own parts – discussed not only in the context of autopoiesis in Luhmann's systems theory and other approaches inspired by it (e.g. Teubner 1993).

To better understand this remark that Tarde's MON puts into doubt, at the very least, this specific assumed character of law, consider how one can approach law in the same vein as that of Tarde. Law can be seen as an instance of the big, in Tardean sense, namely an averaging of abundant relatively smaller entities. If then some entity is merely a simplification of various other objects – "a merely artificial being, a composite made up of aspects and façades of other beings" (Tarde 2012: 47), then it is highly doubtful how such averaging could gain autopoietic properties and be able to (re)create itself practically autonomously. The problem here is not only that Tarde is highly sceptical of discourse in terms of some entity's autonomy or independence, because for him, all that is alone cannot do much, if not even cease to exist. More importantly, when he considers the relations between the small and the big and how the former can give rise to the latter, he appears to assume that the small is already there prior to the big, which can come into existence only once the small elements group themselves in a specific manner. In comparison, beings assumed to be autoreproductive and autocreative, along with having some genesis that involve already present entities, can create their own further parts. If such association of law's autoreproduction and autocreation with its emergent whole status is correct, and under the assumption that law has such specific properties, Tardean MON, with its rejection of emergence, proves to be even more problematic to law.

Trying to be as fair as possible, however, notice another possibility here – that Tarde is right and those who would argue in favour of law's holistic status based on its autopoietic properties are wrong. Ultimately, following Tarde's approach, one can say that law as a composite being out of a plethora of heterogeneous entities cannot (re)create itself, but only some very specific parts of it, like regulations concerning lawmaking, seem to address the creation of new entities, which, once made, will also start partaking in it. Such a move would most likely be faithful to the Tardean motto of explaining the big with the small. However, the discussed framework's outright rejection of law as a holistic, irreducible entity seems to be involved in more problems than the ones highlighted thus far, most directly related to Tarde's take on the issue of emergence.

2.4.2 Law's Utter Fragility

Notice that law as averaging of its smaller parts (monads) proves to be an utterly dynamic and fragile entity. Practically, any move and action of its monads just cannot remain neutral with respect to it, for law in the monadological framework would somehow change with each instance. This is because, being nothing more than the averaging of its elements, an entity will always react to their alteration. Consequently, law as Tardean big would be a mere facade, to refer to the earlier quote from *Monadology and Sociology*. Of course, the idea of the merely apparent existence of law as a separate and stable entity, whereas it is just an everchanging averaging of similarly dynamic elements, is faithful to the commented treatise.

There is, however, a specific tension between the monadological vision of utter superficiality and pretence of the figure of law as a durable object, and what we can observe – all that is involved in law changes, yes, but law still somehow is. Such observation can be addressed through a differentiation between relevant and irrelevant changes – the ones that somehow alter law and those that are of much lesser-scale repercussions. However, more interesting in the discussed context is another possibility. Namely, the degree of maintained stability of law can be explained by its holistic, emergent characteristics. In other words, the fact that relevant things come and go, move and stay and change to various degrees, while law maintains its identity, may be because law is something more than the mere sum of its parts. As anticipated, the issue of emergence returns. Its potential value in addressing the stability of law can be read as another argument showing the problems with adequacy to the law of Tardean MON, a vehemently anti-emergentist framework.

However, as with the issue of autopoietic properties, we can look at the issue in question differently, in a way that will not result in discarding Tarde's framework for its inadequacy. Ultimately, one can say that he is, after all, the one who is right here. Law is utterly unstable, and we should be using frameworks that can do justice to such constant dynamism and not render everchanging, objectively speaking, entities as durable more than they actually are. Notice, though, that the opposition here between law's utter dynamism (fitting anti-holism of Tarde) and its considerable stability (in hand with the emergentism of those who like to think of law as something more than the sum of its parts) is rather difficult, to say the least, to be conclusively resolved. That is why one can feel the need to try to address some stability, after all, of law, differently, yet more in line with Tarde, at least at first glance.

Perhaps this stability can be accounted for in the following way. Let us imagine that some parts (monads) of law significantly change or even somehow move beyond law they co-constitute. Consequently, in accordance with the principles of being assumed by Tarde and the big-small dynamics illustrated earlier using Venn diagram, in such a situation, law would change as well, even similarly significantly. However, the possibility of such far-reaching alteration can be mitigated by some other law's monads. There is then the hypothesis of one monad or even a few monads compensating some broadly understood changes among other elements involved in a relatively bigger entity, for the sake of stabilising it. Notice, though, that such an idea, suggesting some rather classical insights from functionalism in social theory, appears not to be even implied on the pages of *Monadology and Sociology*. Maybe it is its functionalist undertone, and everything that functionalism entails, which is responsible for the absence of such an idea in Tardean framework. If so, then the considered idea of accounting for stability would amount to an even clear deviation from Tarde's ontology. Assuming that one should account for law's stability, despite undergoing various changes, Tardean MON's problematic character for law becomes even more evident when its potential way to address this issue appears to ultimately be in tension with its main sentiments.

2.4.3 Independence of Law's Small

In accordance with the discussed framework, the entities of a relatively smaller scale that can be said to partake in giving rise to a bigger entity can exist beyond it. Of course, such abandonment of the big by the small can be significantly altering or even destructing the big, which is also crucial for law from the monadological perspective, as we just addressed it above. Now, let us focus on the possibility of what can be considered law's monads to function beyond that law, clearly implied by Tardean MON. This problem can be put into the following question: Is law constituted only by entities that simultaneously partake in giving rise to some other objects and can even exist completely outside law?

On the one hand, this idea seems correct. Indeed, we can easily imagine, for instance, law's addressees that not only co-constitute law but also partake in many other societies, in Tardean sense. These people's actions are not only legally but also economically or religiously relevant, legal institutions buildings are involved in water supply networks and others, like electric or heating, or some wildlife – the common object of legal regulations – partakes in the relatively bigger entities respective for their species. In short, the simultaneous participation of law's monads in some other objects does not appear to be a problem.

Then, what about law's monads outside law? If law would be a Tardean nonholistic entity, merely an averaging of what gives rise to it, then its monads could easily "defect". But is it really the case? Here, we will again encounter some ambivalence. Namely, one can argue that there are some monads of law that can enjoy practically to the fullest the possibility assumed by Tarde. However, even after a moment of more careful reflection, Tardean suggestion of freedom of law's parts to leave law reveals its much more questionable and controversial character.

Consider some examples. Some wild flora and fauna can exist with no legal regulations meant specifically for them or can move across various jurisdictions, but such changes can even have an existential impact on them when they get to a more or less protective legal regime. Moreover, their seemingly natural mobility and transgressing spatial boundaries made by humans are nothing truly outside law, but within law, which, for instance, does not regulate such migration explicitly, clearly allows it or does not forbid it. This, to a certain extent, is also the case of more usual human monads of law. As a rule, people can move across jurisdictions or even change their citizenships. Consequently, one can say they leave the law of one jurisdiction or entire country and start partaking in another. However, such a move still happens under the conditions of the first law in question. Let us think now, for a change, about a nonorganic yet manmade element that can be said to partake in law. Material infrastructure meant for some legal agendas can be relatively easily repurposed (e.g. rearranging a court building into a school or hospital and thus moving it beyond an explicitly legal context). However, notice that school or hospital buildings most likely have their own specific legal regimes; thus, despite not being a court building anymore, one cannot seriously say that they are outside law. Finally, what about textual legal provisions? If it can be considered a smaller element (monad) for the big – law – then it should also be practically independent of what it co-constitutes. But is it really the case? For instance, a formally derogated legal provision – moved quite literally outside the valid legal system – can still exist as some utterance, but it would appear as ungrounded to insist that its meaning – not social relevance but linguistic meaning – remains perfectly the same if its ties with the rest of the text of law have been severed. It would be similar in some other hypothetical, if not outright speculative, scenario of somehow extracting specific provision out of law it co-constitutes.

Not going any further into other examples, it appears that the following remarks are in place. First, Tarde assumes that the big constituted by the small has some boundaries that can be transgressed by the small, and through such transgression, monads can stop co-constituting the big. However, we can already wonder whether law, even when considered a Tardean averaging of smaller entities, has some boundaries. Second, Tarde does not problematise different senses in which a monad can be outside the big it co-creates. Even if one would argue that law is not boundaryless, then there is the issue of the most likely different ways in which an entity can be said to transgress law's boundaries and be outside of it. Third, there is also the question of what it means for specific law's elements to go outside law, what are the consequences of such a move, or its particular kind, for the element engaged in it.

These general issues – law's boundaries or boundarylessness and the consequences of reaching outside of law, if there is one – will return in specific contexts of the following two chapters. Here, let us attempt some conclusions of the discussed thread for investigating Tardean MON. If law is a boundaryless entity, and Tarde's framework assumes that the entities have some outsides, then there is quite clear inadequacy of this framework with respect to the specific being of law.

There is another more complicated scenario. If law has some outside, but what can be regarded its parts cannot reach it so freely, as suggested by Tarde, and can be even significantly altered in the process, like gaining or losing some broadly understood status (consider once again the above examples of flora and fauna, people, buildings and provisions), then the following question arises: Why is it like that? Once again, we have here two possible interpretations: one in favour of law as an emergent whole and the other in favour of law as a mere averaging of its monads. With respect to the former, entities that somehow reach law's outside can stop being in the range of law's specific emergent qualities, not found among its components, but arising out of their particular interactions and arrangements. It would then be a situation like a hypothetical scenario of a person or an entire group escaping the coercive influence of Durkheimian social fact, an archetype of a holistic social entity.

When it comes to the latter, one can say that monads somehow leaving law in which they previously participated – detaching themselves from this specific society, in Tardean sense – stop possessing other monads involved in law. Consequently, and in accordance with Tardean principle, according to which one's properties come from one's possessions, the properties of those leaving simply must change, even to such a degree that the mere prospect of a specific alteration may act coercively, force to rather stay within law and just enjoy the properties acquired by possessing other monads that co-constitute law. On such a reading, we can avoid slipping to the opposite, to Tardean MON, position of law's emergent, holistic status as explaining the significant impact abandoning law can have on its "defecting" elements.

From this perspective, the discussed issue is less involved in the problem of (anti)emergentism, which, as we saw, was much more crucial in the case of the previous two subsections. However, Tardean commitment to the idea of monads being independent from the big they co-constitute, to an extent that they are supposed to be able to move beyond that big, is problematic from the perspective of law. Namely, it quite clearly assumes boundaries and treats rather lightly transgressing them by monads. The latter issue can still be addressed in line with Tarde's thought, but bearing in mind the problems suggested above, especially the one concerning the legal provision outside of the law scenario. Nevertheless, it must be stressed once again that it still is tightly connected with, if not even dependent on, the former issue – boundaries and whether law has them to be transgressible by its monads.

There are, then, important controversies in Tardean MON that seem to put the prospect of its application to law in serious doubt. It would just be unfounded to treat lightly his anti-emergentism, emphasis on practically constant dynamics and the idea of boundaries, as well as monads' far-reaching independence from the big and their implications for law.

2.4.4 Heterogeneity of Law's Composition

However, Tarde's many points are at the very least interesting, if not intriguing, for law, some of which also seem of practical value. As such, let us then bring them to the fore, of course, still having in mind the crucial problems in which they are involved and which we highlighted above.

Law, from the Tardean monadological perspective, is of compositional character, as practically everything is in accordance with this framework. Such general compositionality can, indeed, provoke to wonder whether law is co-composing something even relatively bigger than itself; however, for ontological investigations about law, the following is more important. The posthumanist, anti-anthropocentric sentiments of Tarde support the standpoint that, among all relatively smaller components of law, there are not only humans, their ideas or variously communicated utterances but also far-reaching heterogeneity, which may even blur the nature-culture or law-society distinctions.

This heterogeneity alone provokes us to wonder the following issue: Among law's monads, is there some leading element, some entity that can be regarded as stronger than the rest involved, or perhaps law is nothing more than a specific balance achieved among relevant smaller entities with no clear advantage? Not only in the latter scenario, Tarde can be read as trying to convince us or remind us that law is utterly dynamic and even fragile (but, again, mind the tension with its stability). If it is a mere averaging of relatively smaller entities, being simplifications of their own respective monads, then one must consider constant fluctuations of law, many of them may prove to be socially significant, not only for the sake of mere thinking about law.

Namely, such a position inspires or confirms that in order to make a deliberate successful change for the better in some respect, one should not be so focused on altering some official legal texts in respective acts through parliamentary procedures in the hope of achieving some goals. Due to some configuration of things that are to be subjected to a regulation and all that is relevant to them – recall the infinitesimality thesis and the relational character of properties – the regulatory intervention may be ineffective or even counterproductive, as it might miss what is crucial for the phenomenon subjected to intervention. In short, Tardean MON seems a good device for recognising the immense complexity of reaching an intended change in and through law and the high risk of unintended consequences following some actions. The ideas of downward infinitesimal reduction of things and the relational character of their properties are then interesting for both investigating what law is and how to better regulate.

However, as mentioned earlier, we should be wary of the strong anti-emergentist commitment here. Returning to the issue of law's heterogeneity, implied by Tardean MON, it is also consistent with Tarde's general remark that, to achieve anything, one cannot act alone; thus, to a certain extent, the more the diversity, the better. This also holds for law.

2.4.5 Law's Avidity

In this context, the Tardean concept of avidity appears to fit law in the following way. Law, like everything else in Tardean reality, wants to have as much as possible (Tarde 2012: 55; see also Lange 1904: 23). In this light, the proliferation of legal regulations and the problems with finding a piece of the world that is not touched in any way by law can be seen as proof of law's avidity. Through its regulations, law can be said to have, in a peculiar sense, the very broadly understood objects of its regulations. However, it appears that law is not a unilateral possessor, because everything subjected to some regulations also has them (reciprocally) and, as a result, gains some properties, like a recognisable status, rights, responsibilities or protections.

The rather undeniable spread of law – avidity in Tardean terms – can also be interpreted in at least two quite different manners. On the one hand, we can see a hypothetical highly specific function of law – to restrict avidity of all other beings, which, in the absence of some legal restrictions imposed on them, could most likely be much more expansive and detrimental to others (Tarde 2012: 60). In other words, law can be said to gain, from Tardean inspiration, a quite important and uncommon role to play. In the end, it is not easy to come up with a long list of entities that could be said to be, similarly, the controller of possessive urges of everything there is. On the other hand, law's avidity, impressive in its achieved scope, can be just a measure of its own expansiveness, not some honourable function. On such a reading, law is just an entity that proves to be more successful in grasping others, which, let us recall it, are also possessive, but their appetites happen to be more clearly restricted.

If that would be the case, then another rather deep implication of Tardean MON can be uncovered here. To a certain extent, Tarde renders law and all beings as nothing fundamentally special. If avidity is common in things, then it is also common in law. Law's avidity is then perfectly ordinary. Of course, any ontological framework of universal ambitions and proposing some fundamental principles or dynamics to be found in all there is can be said of rendering everything ordinary in a specific sense.

There is, however, another, more interesting way in which Tardean MON can be said to render law as nothing special after all. Ultimately, in accordance with his framework, law should be nothing more than the mere averaging or simplification of some relatively smaller elements, with no special, with respect to them, emergent properties. Moreover, its elements are supposed to be free and independent from it, in the sense that they can move beyond law and stop taking part in giving rise to it or maintaining it. The Tardean idea of the big being utterly dependent on the small, but the small remaining far-reaching autonomy, projects a highly specific vision of law as something not that serious after all and, in fact, abandonable by those involved. Such an implied standpoint can be said to be in clear opposition to most approaches to and theories of law, but it also is controversial in more practical social terms. Having said that, let us stress once more that these remarks are tightly connected to important Tardean commitment to boundaries and the small's independence of the big, a controversy discussed earlier.

In conclusion, Tardean MON with respect to law proves to be clearly ambivalent, and even somewhat frustrating. On the one hand, it proposes and provokes some interesting avenues of not exclusively theoretical value. On the other hand, many of its commitments, so fundamental that they are practically essential to it, make it either explicitly problematic for law, and even inadequate, at worst, or inconclusive at the moment and thus still debatable, at best.

References

Alliez, Éric. 2009. Gabriel Tarde. In *Deleuze's Philosophical Lineage*, Graham Jones and Jon Roffe (eds), 209–218. Edinburgh: Edinburgh University Press.

Bergson, Henri. 1909a. Lettre [Letter]. In *Gabriel Tarde: Discours prononcés le 12 septembre 1909 a Sarlat a l'inauguration de son monument* [*Gabriel Tarde: Speeches Delivered on September 12, 1909 in Sarlat at the Inauguration of His Monument*], 94–97. Sarlat: Michelet.

Bergson, Henri. 1909b. Préface [Preface]. In *Les Grands philosophes français et étrangers: Gabriel Tarde* [*The Great French and Foreign Philosophers: Gabriel Tarde*], 5–6. Paris: Louis-Michaud.

Bertrand, Alexis. 1904. Un essai de cosmologie sociale. Les thèses monadologiques de Gabriel Tarde [An Essay in Social Cosmology: The Monadological Theses of Gabriel Tarde]. *Archives de l'anthropologie criminelle* [*Archives of Criminal Anthropology*] 19: 623–660.

Braidotti, Rosi. 2013. *The Posthuman.* Cambridge: Polity Press.

Davis, Michael M., Jr., A.B. 1906. *Gabriel Tarde: An Essay in Sociological Theory.* New York: Columbia University.

Durkheim, Émile. 2013. *The Rules of Sociological Method and Selected Texts on Sociology and its Method.* Second Edition. Ed.: Steven Lukes. Trans.: W. D. Halls. Basingstoke: Palgrave Macmillan.

Ferrando, Francesca. 2019. *Philosophical Posthumanism.* London: Bloomsbury.

Gibson, Johanna. 2020. *Owned, An Ethological Jurisprudence of Property: From the Cave to the Commons.* Abingdon: Routledge.

Harman, Graham. 2012. On the Supposed Societies of Chemicals, Atoms, and Stars in Gabriel Tarde. In *Savage Objects*, Godofredo Pereira (ed.), 33–43. Lisbon: INCM.

Herbrechter, Stefan, Ivan Callus, Manuela Rossini, Marija Grech, Megen de Bruin-Molé, and Christopher John Müller (eds). 2022. *Palgrave Handbook of Critical Posthumanism.* Cham: Palgrave Macmillan.

Lange, Antoni. 1904. *Społeczeństwo i historja podług teorii G. Tarde'a* [*Society and History According to G. Tarde's Theory*]. Warszawa: M. Arct.

Latour, Bruno. 2002. Gabriel Tarde and the End of the Social. In *The Social in Question: New Bearings in History and the Social Sciences*, Patrick Joyce (ed.), 117–132. London: Routledge.

Leibniz, Gottfried Wilhelm. 2014. The Monadology. In Lloyd Strickland, *Leibniz's Monadology: A New Translation and Guide*, 14–33. Edinburgh: Edinburgh University Press.

Lorenc, Theo. 2012. Afterword: Tarde's Pansocial Ontology. In Gabriel Tarde, *Monadology and Sociology*. Ed. and trans.: Theo Lorenc, 71–95. Melbourne: re.press.

Marrero-Guillamón, Isaac. 2015. Monadology and Ethnography: Towards a Tardian Monadic Ethnography. *Ethnography* 16 (2): 240–261.

Mirek, Franciszek. 1930. *Metoda socjologiczna: Przyczynek na podstawie analizy krytycznej metod Tarde'a i Durkheima* [*Sociological Method: A Contribution Based on a Critical Analysis of the Methods of Tarde and Durkheim*]. Poznań: Jan Jachowski, Księgarnia Uniwersytecka.

Tarde, Gabriel. 1899. *Social Laws: An Outline of Sociology*. Trans.: Howard C. Warren. London: MacMillan Company.

Tarde, Gabriel. 1901. Réponse a M. Espinas [Response to Mr. Espinas]. *Revue Philosophique de la France et de l'Étranger* [*Philosophical Review of France and From Abroad*] 51: 661–664.

Tarde, Gabriel. 1902. *Psychologie économique* [*Economic Psychology*]. Two Volumes. Paris: Félix Alcan.

Tarde, Gabriel. 1903. *The Laws of Imitation.* Trans.: Elsie Clews Parsons. New York: Henry Holt and Company.

Tarde, Gabriel. 1905. *Underground Man.* Trans.: Cloudesley Brereton. London: Duckworth.

Tarde, Gabriel. 1912. *Penal Philosophy*. Trans.: Rapelje Howell. Boston: Little, Brown, and Company.

Tarde, Gabriel. 1999. *Monadologie et sociologie* [*Monadology and Sociology*]. Ed.: Éric Alliez. Paris: Institut Synthélabo.

Tarde, Gabriel. 2012. *Monadology and Sociology*. Ed. and trans.: Theo Lorenc. Melbourne: re.press.

Terrier, Jean. 2011. *Visions of the Social: Society as a Political Project in France, 1750–1950*. Leiden: Brill.

Teubner, Gunther. 1993. *Law as an Autopoietic System*. Trans.: Anne Bankowska and Ruth Adler. Ed.: Zenon Bankowski. Oxford: Blackwell.

Thomsen, Mads Rosendahl, and Jacob Wamberg (eds). 2020. *The Bloomsbury Handbook of Posthumanism*. London: Bloomsbury.

Toews, David. 2013. Tarde's Sociology of Difference: Its Classical Roots and Contemporary Meanings. *Journal of Classical Sociology* 13 (3): 393–401.

Tonkonoff, Sergio. 2017. *From Tarde to Deleuze and Foucault: The Infinitesimal Revolution*. Cham: Palgrave Macmillan.

Tosti, Gustavo. 1897. The Sociological Theories of Gabriel Tarde. *Political Science Quarterly* 12 (3): 490–511.

Wolfe, Cary. 2010. *What Is Posthumanism?*. Minneapolis: University of Minnesota Press.

Chapter 3

Bruno Latour's Actor-Network Theory (of Law); or, What About Law's Outside (Plasma)?

3.1 Not ... a Winemaker

3.1.1 After Tarde

As is quite commonly commented, Tarde's thought can be said to have lost with Durkheimian propositions. Perhaps this is one of the reasons why we had the broadly understood social sciences we had in the twentieth century. If Tarde had come to prominence at the turn of the nineteenth and twentieth centuries, then our thinking about and actions in the world most likely would have been different than how we came to be educated and to what we intellectually and practically accustomed ourselves. Tarde has simply been forgotten, including the possibilities, as well as some problems in his MON, that most definitely fits the description of a flat ontology.

It would be an exaggeration, though, to say that in the wake of Tarde being defeated and falling largely into an oblivion for a considerable time, one cannot find any instances of flat ontologies from the later years of the twentieth century. Ultimately, one can wonder whether such a classification is not adequate to the thought of Alfred North Whitehead or Deleuze. However, let us notice that only recently some (e.g. Jones 2014; Tampio 2015: 56) have started to consider their works – Whitehead's mostly from the twenties and thirties (Whitehead 1978) and Deleuze's from the sixties to eighties (especially Deleuze and Guattari 1987) – in the light of the idea of a flat ontology and its representatives, some of which are covered in this book.

Meanwhile, nearing the end of the twentieth century, Tarde's fellow countryman, Latour, engaged in a very original intellectual and empirical project that perhaps most commonly comes to mind in the face of the concept of flat ontology. This is one of the reasons we are considering him in our investigations.

Despite coming from a family of winemakers, Latour himself did not follow the noble path of the art of winemaking. He not only moved beyond that very path, but transgressed many more. Even though his educational background was in philosophy and Christian theology, a large part of his later intellectual output was either explicitly empirical – in a qualitative, anthropological

DOI: 10.4324/9781003440963-3

fieldwork sense – or very often returned to lessons learned from such research practice and its further implications. In fact, when looking carefully at his impressive oeuvre, the following questions may easily come to mind: Who was he, in intellectual, academic terms? A philosopher, sociologist or anthropologist? An empirical social scientist who happened to engage in some fundamental philosophical, especially metaphysical, problems, or a metaphysician who just had some occasions to do some fieldwork? A writer of separate, independent of each other, works or a thinker of considerable consistency, even when engaging clearly different objects of inquiry and changing vocabulary?

3.1.2 A Bird's-Eye View at Latour's Oeuvre

Just consider some more notable directions of Latour's research and note that the following is still a selective overview made in very general terms. Latour's exposition can begin with his empirical studies on scientists, who Latour carefully observed, including their interactions with various measurement technological instruments, and listened to, in order to get a better understanding of science, scientific facts and researchers' successes and failures. In addition to being among the scientists, whether in their highly sophisticated laboratories (Latour and Woolgar 1986) or in the Amazonian jungle collecting soil samples with them (Latour 1999b: 24–79), Latour utilised some more strictly document-oriented methodologies. These were used not only on the occasion of his well-known historical study concerning Ludwig Pasteur (Latour 1988: 1–150) but also, for instance, in his work addressing the question of why some innovation in public transportation planned for Paris ultimately failed (Latour 1996a). Namely, one of Latour's main interests was not only science but also technology. In both these areas, he proved to be very meticulous and detailed. To acknowledge this, it suffices to notice how much space he devoted to analysing something rather trivial and seemingly not serious enough to pay attention to, like the question: How to make the hotel guests return their keys to the reception (Latour 1991)?

Although Latour is correctly associated with the broad current of science and technology studies (e.g. Sismondo 2010), he appears to draw from his more concrete individually conducted empirical studies and analyses of various real-life cases far-reaching conclusions and implications of much more general, philosophical and socio-theoretical significance. He (Latour 1993) famously diagnoses modernity as a somewhat two-faced intellectual project that, on the one hand, argues in favour of clear opposition between culture and society and nature, and, on the other hand, leads to multiplication of entities that do not fit the implied either-or logic but are instead socio-natural or natural-social hybrids. Latourian interest in modernity leads him not only in the direction of some (re)descriptions of certain thinking patterns or tendencies in the broadly understood Western or Global Northern context. He also proves to be a prescriptive thinker. Following his diagnosis and critique of the way of thinking about and acting in the world called modernity, he (Latour 2004) comes up with the vision of an entire procedure of establishing the composition of reality that would avoid the previously identified shortcomings of modernity or, to be more precise, the so-called Modern Constitution – the complex of ontological, often strongly dichotomising propositions argued to be characteristic of modernity.

Even though the project of analysis and critique of modernity and of proposing some alternative to it can be regarded as significantly broader than, for instance, tracing step-by-step the genesis of some scientific facts, right from the collection of empirical material to the fate of an ultimately published paper in an academic journal or meditation on a peculiar type of key and door lock, Latour also engages more general issues. Already at the considerably early stage of his career, he (Latour 1988: 151–236) presents his philosophical commitments in a form that resembles Baruch Spinoza's *Ethics* (2018) or Ludwig Wittgenstein's *Tractatus Logico-Philosophicus* (2001). A quarter of a century later, Latour (2013) reveals another attempt in grand philosophising. Meanwhile, among various other intellectual enterprises, he (Latour 2005) decides to reflect on the specific way of doing research in the social sciences that he argues he followed in previous research and proposes others to do as well.

3.1.3 "Latour and Law? Just Not That Again!"

Even without explicitly addressing what can be regarded as the last phase of Latour's work – original yet anticipated already in the early stage, interventions in discussions on ecology (e.g. Latour 2017) – one already sees that there is much to draw from when attempting to investigate what can be regarded as Latourian flat ontology from the perspective of law. Moreover, Latour himself engages in law on many occasions. Just consider a few instances, which are addressed in more detail later.

In his early philosophical intervention (Latour 1988: 204, §3.4.3), law is briefly, yet intriguingly, addressed. In his later grand philosophical book (Latour 2013: 357–379), law, yet very specifically understood, becomes one of the many themes to which Latour devotes considerable space and attention. Latour (2010) is also known for conducting largely qualitative observational research in a very important institution for the French legal order – *Conseil d'État*. One must add to this that Latourian propositions, both explicitly devoted to law and others, have already interested many legal scholars (e.g. McGee 2014, 2015; Cloatre 2018).

In light of this, the obvious question is: Why propose a return to the issue of Latour and law? Is what Latour himself says about law and various other legal scholars utilising his work not enough? The present chapter ultimately addresses this part of Latourian thought that has not been sufficiently considered and appears crucial from the perspective of its adequacy to law. However, before we investigate it, we must address some crucial underlying assumptions and provide some reconstruction of what can be seen as the basic unit for ontological inquiry for Latour.

But, again, which Latour? So far, in this chapter, we did not say this explicitly, but most of Latour's work can be associated with what came to be known as ANT. However, Latour's (2013) previously mentioned grand philosophical work, despite coming from the very same person, is somewhat different from the earlier (due to publication dates) complex of ideas and research practices Latour is most well known for. In other words, we should first prepare the ground with respect to Latour's ANT and an inquiry into the modes of existence (AIME) project, fully revealed in the last decade of his life. While in Tarde's case, the selection of relevant material for our discussions here was rather unproblematic, in Latour's case, it is much more complicated, and we must devote some space and effort to it.

3.1.4 Actor-Network Theory or Theories?

Let us first address the ANT issue. Indeed, it can be said to have its beginnings in the science and technology studies field, especially empirical research, but no, this is not a proposition of Latour only. There are a few original actor-network theorists, Latour being only one of them. Despite the fact that Latour, Law (already mentioned, in the Introduction), but also Michel Callon and Madeleine Akrich have all worked with each other and identified themselves with the name (e.g. Akrich et al. 2006), one can doubt whether there is one ANT (see also Kanger 2017). In fact, Latour (2005: 243) himself acknowledges this when, for instance, he says about Law's own ANT "perspective".

Moreover, when considering the various writings of scholars originally associated with the name, we can see some considerable differences or tensions between them. Notice, for instance, that in one of the most iconic early texts of Callon (1987: 100–101), he suggests that actor-networks differ from systems in that they are not involved in a clear demarcation between themselves and their surroundings. While Latour (1983: 153–156; see also Latour 1996b: 372) himself, in an even more well-known text, argues similarly about the deconstruction of the inside-outside (of some entity) dichotomy, he also suggests in some other texts, also early ones, that actor-networks have some outside to themselves (Latour 1988: 171, §1.4.2; 1999a: 19). Consequently, an unsubtle tension is noticeable among prominent actor-network theorists in some of their important writings.

We will come back to the issue suggested here – the existence of some limits or boundaries and, thus, outside, to actor-networks. Now, let us just say that, although uncovering similar differences and tensions in different renditions of ANT would most definitely be an important learning experience and clarification, this is a task we will not be taking up here. We focus on what can be regarded as the Latourian version of ANT (or simply ANT for sake of brevity here), not only because it is one of the original renditions that is also most well known, yet with some issues not discussed enough in literature, but also given the already suggested very strong and explicitly expressed philosophical underpinning.

If one can have doubts about whether there is one ANT among many scholars originally identifying themselves with it, then what about Latour himself? Is there one ANT in his oeuvre? On the one hand, one can respond to this negatively. Notice that we already pointed at some tensions in his writings concerning the existence of some outside to actor-networks. In fact, Latour is, at least, labile with respect to his intellectual output on a much greater scale. He does not only engage in what can be named obstinate synonymisations – instead of sticking to a concept, he often multiplies the expressions, but still grasps one thought (e.g. Latour 1988: 159, §1.1.7). He also navigates the meaning of very specific concepts in his oeuvre differently, which appear to have passed the test of time and are still within the vocabulary he uses (e.g. translation, compare Latour 1983, 1988: 151–236, and Latour 1993). Moreover, even in a single work, Latour can somewhat deviate from the once established meanings of some concepts, even those that are meant to function as opposites (e.g. mediator–intermediary; compare Latour 1999b and Latour 2005). To a certain extent, it is all in character with Latour (2004: 67), who, for instance, self-reflecting on some rather difficultly presented formula, still says that "a speech impediment is preferable to an analytic clarity". He (in Latour et al. 2011: 42) even happens to say that his various book-length "works are of a very different status" and that he is "not homogeneously serious" thinker. Such a suggestion that there is not much continuity in his oeuvre may make the idea of some core of ANT pervading throughout his work even more questionable, also in the light of the following situation. Namely, in the nineties, Latour happened to offer some valuable authorial reflection on ANT (Latour 1996b) and call to cancel the name, enlisting what he considered to be crucial problems with it (Latour 1999a).

However, there are some reasons to consider the presence of a relatively defined ANT in his works, despite this rather conflicted approach to it, visible also through, for instance, Latour's infrequent use of the actor-network concept. One should recognise not only that just a few years after recalling ANT (Latour 1999a), he returns to it, to its very name and devotes to it a specific reconstructive book (Latour 2005) or that when anticipating some wonderment, how it happened that he, an empirical researcher of scientific practices, decided to conduct fieldwork in *Conseil d'État*, he (Latour 2010: viii–ix) says he has been practically doing the same all along, at least since *Laboratory Life* (Latour and Woolgar 1986) – one of the crucial works for science and technology studies as well as ANT. More important is to notice that there is a significant continuity of motifs, concepts and general sensibility and approach throughout the majority of his works, which allows us to say that, after all, there is some single ANT in Latour's oeuvre. Sure, it is often covered by sometimes overly varied and fluctuating conceptual decisions (or undecidability) of Latour, some tensions and inconsistencies across his works, even quite frustrating, as we will see below, but most definitely we can bring to the fore its most crucial aspects, at least with respect to the agenda we set for this book.

Even if this can still be said to be possible, it does not mean it is an easy task. Ultimately, considering his ANT as a flat ontology, we somewhat transgress what Latour says about ANT in some of his later writings on it. Namely, in his clear engagement in social theory, Latour (2005; see also Latour 1999a: 15) insists that ANT should be treated as a method, not theory *tout court*. However, despite such declarations, he can be said to be proposing quite developed vocabulary and principles of general, if not universal, ambitions. In other words, there is some predictable tension between the reading proposed below and how Latour himself would probably react to it. For instance, we sometimes use the concept of framework in reference to his version of ANT, despite his (Latour 2005: 143) dislike of the concept, driven by the insistence to consider his work as largely methodological, not theoretical. It is also difficult to see in the investigations below the evident realisation of the "follow the actors [and let them speak their own language]" principle (e.g. Latour 2005: 11–12, 68, 227, 237). In the following, as with Tarde and the rest of the chosen flat ontologies, ANT is treated – with good reasons for it, despite some contrarian remarks by Latour himself – as an ontological framework that is reconstructable and possible to be confronted with more specific instances of some entity, law in the case of this book. On the other hand, as is clear below, much effort is put into trying to stay true to many other Latourian themes, like multiplying mediators in accounts concerning some entity (e.g. Latour 2005: 61, 128).

3.1.5 On an Inquiry into Modes of Existence Project

Before going into the assumptions of ANT, its basic unit for ontological inquiries and juxtaposing them with law, we must address the already mentioned project of inquiry into modes of existence. It is motivated by Latour's self-criticism raised against what he considered as significant indistinctiveness of ANT (e.g. Latour 2013: 27, 35), which can be read as rendering everything, whether science, technology, law or religion, as very similar to each other as following basically the very same "logic".

In addition to doubting whether discovering the regularity or regularities that is or are so universally adequate would actually be a bad thing, there is the following, even more important reservation to make. Latour's ANT writings do not, in fact, preclude distinctions and differentiating entities. Of course, there are some passages in his (e.g. Latour 1996b: 380) oeuvre that render ANT a framework incapable of differentiation, but they can be read as a peculiar instance of forgetting what was said with respect to it earlier. In the end, Latour (1991: 130) also happens to say that the analysis method he is proposing does not preclude making some distinctions. Moreover, he (Latour 1993: 107–108, 114) says quite clearly about some criteria for difference, such as the mere size of entities, which, as we will see, proves important for our investigations concerning the adequacy of ANT.

AIME, in addition to being based on what can be regarded as some exaggeration in self-criticism against ANT, is indeed a project that, to a certain extent, is separable from ANT. AIME can be understood as founded upon Latour's (2013: 32) stressing of the distinction between network and what can be said to be passing through it. That entire project can be read as a result of an attempt to do justice to the latter while not severing entirely from the former. In the end, when Latour (2013: 27–46) speaks in AIME of networks as a separable mode of existence, even meta-mode (in Tresch 2013: 306), he is close to the somewhat previous major concept of his ANT. In this light, some may be tempted to say that AIME is interesting for our purposes here and should be more fully covered. This would be the case if not for certain issues that need to be revealed.

First, with reference to the already raised issue of networks in AIME and ANT's sense of the concept, one can say that what Latour presents in his ANT writings is much more nuanced and detailed than those in AIME. His pre-AIME work often contains a conceptual apparatus concerning networks that is incomparably richer than some rather superficially corresponding remarks in AIME. Second, indeed, Latour (2013: 357–379) devotes in AIME considerable attention to what he terms law. However, one can say that his understanding of it is, on the one hand, significantly narrower than what we set to be our point of reference and, on the other hand, addresses some processes that, in fact, can be associated not only with law. Let us explain this crucial point.

Latour's reflection on what he names law in AIME is strongly based on his (Latour 2010) already mentioned ethnographical study of *Conseil d'État*. Given that he was quite extraordinarily granted access to some official meetings and deliberations of this institution's officials, his observations allowed him to analyse and reconstruct their broadly understood adjudication practice. In other words, the legal institution Latour investigated can be classified as mostly focused on the application of law, on linking some situations with legal consequences. Of course, such processes are crucial for law, but it would be controversial to assume that they constitute its entirety. In turn, one can get the impression that Latour extrapolated from what he saw in a single, quite peculiar, mostly precedent-oriented institution out of an ultimately statutory law-based country, a far-reaching conclusion on law as such. The Latourian rather narrow adjudication-centredness in most of his clear statements about law can be said to be responsible for how he understands law in AIME (e.g. Latour 2013: 54, 60, 66).

What he (Latour 2013: 38–39, 371–372) terms law in this project is basically establishing and maintaining a connection between the action and the actor responsible for it. Of course, what is usually understood or identified as law can indeed be associated with such a specific function, especially when one is having in mind, just like Latour, the activities of such legal institutions as courts or public administration offices. Namely, through their various decisions, they connect and simultaneously record the connection between, for instance, some action deemed crime and its perpetrator. However, one can wonder whether grasping law, or at least what is termed law, with such a function is correct. In the end, the action-actor connection can be said to be established by something other than the law commonly understood. In other terms, Latourian association of law with that connection in AIME, although understandable in light of Latour's personal fieldwork experience in *Counseil d'État*, appears to fall to the fallacy like that of the functionalist definitions of law, as described by Brian Z. Tamanaha (2001: 176, 179, 180). Namely, if one tries to define law with some broadly understood function it is supposed to realise, it can turn out that such a definition misses the intended mark, as the function in the proposed definition can or is realised by entities other than law. Such a critique of Latour and his AIME approach to law is justified, given the fact that Latour (2015: 331, 349, note 1) himself admits that when he refers to law in the commented project, it can be misleading. Moreover, he admits that some other names were considered for the actor-action connection and indeed names such as assignation, instead of law, would be much more adequate. He adds, with his not that uncommon tongue-in-cheek manner, that he did not decide for such name as its first three letters abbreviation – distinctive for the AIME project – would be rather inappropriate.

Finally, let us notice that the AIME project is quite different from the basic sentiments underlying the mere idea of a flat ontology. Its representatives propose their specific single sets of concepts and principles that are meant to address practically all there is and thus are wary of some *a priori* hierarchisations and dividing reality into various domains. Such ambition just begs to be verified with respect to concrete entities, with law being one of them, hence this entire book. In comparison, AIME can be said to offer not a single framework but few parallel frameworks, each devoted to some specific subject, like politics, technology or religion (Latour 2013: 207–232, 295–325, 327–355); thus, their verification is of a completely different weight than that of some flat ontology. As we will argue below, ANT can be regarded as one. Although we focus in this chapter on it, some references reaching Latour's AIME writings will appear, when necessary. However, just as the entire book can be deemed as a specific back-to-basics when it comes to flat ontologies, a similar move is proposed here with respect to Latour. We return here to his ANT deemed as an ontological framework.

Despite what is implied by the word "return", the proposed reconstruction of ANT's basic sentiments and the assumed unit for ontological inquiries can be regarded as different from other comparable reconstructions. Nevertheless, the most important here – in our focus on law through ANT, and not on what Latour happens to name as law in AIME – is that while a significant part of what can be considered ANT seems quite adequate to law, Latour's (2005: 132, 241–246, 253) idea of plasma or simply actor-network's outside (see also Sutter 2015) – having some anticipations even in early writings – and its connection with Latour's main criterion for existence is problematic. We will see this in the last section of this chapter. Now, after this complicated field clearing – in the following chapters, it will be easier and take up less space – let us bring to the fore ANT's assumptions and sentiments.

3.2 Stepping into … Latourian Actor-Network Theory

3.2.1 To Exist by Actions, to Act and Become Stronger (and Weaker) Thanks to Allies

One can venture to say that the majority of defining sentiments for ANT are already concealed in the actor-network concept and can be unpacked from it. Before considering other fundamental motifs that cannot be easily associated either with the "actor" or with the "network" aspect, let us notice the following. When it comes to the former aspect, ANT can most definitely be said to be an ontology that is action-centred. For Latour, the criterion for the existence of practically anything is whether the entity we are interested in can be said to act on others (e.g. Latour 1991: 109–110; 1996b: 373; 2004: 75, 237; but see also Latour 1988: 158, §1.1.5, 227, §4.5.9; Latour 2005: 137). Action is understood here as broadly as possible. Whenever some entity makes a difference, even the slightest and most mundane, for anything else, then it can be said to exist. Notice that this principle "to exist means to act" can account for both very big and significant entities of an overwhelming influence on a plethora of other entities and for something so delicate and potentially easily fleeting, like a nursery rhyme repeated in the playground.

However, ANT should not be seen as taking interest in merely stating whether something exists, somehow acts or not and thus is inexistent. Notice that speaking about action also implies some practically necessary interest in broadly understood strength and power. It does not seem to be far from common sense to say that some entities appear to influence others to a greater extent, while other actors are much less influential. Why is it like that? To address this, the second aspect of ANT – "network" – should already be considered. Namely, in ANT, there is practically one recipe for becoming stronger, acting better and, in effect, marking one's own existence more decisively and concretely. One must simply make alliances with other entities. Only through relations with others can one become more powerful (Latour 1988: 160, §1.1.9).

We will return to the issue suggested here between the lines that there is practically no innate strength to anything, and that alone, there is not much to achieve whatever given entity is or appears to be. For now, let us notice that the necessity of some alliance-making stressed on many occasions by Latour also works in the opposite direction. In the end, any alliance, any gathering of resources that can be said to endow some entity with more strength, can be significantly weakened by just one specific ally somehow malfunctioning or detaching oneself. Think then of the figure of chain, which is as strong as its weakest link (e.g. Latour 2013: 61–62). There is a strong sense of strength-weakness dialectics in ANT (e.g. Latour 1988: 201, §3.3.6). What is co-responsible for some entity's strength is also the spot of its weakness and even futility.

Although one can find some more nuanced reservations in Latour's oeuvre (e.g. Latour 1988: 191, §3.3.1), most usually he suggests, in the discussed context, quite unsubtle quantitative, additive logic, according to which the more, the better (e.g. Latour 2005: 237). Of course, one can see here some tautology: the more allies one has, the more one can do, making further allies included. This is not the most important here, though. Notice that the talk about gathering allies, in addition to obvious pluralism, also entails strong emphasis on heterogeneity, even impurity in ANT. The quote from Michel Tournier's (1969) reimagining of the tale about Robinson Crusoe on being wary of purity because it is the poison to soul that is used by Latour twice in his early books (Latour and Woolgar 1986: 8; Latour 1988: 201, §3.3.4) speaks volumes here. To be stronger, to act more and better, one must ally oneself with other entities very often significantly different from oneself, even up to the point of coming from what usually is considered completely different spheres or domains of reality.

3.2.2 *Against Domains, Hierarchies and Critique, For Descriptivism*

Speaking of them, ANT is strongly against thinking about the world in such terms, most usually entailing dichotomies and inequality between their involved terms. Perhaps most famously, ANT wants to disrupt such binaries like nature-culture/society, as well as macro-micro or global-local (e.g. Latour 1993, 2005). The word "disrupt" is more important than it may seem at first glance. Namely, Latour argues not in favour of some mitigation or compromise between the extremes in such dichotomies, trying to find some middle ground between them. Instead, he advises us to symmetrically disrupt or abandon them. Notice that when one considers various entities in terms of their actions and influences that, as said, depend on the diverse allies, rendering back the entities one starts the analysis with as, in consequence, transgressing the suggested usual distinctions or, to be more precise, not truly belonging to any one of them, such symmetry is quite understandable and can be said to be just flowing from previous sentiments.

However, we should stress that the symmetry in ANT also has another, yet connected with what was just said, meaning. Just as anything that exists, whether human or nonhuman, can be said to somehow act on others, we should also get rid of any separate vocabularies, each devoted to some type of entity (e.g. Latour 1991: 108). ANT itself can be seen as a conceptual framework at this level of generality that it can address everything there is, what typically is seen as human, but also even utterly nonhuman, without any sense that anything or any type of entity is more worthy or important than others. The anti-domain or anti-dichotomies symmetry entails what can be named far-reaching descriptivism and anti-criticality of ANT, while human-nonhuman symmetry – anti-anthropocentrism.

With respect to the former, Latour (2005) opposes the distinction between the mere description and explanation concerning what was observed and described.

Very often, the research practice in broadly understood social sciences consists of some account of the case under scrutiny and a subsequent explanation that may frequently utilise concepts such as "context", "culture" or "economy". In turn, Latour proposes that any description of whatever we are interested in that is truly complete, brought to its end, can also be said to provide an explanation of the case, and, consequently, any reference to the concepts like those just mentioned is just unnecessary. For Latour, that which can be said to explain some phenomenon is immanent to it, not transcendent, similarly as for Tarde. Moreover, Latour is ready to call the practice of making references to such grand notions the symptom of research laziness and taking shortcuts. In turn, the research practice model suggested by ANT is to be as patient, focused on details and ready to follow even the most seemingly miniscule or mundane aspects of the case wherever they may lead, as possible. Notice that here Latour presents himself as an opponent to any cutting corners in research and practically costlessly coming up with the explanations of some observed phenomena by just drawing some concepts like the above-mentioned or similar (consider, for example, "capitalism"). However, Latour is also specifically against costlessness in more clearly ontological accounts or diagnoses of various entities when he (Latour 1988) talks about the potentiality. We will address this issue below. For now, let us just recognise that often the concepts used for explanation – in its mode criticised by Latour – also suggest some different and objectively separable domains of reality, some of which may be even thought of as involved in some hierarchies between themselves. ANT's programmatical disruption of them and the prescribed time-consuming, even painfully meticulous, utterly descriptivist (but at the same time explanatory) methodological ideal simply go hand in hand.

In addition to the connection between anti-domain symmetry and descriptivism, there is also a relation with Latour's anti-criticality, in the sense of his opposition, sometimes even bordering with ridicule, to what can be regarded as critical theory (e.g. Latour 2005: 85, 101–102). Notice that one can associate investigations that identify themselves with that notion with imagining some level structure of reality, where layers regarded as somehow more important or fundamental exert their influence on other levels; thus, reference to them is required to account for what is happening on minor or derivative layers. Obviously, Latour is against that.

However, he is also opposed to the critical-theoretical manner of practically arguing that those involved in an analysed situation or phenomenon are wrong in their grasp of it, that their perception and thinking are distorted by some form of false consciousness which prevents them from seeing the entire relevant reality and, thus, should be enlightened, made more reflective by researchers. Once again, ANT wants to counter that by stressing the need to listen to the involved actors themselves, seriously treat their accounts of the relevant case and not dismiss them as, for instance, the results of some deception or low cognitive competences. Not only meticulously following the actors but also carefully listening to them may, as a result, thoroughly disrupt any underlying belief in more or less important levels of reality and dichotomies said to be fundamental, but for Latour, way misleadingly convenient for researchers.

3.2.3 Nonhumans as Actors, Delegates, Mediators and Intermediaries

Having reached this point, let us now move to human–nonhuman symmetry and anti-anthropocentrism of ANT. If it can be said to begin with the mentioned action-centred criterion for existence, then we can most definitely say that it specifically equalises humans and nonhumans, for both can be said to exert some influence on others. Of course, associating humans with actions is somewhat easier, but perhaps only because it is us, humans, who make such an association. Nevertheless, just as some humans can cause some difference for other entities, their fellow humans and everything else, nonhumans act on us and among themselves (e.g. Latour 1992).

I, the author of this book, through its contents, cause some change in you, dear reader, just by occupying your attention (hopefully effectively and with some satisfaction for you). However, to reach this point, I had to, among other things, use specific computer hardware and software – though human-made, themselves not being humans – just to prepare the book's manuscript. These nonhumans influenced me back because I had to adjust myself to their requirements and characteristics.

Of course, some may react that humans' actions cannot be equalised with that of nonhumans because we are endowed with intentionality, whereas it cannot be identified in a plethora of nonhumans. However, let us recall that ANT's sense of action is very general as it basically addresses any difference that one entity can make to another. This is, though, merely one aspect of Latourian anti-anthropocentrism.

In addition to saying that not only humans act and, thus, in a specific way undermine our supposed exceptionality with respect to all the rest of being, Latour also devotes much space to showing how much nonhumans do and how much we would not be the way we are if not for them. In short, we can say that ANT's another important tenet is the appreciation of nonhumans, especially materiality. Ultimately, a distinctive feature of the analysed framework is Latour's engagement with even the most seemingly trivial material entities, such as doors, keys and locks (e.g. Latour 1991); seat belts (e.g. Latour 1992); speed bumps (e.g. Latour 1999b: 186–190) or a plethora of scientific devices, from really sophisticated laboratory equipment (e.g. Latour and Woolgar 1986; 1988) to really basic, yet practically highly significant, such as a cardboard box divided into many smaller cubes – containers for soil samples (Latour 1999b: 47–67). Taking many remarks and passages in Latour's work, we can say he considers material entities, both relatively big and small, in a plethora of contexts or from the perspective of many roles and functions realised by them.

First, as already anticipated, Latour is ready to stop treating material entities as passive objects destined to be moved by others, especially humans, and not to move them in return. The agency is given here to material things as they often are noticed to exert their influence even on humans, who, when confronted with a given entity, are faced with the following alternative: either step up and adjust oneself to what seems to be required by a thing to be used or face various consequences, such as lack of possibility of reaching one's own intended goals or having to cope with a negative outcome. However, this does not imply that, in the Latourian perspective, material things cannot be employed for a human agenda. They can and actually are utilised for what Latour calls delegations (e.g. Latour 1992: 229), but their use always comes at a cost for the user. Moreover, just to be clear, instances of what are named delegations do not necessarily have to involve humans.

When it comes to the concept of delegations, even though we will return to it later, when discussing the mere basic unit in ANT – that is, actor-network – we can already say the following. To get some basic grasp of the concept, consider that you would like to have your political or ideological message better heard and recognised. Obviously, you cannot stick to merely speaking about it in person in some face-to-face situations, because your voice alone will reach a small portion of the quantity of people you would like to influence. In this light, you can, of course, write down your ideas and distribute them among many more addressees. With even something so trivial like a written or printed document, its author's physical presence is not needed, but the ideas can gain much wider recognition. Various material entities can play the role of that to which some action is delegated to be passed on.

Speaking of passing on some action – whether some idea or much more explicitly tangible force – notice, in reference to our political-ideological message example, that whatever device or technology we could use to help us expand our reach cannot be said to be neutral with respect to our idea. Of course, many of us are probably accustomed to thinking that writing, print or digital text edition possibilities are perfectly transparent with respect to what is transferred to paper or screen. However, anyone who has written anything in their lives may now realise that the mere perspective of writing down what one has in mind, heart or soul alters that message. Perhaps this alteration is often quite subtle, yet it still happens.

In light of this, one can say, in just another anticipation of what we will discuss below: material entities, in addition to being delegates, very often function as mediators. Namely, Latour appears to be quite strongly and faithfully – noteworthy in the context of his often dizzying habit of changing vocabulary – attached to the distinction between mediators and intermediaries (e.g. Latour 2005; but see Latour 1993: 38). The former is the name for entities that are not neutral with respect to what they carry or pass on. Mediators always modify that for which they are specific vessels. In comparison, the intermediaries concept is meant to denote that which perfectly neutrally, without any additions and without any losses with respect to what they carry, pass it on. To put it differently, that which is transferred by an intermediary stays the same when comparing some destination point it reaches with the point preceding being put into intermediary. As suggested earlier, ANT generally advises to be detail-focused enough in one's investigations that one multiplies mediators – treats entities involved in some analysed situation or phenomenon as those that do not remain neutral with respect to what they transfer. Of course, it is possible to regard various entities as intermediaries only, but for Latour, a good, in ANT's sense, description is the one with as many mediators as possible.

Returning to our example here, we might treat the involved material devices allowing us to pass our message further as intermediaries, but it could be regarded as us not paying careful attention enough to see in them the actual mediators. This is, though, still not the entire image of the most crucial points from ANT that show its treatment of nonhumans, and, at the same time, anti-anthropocentrism – in the end, the statuses of delegates, mediators and intermediaries are not restricted to nonhumans only, but we can also play such roles, which is just another way of equalising humans and nonhumans.

3.2.4 Scattering of Action

To show that another point, just think once again of our example of disseminating some political or ideological message. Let us suppose now that we succeeded – more and more people are starting to think in the terms we proposed. In such a situation, most of us would be ready to celebrate our success as if only we personally were responsible for our achievement, right? However, notice that in ANT's terms, it would simply be unwarranted, because strictly speaking, we alone did not achieve our success. It happened due to, among many other circumstances, our usage of the chosen dissemination technique, which can be regarded as our ally that enhances our power, our action. ANT, in fact, invites us to consider how much of anyone's or anything's actions are not that very entity's achievements but can be said to be the result of various external entities. In reference to this point in his framework, Latour (2005: 45–46) uses different concepts, such as dislocation, distribution or overtaking of action. It appears that it will not be unjustified to use the concept of scattering of action instead.

Before moving on, two issues should be highlighted. Of course, material entities, various nonhumans can and most often are involved in such scattering of action, but so can and are humans, depending on what is analysed at the given moment. Perhaps even more importantly, notice that the word "external" used a few lines earlier can be somewhat misleading in the discussed context. In the end, the action of even seemingly easily identifiable in space and time entity is not its alone but scattered across a plethora of other entities. However, given "to exist means to act", these entities are not truly external to the action and, in consequence, the existence of the entity one analyses or, to be more precise, the part of its existence that is due to the action in question. In short, one can say that, for ANT, the following is true: "X is, because X acts, but X's action is due to others, yet specifically internal to that action". Notice also that this is consistent with what we said at the very beginning of this section. An actor's power is not that actor's itself but of the network of allies it manages to make.

3.2.5 Significance of Nonhumans for Humans

In addition to the importance of the connection between the threads of scattering of action and the actor-network nexus, notice that what we said is crucial not only in the context of nonhumans appreciation but also for anti-anthropocentrism we are still addressing here. From the above flows the confirmation of what Latour (2004: 263, note 21) himself says: humans, we are ourselves not thanks to some innateness but thanks to a myriad of nonhumans. This holds not only in relation to our mere somaticity, biological existence – just consider the importance of our intestinal bacterial flora and how we ought to take care of it, for instance, taking some probiotics while undergoing antibiotics treatment. We also take our shape in other, interpersonal, social and professional terms due to nonhumans, which, as said earlier, require from us certain skills to make use of them. If we succeed in that, we can expand our social network, gain broadly understood status or, more concretely, better professional positions, that all can be said to feed back into us.

Reaching slowly the end of this significant thread of ANT, we should add that nonhumans, especially materiality, appreciation is related not only to the individuals we focused ourselves to this point but also to the entire populations or societies. Namely, for Latour the fact that humans managed and still manage to have among themselves some relatively stable social structures that can expand themselves up to the point of embracing even millions of people would simply be impossible if not for materiality (e.g. Latour 1993: 54, 111, 120). Just as we already brought up in the Introduction, Latour likes to juxtapose the social structures of humans and baboons (e.g. Latour 2005). The latter are quite literally bare in their relations, and thus, any order and stability in their groups must be constantly maintained by various activities in their interindividual interactions. In the case of us, humans, a lot of work required to have stable structures and institutions can be said to be quite successfully delegated to a plethora of nonhumans. To recognise this, just try to imagine any contemporary organisation, of the public or private sector, without any nonhuman materiality, like office buildings, computers, other relevant hardware or internet and electric power infrastructure. Without them, all that would be left are humans, who without any aid from these and other materiality could be able, at best, to have some relatively small meeting but not to run even a medium-sized enterprise. Of course, the similar regularity applies to all structures, organisations or institutions, including the level of entire states and international and transnational entities.

In short, in ANT, even that what can be regarded as perfectly human – various institutions, enterprises and entire political organisations – are not and could not be entirely human. Endowing nonhumans with a value, doing them justice and increasing their status in broadly understood social sciences can then be regarded as a strongly deanthropocentric move. However, one should notice that Latour's interest in material entities is largely the result of wanting to account for big human societies and their stability, on the ground that bare humans just could not achieve them. Of course, there are some small remarks of Latour on exclusively nonhuman–nonhuman relations (e.g. Latour 1992: 258, note 23), but still he is not against anthropocentrism as strongly as possible because his ANT devotes little attention to situations where no human being is involved or even only present.

What is more important here, though, is that the above discussion concerning Latour's nonhumans appreciation illustrates well his commitment to specifically understood heterogeneity and impurity. Even our bodies are not entirely human, given the above-mentioned intestinal flora. Our ideas, just like the ones in our example above on the political message, are not purely ideational, given their entanglement in various material entities. The same is true for various social organisations and institutions. Although some may still be tempted to consider them as, for instance, beings of purely human, interpersonal agreements, just like many contemporary analytical social ontologists we draw attention to in the Introduction, they are much more than exclusively agreement-based. This is because the agreement between people that would not be materially mediated is just not enough to maintain entire contemporary social structures, even those of a relatively small scale.

3.2.6 Issue of (Anti)Essentialism, Translation and the Irreduction Principle

Having followed what is specifically packed in both aspects – "actor" and "network" – of the main concept of ANT and covered in many different passages in Latour's relevant works, and slowly reaching the end of discussion on the most crucial sentiments and assumptions, we should address the following issue. Given all that we covered above – especially Latourian regularity, that to exist means to act, but one's actions are due to various allies and, consequently, do not entirely belong to the one that can be said to be acting at some analysed moment – Latour may be considered as a quite vehement opponent of essentialism. However, such a classification is way too hasty.

As we will see below, there are some traces of essentialist thinking in his ontology, especially when he (Latour 1988: 159, §1.1.8) says that there are no actors that would be so weak that they cannot make alliance with some other entity. In short, he assumes some basic capacity for making alliances with others, even in the seemingly weakest, the least allied objects. Moreover, he is not against the idea that there are some characteristic features to things out there that make them what they are. He just proposes not to assume any such essences in a way that would suggest that these features were present in the object in question since its very beginning. Latour adheres to the vision that essences are possible, but they uncover practically simultaneously with the stabilisation of a given entity, its maturation, which, one should add here, is done not only by, for instance, human scientists investigating a given object (whatever it is) but also by everything else that somehow relates to it. In other words, while Jean-Paul Sartre's (2007: 20) famous "existence precedes essence" – itself having some similarly famous predecessors – is expressed in an explicitly anthropocentric context, according to Latour (1991: 115; 1993: 86), it gains much more general, posthumanist meaning. Nothing is by itself, from its very inception, with an essence specific to itself. Essence reveals itself only later (Latour 2004: 167) because "we never work in a world filled with actors to which fixed contours may be granted" (Latour 1991: 109). In short, we can characterise ANT's position as *a posteriori* relational essentialism.

To understand this point better, it suffices to remind one quite humoristic, yet informative, tale about toads that Latour (2004: 87) presents in one of his books. He refers to an ethological expertise according to which specific species of toads come back to their birthplace pond to lay eggs for another generation. In accordance with such a thesis, building highways had to be somewhat complicated to take into account dedicated tunnels for toads to allow them to safely reach such a destination. However, once highways with toad tunnels in embankments were in place, the toads did not follow the theses of ethologists and did not use the painstakingly built amenities dedicated to them. Instead, it appeared that, basically, any water reservoir in some vicinity proved to be sufficient for the toads' needs as they laid their eggs there. Latour's commentary on this can be summed up as follows: what was considered as an inherent and unchangeable essence of these toads – egg-laying behaviours – proved to be nothing truly innate and stable. Even the practices of organic nonhumans, which some may be more prone to consider in essentialist terms, prove to be nothing more than a derivative of the relations in which they currently partake. To put it differently, in ANT, the specificity or singularity of existing entities is not due to themselves but due to other entities.

However, ANT's existential principles, we began this section with, are still in force. Namely, there is a practical necessity to relate to others, to make some alliances in effect of which one becomes stronger and can act more and better. In short, entities must interact with each other. How can it happen, though, if they are assumed to be utterly specific (Latour 1988: 158, §1.1.1)? Latour (in Latour et al. 2011: 43–44) argues that any relation between entities is the translation they make of each other. They engage each other and grasp each other, but, as with more usually linguistically understood translation, they do not and just cannot do justice to their entire specificity or singularity. Something is always lost in translation – any relation can be said to be also a specific distortion of its terms, or, to be more precise, the relating terms distort each other.

All these crucial threads – relational, derivative, not innate character of entities' features, yet still some incommensurability of things that necessitates that any relations between objects are only translations, with all their possible imperfections – are put succinctly, perhaps too succinctly, by Latour in various propositions in *Irreductions*. Latour says, among other things, that "[n]othing is, by itself, the same as or different from anything else. That is, there are no equivalents, only translations" (Latour 1988: 162, §1.2.1), "[s]ince nothing is, in and of itself, either equivalent, or not equivalent [...], two forces [one of many Latourian synonyms for entities – M.D.] cannot associate without misunderstanding" (Latour 1988: 168, §1.3.3), and that "[t]here are acts of differentiation and identification, not differences and identities" (Latour 1988: 169, §1.3.7). Notice Latourian emphasis on how things are not any by themselves but always thanks to others.

This emphasis can be said to flow directly from the so-called Irreduction Principle, with which Latour begins the mentioned *Irreductions* – one of his most dense and challenging texts, especially in the first contact with it, which is also one of the most important for the task set in this chapter. According to this principle, "[n]othing is, by itself, either reducible or irreducible to anything" (Latour 1988: 158, §1.1.1). In light of all that was said earlier, it can be somewhat unpacked in the following way. Everything is the way it is. By itself, an entity is neither, for instance, reducible to something else nor irreducible. It may prove to be just like that only by some other entity that relates to it in a specific way or, to be more precise, translates it and modifies it. Something that, according to the Irreduction Principle and its derivatives quoted earlier, is by itself neither reducible nor irreducible is specifically altered, changed, as some entity that relates to it renders it reducible or irreducible to, for instance, its components. Once again, then, the derivative, relational character of entities' specifics comes to the fore, which, it must be also remembered, is specifically coupled with the idea that anything by itself is just the way it is.

3.2.7 What About (Anti)Emergentism?

The Irreduction Principle is mentioned here not only to provide a better insight into a crucial sentiment in ANT but, more importantly, to address another aspect of how Latour characterises that which exists. Namely, notice that here Latour proves to be difficult to classify in terms of emergentism-anti-emergentism. On the one hand, the principle suggests that, for Latour, both possibilities are still on the table. In fact, Latour can be regarded as, for a lack of better description, an abinary thinker, meaning that he often appears to make his point of reference some binaries or clear polar oppositions. However, he does not adopt for himself the necessity to choose of the relevant extremes, and rather sticks to abinary thinking of "neither ... nor ...". On the other hand, Latour's (2005) scepticism towards big social entities and his criticism against Durkheim flowing largely from his admiration for Tarde, including the latter's rejection of holism, may put Latour in a different light – as an opponent to emergentism and what it entails, such as the nonreducibility of a holistic entity to its components.

This can be read in at least two ways. First, Latour, by revealing his strong disagreement with holism, may be regarded as contradicting his Irreduction Principle, because here he seems to prejudge the characteristics of various beings. Second, though, he can be defended against such an accusation. One can argue that Latour does not say that entities are by themselves reducible. Instead, he just renders entities reducible in his anti-holistic approach. In this light, there is no "by itself" aspect in his disagreement with emergence and he remains, at least in the discussed context, still in line with the Irreduction Principle, even though he expressed it over fifteen years before his (Latour 2002) clear engagement with Tarde and his anti-holism. However, let us not delve into this potential controversy anymore – as Latourian oeuvre is full of various similar tensions, some of which we will see below. Practically, at the end of this exposition of ANT's key assumptions and sentiments, we have come to the Irreduction Principle, with which we could have also begun this section.

3.2.8 (Claim to) Universality

Before focusing, for a moment, on the actor-network itself – arguably as a basic unit for ontological inquiry in ANT – let us just illustrate here the assumed universality of this approach. First, let us return to the nursery rhyme example above to illustrate how ANT can account for linguistic entities, obviously important for our interest in law.

Children's rhymes most definitely can be said to act given the fact that they attract children and their caretakers, who may end up repeating a catchy rhyme or song themselves, often against their conscious will. If it happens, then it can be said that all those who repeat the specific string of words are its allies. The more people say it, the stronger it is. Notice that already here the important point made by Latour (1988: 183, §2.4.2) with respect to language comes into play – that words alone cannot do much and they must be surrounded by other kinds of entities. In our example, these other entities – rhyme's allies – are human beings who keep in their minds the words and say them aloud. However, as Latour (1988: 183, §2.4.2) explicitly says, words can associate themselves with "anything". As practically any linguistic entity, our rhyme can become more stable than what human memory and children's interests and trends allow by being written down, published and distributed using various media, both analogue and digital. Obviously, all involved entities can be considered through the conceptual lenses of delegations and mediators or intermediaries. By associating with many such entities, very often quite different from itself as, for instance, tangible, concentrated in space, like a printed booklet, or more expanded, like server rooms, electric power and internet connection infrastructure, the rhyme becomes stronger but also appears much less pure and more heterogeneous. In the end, what could be considered a linguistic entity is not purely linguistic and, for Latour, cannot be, for its weakness resulting from its potential purity would risk its nonexistence. Obviously, this impurity of the rhyme entails the other crucial threads we covered earlier, as they prove to be applicable to our example as well. Not only materiality is appreciated here, but something that could be seen exclusively in anthropocentric categories reveals to be much more ontologically ambiguous. Consequently, some domains and dichotomies that may come to mind when considering linguistic entities, like ideational-material, cultural-technical or even cultural-somatic, are disrupted or, at least, put into doubt.

ANT's approach to language is more than the mere reiteration of its general principles with respect to what can be seen as specific, because linguistic, entities. For instance, when addressing the issue of true statements, crucial for Latourian involvement in the problems of science and its practices, he says:

> A sentence does not hold together because it is true, but *because it holds together* we say that it is "true." What does it hold on to? Many things. Why? Because it has tied its fate to anything at hand that is more solid than itself. As a result, no one can shake it loose without shaking everything else. (Latour 1988: 185–186, §2.4.8)

In other words, the truth of a statement can be understood as a function of everything that a very sentence is connected with and refers to. For instance, a sentence without any referents that would be more durable than that sentence cannot be considered true. However, as soon as it gets some referents – be they contents of other statements or something tangible in the physical world – it can be said to gaining allies, becoming stronger and acquiring the status of truth.

Without delving into these and other comparable passages, our rhyme example should already illustrate ANT's universality or, at least, its promise that, after some more details on the actor-network itself, we will try to verify with respect to law. This promise is serious, given the fact that Latour (2005) basically proposes to apply the very same ontological principles to human beings in one of his most focused and lengthiest interventions in social theory.

Just like anything in his framework can be said to be compositional – just think again of our rhyme or organisation examples – so humans are explicitly said to be the same (Latour 2005: 207). Interestingly, he does not have in mind in relevant passages the intestinal flora we referred to earlier but something more stereotypically and intimately human – our thoughts, competences and actions, including those clearly related to other humans. Latour's point seems to be summarised in the following question he (Latour 2005: 209) asks: "[h]ow many circulating clichés do we have to absorb before having the competence to utter an opinion about a film, a companion, a situation, a political stance?". We are what and who we are – including our social identities and how we manage ourselves – not thanks to us ourselves. We become what and who we are thanks to a plethora of other entities of diverse specifics that, even if not entirely external to us (think again of why we take probiotics with antibiotics), are nevertheless somewhat foreign.

Latour gives a few examples. First, "official and legal papers which designate 'you' as being someone" (Latour 2005: 208). Indeed, our identity, subjectivity and singularity come from beyond, even something so trivial like various public administration records. Second, "[c]ognitive abilities do not reside in 'you' but are distributed throughout the formatted setting, which is [...] made of [...] many small intellectual technologies" (Latour 2005: 211). Even our intellectual powers are not entirely ours or confined to the contents of our skulls but the functions of a plethora of entities way beyond our bodies, from pen and paper, through calculators, to various internet databases.

On a side note, it is telling that Searle (2014), who can be classified as a materiality belittler, said in one interview that "the theory of extended mind makes me want to throw up", while Latour (2005: 11, 60, footnote 66), a clear instance of a materiality immodest equaliser, speaks favourably of the earlier distributed cognition theory and, in fact, touches upon the very same issues as extended mind proponents.

Third, and finally, even the most personal emotions and their expressions are not entirely ours but can come from, among other sources, the pop culture we consume. Just think about another question of Latour (2005: 209): "[d]oesn't reading novels help you to know how to love?". In conclusion, Latourian ontological action-centredness, and the plurality of seemingly external and foreign entities – allies – contributing to the strength of the given entity, its actions, actual impurity, heterogeneity and all the features that most usually are regarded as innate, essential in *a priori* way, can be noticed not only in specifically nonhuman beings but in us as well.

3.2.9 Latourian Actor-Network Theory as Flat Ontology

Having reached this point, we can safely say that ANT fits the conditions of a flat ontology as proposed in the Introduction. In reference to the pluralism aspect of the mere idea of a flat ontology – ANT most definitely tries to do justice to a myriad of entities, no matter how mundane or trivial they appear to be, with as less ontological prejudice as possible.

As such, ANT adheres to nonhierarchy. However, its approach towards hierarchy is more nuanced. Namely, hierarchies are possible, but they must be achieved by involved entities and properly accounted for in the analyses, not presupposed (e.g. Latour 1996b: 372). In turn, when it comes to what can be considered an internal structure of a given analysed entity, the possibility of hierarchy seems more debatable. For instance, there is a passage where Latour (1988: 233, §4.7.6) slightly suggests that one should avoid thinking in terms of one component ruling, towering over others, but, again, if one element proves stronger than others, it is unclear why rendering the situation in which it is involved in hierarchical terms ought to be prevented. Nevertheless, what is much more certain is that ANT is strongly against the idea of largely clear-cut, often opposed to each other, domains or levels of reality and other usual dichotomies in social sciences.

The time has come now to focus on ANT's basic unit for ontological inquiries. As in the case of Tarde's MON, a lot of specifics of Latourian actor-network were already covered in this section. In consequence, below, our discussion will be somewhat more concise. However, we will not merely reiterate, as we will address some more detailed issues, which simply are unfit to cover when dealing with general sentiments and assumptions, but which prove to be still crucial in light of our research questions.

3.3 Focusing on … Actor-Networks

3.3.1 Not Only Synonyms

First, before we bring to the fore ANT's understanding of being, of what there is, let us notice that also here one can witness Latour's obstinate synonymisation. Namely, it appears that in his oeuvre to denote that what exists, he uses, among others, the concepts of force, weakness, entelechy, monad (Latour 1988: 159, §1.1.7), hybrid (Latour 1993), association, actor, actant and network (Latour 2004). Despite that and some varying approach of Latour himself towards it – as mentioned earlier – we will stick to the actor-network concept, most importantly because the two terms involved already cover some of the crucial specifics of the commented framework.

However, such a decision for the sake of the analysis here should not be understood as a statement that every Latourian concept that appears to denote what exists means perfectly the same. His vocabulary, in addition to being rather far from stable across various works, is rich in what can be regarded as various distinctions concerning what exists, made based on diverse criteria. Just recall the already introduced crucial differentiation between mediators and intermediaries. However, there is much more to this. For instance, in *Politics of Nature: How to Bring Sciences into the Democracy*, he (Latour 2004: 22) introduces quite interesting, yet somewhat neglected in various commentaries (e.g. Harman 2009; Blok and Elgaard Jensen 2011; McGee 2014, 2015; Schmidgen 2015; De Vries 2016; Michael 2017; Blok et al. 2020), distinction between risk-free and risky objects. The former are basically understood as well-defined entities, endowed with some concrete essence, whose all preceding factors that gave rise to them are practically invisible; their significance for the object became unnoticeable. The latter are obviously opposite of such characteristics. As an instance of the former, one can give something so mundane like a brick, while for the latter, one can give a genetically modified organism (GMO). In the end, practically everyone knows what a brick is and what it can do, but no one has in the picture brick producers, the technologies they adopt and the materials they use. In turn, a GMO, when it comes to its specifics, is uncertain, fluctuating; it may reveal its further aspects only in more or less distant future, and its creators are not moved into the background of it.

In short, then, in ANT, one can find various differentiations of entities, in accordance with some aspect of them or a role that is put into the fore. With full acknowledgement of this, we will still stick to the back-to-basics approach, revealed earlier, and will focus on the actor-network itself. Before doing that, however, let us just notice that, especially in the mentioned work of Latour (2004), there is also suggested an entity that rather cannot be considered just another type of actor-network, but something else, which can also be regarded as the largest category in Latourian vocabulary. As already mentioned, Latour's anti-domain and anti-dichotomies commitment, connected with his anti-anthropocentrism and critical stance towards modernity, leads him to be critical of the concepts of culture and society. To free oneself from their human-centredness, counterfactual due to the already discussed role of nonhumans and materiality, and the implied opposite figure of nature, Latour proposes the concept of the collective. Basically, it is meant to be a substitute for society but involves a whole myriad of different entities, including nonhumans. The exact composition of the collective – who and what is recognised, and who and what is (still) not allowed in it (just think of, for instance, artisanal cheeses and faeries, not as creatures of fiction but as real sprites of forests and brooks, in the contemporary context) – is to be established in accordance with the procedure imagined by Latour. We will not delve into it, as it is unnecessary for our purposes here. Nevertheless, it is mentioned here for the mere sake of raising awareness that one can identify in Latour somewhat different entities than actor-networks and the various roles they may play in the phenomena under scrutiny.

3.3.2 Broad Sense of Action

When dealing with actor-networks, let us notice here first that Latour (e.g. Latour 2011: 796, 799), on the one hand, appears to use the concept in a strictly methodological sense, as a specific figure that accounts of various entities and phenomena should adhere to. On the other hand, though, there are many passages in Latour's relevant works where an actor-network is treated as a formal basic unit for ontological inquiries. Here, we largely follow this second line of interpretation, having considerable support in various Latourian writings.

An actor-network can denote any entity that acts. In accordance with the already mentioned action-orientedness of ANT, only that which somehow acts can be said to exist. "Somehow" is the key here because Latour adopts a very broad sense of action. Namely, anything – also something clearly nonhuman, even nonorganic and seemingly inert – that makes any difference to something else can be said to act and thus exist. Even the mere upholding of something else can be considered as acting enough to classify a seemingly perfectly passive supporter as a true actor and existing entity. Considering this, the brick in the wall can be said to act as it upholds the entire relevant construction. Love poem may cause various emotions or, at the very least, occupy its listeners' or readers' attention for a moment. Moreover, for Latour (1992: 241), even something utterly non-figurative and abstract as some geopolitical abstractions like West or East still specifically act.

Such inclusive action-orientedness has not only the consequence that ANT most definitely can be regarded as raising the claim to be a universal ontological framework. It also is tightly connected with a thread we did not have heretofore a good opportunity to address – Latour's approach to potentiality.

3.3.3 Against Potentiality

Latour (1988) is against giving or ascribing to some entities the features, possibilities, range or worth they currently do not actually have but merely appear to have or appear to have some prospect to get. If to exist means to act, then one should stick to in one's investigations only to that what is really done or achieved by the entity under scrutiny. Anything that could be said to be merely potential for a given object should be regarded as actually not within its grasp – something not had, not achieved and thus not allowed in its ontological profile made in accordance with ANT.

There are a few additional remarks to make here. First, despite what the largely anti-potentiality stance of Latour may suggest, he is not against the idea of some entities having various possibilities to act, but, for whatever reasons, not actualising them at the moment. Possibilities are not rejected in ANT, but one cannot just take them for granted (Latour 1988: 174, §1.5.1.1). Namely, any possibility of acting always necessitates some costs for the actor, who or what is analysed. If that actor can be said to have the necessary infrastructure to move somewhere, but it does not use it in some considered moment, then one can say that the anti-potentiality position has not been transgressed. However, if some argue of a certain entity that it can achieve some goal, but it does not have that what could account for the presumed possibility, then one falls into potentiality. Think of one of Latour's most favourite figures – train and tracks (e.g. Latour 1988: 220, §4.4.2, 226, §4.5.7.1; 1993: 117). Basically, trains can move only on dedicated tracks. When the tracks are expanded, trains can reach some new destinations. However, it would be unfounded to say that a train can travel anywhere. In other words, ANT is strongly against taking shortcuts in reasoning and taking for granted that which requires much work to become possible to realise by some entity. This is why we had already anticipated the commented thread while talking earlier about Latour's critique of costlessness. Possibilities that were created, their costs were incurred, even when not realised by some entity at the moment (when some of its other possibilities are taken up in some action), are not against action-orientedness and anti-potentiality. In turn, that which cannot be accounted for (the economic connotation is most definitely intended here) in any way deviates from the emphasis on action and falls into potentiality. Having said that, there is a second important reservation to make.

Although Latour's anti-potentiality can be summarised in the following way – disagreeing and criticising claims that a given entity has something or can do something while it has not or cannot – he sees some perhaps somewhat perverse and deceitful sense in arguing by some entity that it has or can do (what it does not have or cannot). Namely, when dealing with potentiality, Latour (1988: 174, §1.5.2) also treats it in terms of a bluff. As anyone who has played Poker or any comparable card game knows, even if one does not have a strong hand, but just comes across like they have among the rest at the table, can still win. The same is the case with the Latourian sense of potentiality. Indeed, potentiality is merely apparent, nothing real. However, if a given entity constantly tries to show off as specifically bigger and stronger than the rest because it claims to have more and be able to do more, then some of that rest may simply believe in it. In consequence, that what begins with a bluff, impression (objectively false) can end up with becoming real. Just think of a person who claims to know everyone important in some area (but they do not). They still may end up knowing some important people, who themselves want to be even more well-connected via that bluffing person.

3.3.4 (Scattering of Action and) Basic Features of Interactions

Returning to the main thread of action-orientedness and anti-potentiality, it should then be understandable that Latour (1988: 174–175, §1.5.3) says, for instance, the following: "[p]ower is never *possessed*. We either have it 'in potentia,' but then we do not have it; or we have it 'in actu'". However, what means the part that follows the one just quoted: "but then our allies are the ones that go into action"? To address it, we must think once again about the actor and its action. Despite the action-oriented criterion for existence, which can imply that the identification of the very source of action and difference from other beings is simple, Latour basically argues the opposite. Recall what we named scattering of action and what Latour called its dislocation or overtaking. In accordance with this idea, any action of practically any being does not come exclusively from it but from a configuration of a myriad of other entities.

Consider the action of a usual household printer – printing some document – and notice how many different entities are involved. The engineers, programmers and various components (and their providers) to produce the printer and make it functional, from different types of plastic, glass, wires and insulator materials, through ink, and to microchips. This is still the tip of the iceberg, because for the printer to actually print, there must be a computer with proper hardware and software to provide the document to print. Of course, there is most likely some human being behind the click "print", but one can say that they still do not do much here. This impression is only deepened when we acknowledge something even more in what seems to be a background of this situation – electric power and internet network (if the printer works without a physical wire connection to the computer). Perhaps already frustratingly to some of us, we can say that this is still not everything. For instance, the utilised microchips depend on something so ancient like silicon (in the sense of a chemical element), and the quality of the printed piece of paper is a function of the specifics of the previous paper production (not the printer itself). In light of this, the following question is not that absurd after all: Who or what acts when the printer is printing? Here, once again, ANT's highly peculiar abinarism reveals itself – the printer prints, but it also does not print.

This idea of scattering of action can be said to be, to a certain extent, developed by Latour when he considers some basic features of interactions, an obviously crucial theme for an ontology so action-oriented as ANT. Namely, in one of his lengthiest and clearest engagements in social theory, Latour (2005: 200–202) argues that interactions are not the way they seem. First, with respect to spatiality, Latour invites us to consider how all that appears to occur during some interaction in a defined place actually comes from different places and actors. Second, in reference to temporality, all that partakes in an interaction also comes from different moments in time. Third, in relation to visibility, in the "here and now" of a given interaction – already problematised in previous points – not all that participates is easily noticeable. Fourth, when it comes to the components of an interaction, Latour obviously stresses its heterogeneity – that differently characterised elements (human, nonhuman, organic, inorganic, etc.) take part in it. Finally, concerning the strength or the measure of influence of all that partakes in the "here and now" of a given situation, the involved elements differ from each other – some are stronger, while some are weaker.

Just think again about a printer printing some documents. Most definitely, it can be said to be an instance of a specific human–nonhuman interaction. However, it actually involves a plethora of entities other than the human who clicks "print" and the used printer. These entities can be deemed in detail as having different importance for the situation in question. Moreover, some are more clearly visible than others partaking, and some come from afar, while others are much closer to the situation in question. Finally, they occupy different moments in time.

One can say that the idea of scattering of action, which is consistent with how Latour characterises interactions and can be expanded with reference to that, is also perfectly well-aligned with what is implied by the mere concept commented in this section – actor-network. Any existing entity – actor – is an entire association of various entities – their network (Latour 1999a: 18–19; 2011: 800, 801, 806) – because any action (proof of existence) is not exclusively of the considered well-identified entity but of the plethora of others, somehow interconnected with the object under scrutiny. In the end, let us remember that, in ANT, there is just one general way to become stronger, to act more and better and thus to mark one's existence more clearly – to associate with others, to make alliances. We will expand this important thread below.

3.3.5 Reasons for the Inevitability of Translations

Now, let us just recall that Latour here does not propose some one-sided, power-focused ontology, but his ANT can be characterised as clearly involved in some strength–weakness dialectics. Namely, if an actor exists because it somehow acts, but its actions are not literally its own but come from a plethora of other entities – hence actor-network – then it should be clear how much actors and their actions are fragile. Practically, any fluctuation among the network can cause the actor to undergo some changes, especially with respect to what it does. Of course, at this point, one should be cautious not to presuppose a clearly reductionist position according to which entities are nothing else than their elements (other actors), whose configuration can be said to allow their actions. In the end, such a reading would be in strict opposition to the mentioned Irreduction Principle. According to it, any existing thing by itself is neither reducible nor irreducible. Reduction or some entity's irreducible status always comes from others, as well as any set of its features. This is why we allowed ourselves earlier to brand ANT as *a posteriori* relational essentialism.

However, one must also keep two important points in mind. First, Latour stresses that there is no entity so weak that it would not be able to make any ally and, as a result, make oneself stronger, which in turn would enable even further associations – the mentioned tautology returns here and some, after all, assumption that can suggest the more usually understood essentialism. Second, and more importantly, Latour argues in favour of the thesis that entities have some specific to themselves singularities. On the one hand, this may be controversial, due to the strong emphasis on the basically relational genesis of specifics of entities. On the other hand, there may be no tension after all. What Latour would consider some entity's singularity may just be a product of a very stable set of relations with other entities our object of interest remains in. On this reading, the singularity would not be timeless but simply relative to the past of entity investigated at the moment – that what is already in a given object prior to some currently considered situation and, thus, being the outcome of previous relations. This is, though, not the most important issue in this recapitulation.

Given the mentioned singularities of entities and, consequently, incommensurability among them, any contact between them, any interaction (that may result in becoming stronger) is a translation (Latour in Latour et al. 2011: 43–44). With full awareness of Latour's fluctuating sense of the concept in his relevant works, for instance, passing on something, hybridising or being practically synonymous with mediation, we focus here on the translatory character of any contact in accordance with ANT. Entities encounter each other, but they ultimately contact mere translations of what they interact with. These, as with all translations, are more or less faithful to what is translated, and never grasp it in its entirety, never do complete justice to it.

It appears that the best way to understand this main sense of Latourian translation is to reflect, even for a moment, on part of the social scientific practice – surveying. Various quantitative data on different social phenomena, even those that deserve the name of detailed and thorough, are still nothing more than a simplification of what they refer to. Of course, the path from the things in the world (that are somehow investigated) and the words about them (in the form of some research report, like in an academic journal paper) is much more complex and involves many more translations than this brief impression here may suggest (e.g. Latour 1999b). After this detour, let us address the anticipated thread of the practical necessity to associate with others, to make allies in order to become stronger entity that can act and acts more, as only through such connections can one's strength grow.

3.3.6 Basic Ways of Becoming Stronger

The exact ways of making allies by a specific entity obviously depend on the entity in question. Namely, the modes of associating of, for instance, some species of social insect and some theoretical concept in physics, are most likely quite different in detail. Nevertheless, ANT as a flat ontology, with characteristic universal ambitions and a formal concept of actor-network, whose example may be both termite and some specific interpretation of quantum mechanics, provides some more general ideas on making alliances and thus becoming stronger. Among many different, often appearing to be synonymous, Latour's suggestions on how to associate with others, let us focus on a few examples (Latour 1988: 172, §1.4.6).

Even though it may sound peculiar at first instance, strength (through alliances) may grow by commanding others and, by implication, threatening them with some negative consequences if they do not comply. Next to such a negative way of gaining allies, one may attempt something more positive and just buy allies – make them, but at some price, cost that must be incurred in the form of something that is given to them in return. Obviously, both modes of alliance-making may be regarded as significantly unstable (in an already far from some default durability "world" of Latour). Any threat against disobeying commands must be backed up with resources to realise it. If these are not sufficient, then threatened allies may go in separate ways. This is also the case with the mode of buying others. However, there is still the scenario we anticipated earlier – potentiality and creating the appearance that one can do more than in reality, which may prove to be convincing to some; as a result, they can associate themselves with such a bluffing actor.

Latour also suggests alliance-making that is based on something more subtle than commanding and threating, buying or some counterfactual appearance. Namely, an actor may make allies by putting the needs of others in somewhat different terms, which would render them as acting for the sake of one purpose positive to all involved. Latour appears to have in mind trying to convince others to oneself. It may sound as a mode of alliance-making that is more respectful to others – in the end, they are here not threatened, bought or lied to. However, even here, some ambiguity can be noticed, for instance, when Latour (1988: 201, §3.3.5) speaks of programming others so that they are not able to betray the alliance. This resonates well with Callon's (1986: 216) remark on silencing others in the name of which a given actor speaks. In other words, convincing others may even end up substituting the needs of others, from before their association with the main actor under scrutiny, with the agenda of that actor, that what is in line with it, or, at least, with something neutral to it.

At this point, one should not be surprised to find a reference in Latour's works to the idea of monopoly, something becoming so necessary that no one will function well without it; thus, others commonly, if not even universally, associate with such a successful actor and make it even stronger (if it is even possible) and stable. This is quite consistent with the figure of the actor that expands more and more, even when it can increase the risk of some dissidents along the way. In the end, with a clear quantitative emphasis on the number of allies, there is also a growing possibility of some relatively decreasing coherence among them. Latour (1988: 198, §3.2.4) appears to be aware of it when he juxtaposes the mentioned figure of an extremely expansive actor with another type, who (or what) decides not to go very far, while taking more care of the consistency among the allies.

In fact, there are some other instances in which Latour may appear as wanting to somehow soften his specific quantitative logic – simply, the more, the better. Indeed, he (Latour 1988: 185, §2.4.6) considers as a measure of an actor's strength the number of other actors that would have to be associated in order to destroy it. However, his fundamental idea of actor-network and the dialectics of strength-weakness we noticed earlier also suggest something clearly different. An actor may be destroyed, even by somehow impacting just one element in its network. Consequently, not only can the mass hurt the big but also the individual can hurt it, which resonates well with the quote from another actor-network theorist, Law, used in the Introduction.

3.3.7 Mediators and Intermediaries

Before addressing the final aspect of actor-network, let us recall some general yet crucial concepts concerning connections between various entities. Of course, the common translatory character of any connection between entities has already been presented in this section. We should add to it the previously introduced distinction between mediators and intermediaries. The former, as their very name suggests, pass on through themselves something else, but in the process, they also alter it. In other words, mediators are not neutral about what they carry. Intermediaries, on the contrary, add nothing from themselves to what they pass on. One can say that what is at their output is the same as at their input.

Mediators and intermediaries are not separate kinds of entities in ANT but are mere classifications of ordinary entities, actor-networks, made in accordance with the criterion of what they do with respect to each other. Obviously, there is a need to address such an issue in an ontology that imagines even the most seemingly mundane and concentrated in space and time entity to actually be an entire network of other entities. Interestingly, although Latour stresses the translatory character of relations and, accordingly, there should be only mediators, he still uses the other concept. Such a decision can be associated with Latour's declared approach to his own version of ANT as not a theory but merely a methodology, way of doing research and writing reports from it. In this light, it is understandable that one and the same element may play the role of an intermediary or mediator in some analysed situation. It depends on how detailed and meticulous the analysis is. The more we are general, the more we will treat various entities in the analysed context as mere intermediaries that do not actually make any difference and, on this account, may be even not mentioned explicitly in the analysis. It appears that materiality is largely treated in this way by those who may be regarded as materiality ignorers and belittlers.

As already anticipated, a good ANT analysis distinguishes itself in that it multiplies mediators – ideally treats all involved entities as modifying, to a greater or lesser extent, what they pass on. In methodological terms, then, mediator and intermediary distinction is a relative matter. Those who make analyses render relevant objects either intermediaries or mediators. However, in ontological terms, due to the translatory character of all connections, we may ultimately say that everything is a mediator. Perhaps this is why Latour often seems to treat both concepts – translation and mediation – as synonyms.

Of course, the mere concepts of intermediary and mediator and some passages in Latour's ANT-relevant writings (e.g. Latour 1996b: 378) may support the reading that the mediator is a separate kind of object that participates and mediates in contact between two entities of different categories than itself (Harman 2009). Notice, however, that such an approach misses the point of ANT. Namely, this framework invites us to consider entire chains of entities and not only simple dyads in which some other entity may participate to make the contact between the two possible. If we are actually considering whole variety of actors, for instance, A_1, A_2, A_3, etc., each actor in such a chain (most likely, constituting some other actor-network) can be said to be a mediator (or an intermediary) with respect to that what precedes it in the chain under consideration.

3.3.8 Delegates

Notice, however, that relations between entities in Latourian ANT are not only treated in light of the question of what entities do with what they pass on. As already anticipated in the previous section, relations can be also considered in terms of delegations, when one entity delegates some activity to a different entity and, as a result, does not have do it individually and while being present in the place where the intervention in question unfolds. Although one may wonder whether Latourian delegation always involves it, to get a better grasp of it, let us focus here on the idea of programmes and antiprogrammes of action (e.g. Latour 1991, 1992, 1999b) and consider the example quite similar to those in Latour's relevant writings.

Imagine some authorities of a considerably big city that is quite popular among tourists globally. These authorities want to make their city even more attractive and, among other things, want to fight with the noticeable practice of people sleeping in public spaces. In short, the programme of action they want to realise is "no sleeping in public". City officials can try to realise this programme by themselves, but the prospect of them individually observing city parks, squares and other similar places is not only quite absurd but also will be largely inefficient. This brief programme of action can then be made part of municipal legal regulations. Obviously, in such acts, the programme of action will be phrased quite differently, which already is a good illustration of Latourian translation and mediation.

Let us imagine a subsequent moment. The relevant regulation comes into force. However, the programme of action that is expressed through it appears to be largely unsuccessful. There are still instances of various people sleeping in public for various reasons. The city's programme of action fails due to some people's antiprogrammes. In the face of it, city authorities have at least two possibilities of delegating the action in question – preventing sleeping in public – even further. First, they may increase the number of patrols of relevant services in specific areas of the city, who by their very visible presence may act deterrently and intervene when needed. Second, the city may invest in various sleep-preventing material devices, for instance, amend the city benches so that lying on them is either impossible or at least highly uncomfortable (e.g. Rosenberger 2017).

Of course, both options have their respective pros and cons. The second is, to a certain extent, more effective than the first. In the end, sleep-preventing benches are constantly at relevant spots, while patrols keep moving and changing their locations. After leaving one place, sleeping in public may still occur. Patrols to which the action in question is delegated may then render it somewhat weaker and more labile, but officers may be more subtle in their reactions to people transgressing the prohibition. In the end, one may lie in some spot in a public space for several reasons. In turn, sleep-preventing benches are incomparably more effective, but they are not able to make some nuanced distinctions between a person who just felt ill and a person who is intoxicated (two different types of relevant antiprogrammes of action).

Notice then that both delegations are not neutral with respect to the programme of action in question. Delegation to nonhumans (benches) renders the prohibition very strict and serious. Delegation to humans (patrols) ultimately makes it somewhat softer. Some activity, some effort is passed on through different entities, each specifically altering it. In other words, chains of delegations are also chains of mediators (which can be rendered by some as merely intermediaries). Of course, we could wonder whether delegates and mediators are so close to each other that they are practically synonymous. However, there is a difference between transporting something with its transformation – mediating (or without any changes – intermediating) and delegating some effort to take to others (delegation). Just think of the entire chains of mediators that allow us to notice and consider some social regularities based on quantitative research that is quite far from doing justice to its object, but is merely its translation. They are quite different from the example of delegation just presented and other similar, noticeable all around us.

3.3.9 Plasma

At the end of this section, let us address the issue that heretofore was merely suggested between the lines – the limits of actor-networks. Although in Latour's early writings relevant to his ANT, one can notice propositions suggesting that actor-networks do not have an outside, he proves to be attached to the idea of their boundaries. One should have here in mind not only a very specifically understood concept of plasma, with which Latour has worked since the nineties. Namely, even in his *Irreductions*, the idea of that what is beyond actor-networks is noticeable, for instance, when Latour (1988: 171, §1.4.2) says that "a network [...] remains local and circumscribed, thin and fragile, interspersed by space". In addition to this, recall that his *Politics of Nature* (2004) is, to a certain extent, focused on the vision of the collective and the entities that are beyond it and their inclusion is to be subjected to a specific procedure of agreeing on the composition of the world. Of course, as said earlier, the collective is presumably a category of different level than that of actor-networks. Nevertheless, it all shows Latour's closeness to the idea that entities have some boundaries to themselves and, in consequence, have an outside. It is especially interesting in the case of actor-networks, because ANT stresses their expansiveness (with some instances of softening this emphasis).

As mentioned earlier, Latour expresses the idea of boundaries with the concept of plasma. However, to be more precise, one should stress that Latour appears to refer to it to denote different issues. First, Latour (2005: 244) considers plasma as the foundation that allows some entity to function or, to put it differently, as something external to the actor that enables it to act and subsist. Notice, though, that such a concept is controversial, to say the least, in light of the rest of the commented principles of ANT. Namely, if existence is action, but action has many sources, in accordance with its scattering, then one cannot say that what enables actions of some entity (actor-network) is beyond it, external, outside. On the contrary, it may be said to be within it. Because of this controversy, already noticed in relevant discussions (Isabelle Doucet in Latour et al. 2011: 140), we may allow ourselves to focus on the second sense of plasma, as that what is not within the actor-network considered, the rest outside of it.

Luckily, Latour provides us with some aid to better understand this highly abstract idea. Namely, he (Latour 2005) invites us to imagine actor-network as having a star-like shape of entities remaining in relations. Following this suggestion, let us look at Figure 3.1. The entire star is an actor-network, and the dots represent entities partaking in it (but if subjected to scrutiny, they also would prove to be actor-networks). Their relations (of ultimately translatory or mediatory character, which may be rendered as merely intermediate, and some of which may be classified as delegations) are lines between the dots. The central dot can be said to represent that actor which appears to be the source of some action (but is actually not, due to scattering of action, which has many sources in other entities partaking in the entire network). Where is then the plasma, the outside of the visualised actor-network? It is all that is left, all white background in Figure 3.1. This is why plasma in its commented sense can be said to be much larger than some actor-network under consideration.

3.4 Law and ... Latour's Actor-Networks

3.4.1 Is There Anything Beyond Law?

Of course, above we did not address many other concepts out of a very rich Latourian conceptual repertoire that are also important for his version of ANT. Nevertheless, what is proposed here can be regarded as the most important and fundamental to this vision and the basic unit for ontological inquiries assumed in it. Even when sticking to our assumed back-to-basics approach, the above exposition is the longest compared to the rest of flat ontologies analysed in the book. It is a simple consequence of the richness and complexity of ANT's

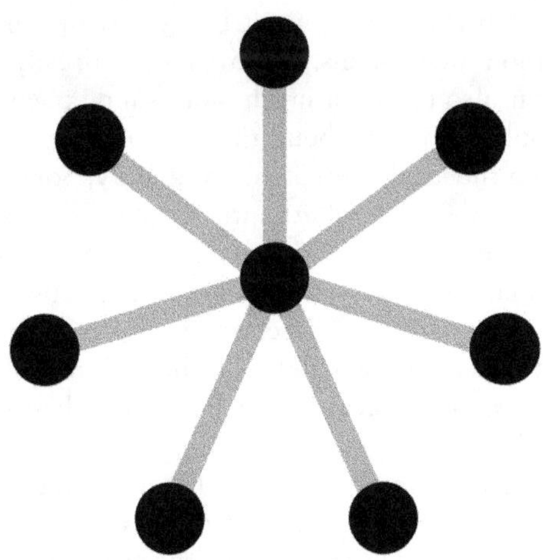

Figure 3.1 Actor-network (with plasma).

threads that, perhaps more than other comparable frameworks, require presenting them largely in the form of a chain of propositions following each other, a form that is not often utilised by Latour himself. However, the above work is already convenient enough to address the problem of ANT and law.

When it comes to the adequacy question that largely guides this book, we can say the following. The majority of what is considered here as ANT seems adequate for law. There is, however, basically one specific idea, the feature of actor-network adopted in this framework that proves to be problematic for law, or, putting it differently, law seems not entirely suitable here. Ultimately, though, the issue referred to here renders the adequacy problem largely inconclusive. We will address it first, leaving the remarks on what seems to fit law for the end of this section and, at the same time, the entire chapter.

As said at the end of the previous section, when dealing with plasma, Latour assumes the limited character of actor-networks, that they have an outside. Despite the entire competitive rhetoric in a significant part of Latour's relevant writings, his idea of plasma means that there cannot be a truly totalising, an all-embracing actor-network, without an outside. At first glance, law, in the sense adopted in the Introduction, can be said to realise this condition as there appears to be much beyond the entities that are somehow within the actor-network of law. Notice that even if law is or consists of all those things we considered when exposing the understanding of law that guides this book, there is still much left in the world, already given the obvious fact that even dynamically proliferating contemporary law in the Western or Global Northen context clearly embraces in its regulations only a part of what there is.

However, there are various diagnoses or lines of arguments in favour of the thesis, problematic for actor-networks' feature assumed by Latour, that law has no outside. Consider, for instance, the largely critical observations about the degree of saturating the world with law in the spirit of the famous Habermasian juridification (Habermas 1987), itself being part of a broader processes of Lifeworld colonisation by Systems. It covers the already suggested issue of overregulation, but it also tackles a much more subtle phenomenon of even the most ordinary people thinking about the surrounding world and orienting themselves in it using the legal conceptual vocabulary. Somewhat similar motifs can be found on the other side of Atlantic in the discourse of Critical Legal Studies movement, especially its notions of categorisation and alienation (Gabel 1980), as well as in empirical research on legal consciousness (in its American sense, which may be regarded as closer to social projections about law than European approaches, see Hertogh 2004). In the end, one of the participants in the work considered to be classical for the latter said that, for him, "the law is all over" (Sarat 1990: 343).

There is also another way to specifically undermine the idea of law's boundaries and outside, which is not so strongly focused on the attitudes and activities of ordinary people but flows from engagement in legal deontic modalities. In line with this, let us focus here on texts of legal acts. We can say that they address the world in different ways. Sticking to basics, they express some prohibitions, forbid something from occurring in the world. They also contain obligations that instruct what should happen. Moreover, one can distinguish in them expressions of competences of subjects, according to which they can do something (and, by implication, subjects other than the one pointed out in a given provision should not engage in it). Even when the entirety of texts of valid law in state jurisdictions in the contemporary West or Global North are enormous, there is still a finite number of issues clearly addressed in these texts. In consequence, law most definitely can be said to have an outside – all things it does not address explicitly.

However, as Latour (2005: 257; see also Latour 1999a: 18) argues, various objects in the world are often co-constituted by various discourses, academic included, concerning them. "Without economics there are no economies; without sociology there is no society; without psychology there is no psyche; without geography there is no space". With this in mind, let us notice, for instance, the well-known jurisprudential idea according to which "everything that is not forbidden is allowed". In other words, there is an identifiable concept that even if law does not address something explicitly in its acts, that what is in such a way specifically omitted can still be regarded as embraced by law. Ultimately, it addresses the world not only through explicit normative statements but also by leaving some of the world's aspects up to individual choices of legal subjects. In short, and drawing from William James (1912: 11), no legal decision is also a legal decision. One can say that even if law does not talk about something, it still talks about it, because what is left after regulations based on basic modalities of prohibition and obligation is also a specific modality of law, permission or indifference (e.g. Ziembiński 1976: 298–299, 407; Zirk-Sadowski 1985: 113, 114; Opałek and Woleński 1991: 341–342).

Moreover, even if something is treated as so fundamental in a given legal order that any intervention in this important, nearly sacred area is practically forbidden due to, for instance, constitutional or international commitments, and even mere talk about possible intervention does not happen in legal-political discourse, one can still say the following. That what lies beyond such rudiments is still specifically accounted for by the law in question. Interestingly, it is this way both despite and because law literally excludes what is beyond some relevant fundamentals from itself.

From such a perspective, law proves to have an all-embracing character. Indeed, it is full of gaps – leaves many issues not addressed explicitly – yet it is gapless. Although there is a world beyond legal acts, parliamentary procedures that create them and the plethora of material entities that are relevant to them – to refer just to a part of what we considered in the Introduction – law can be said to spill itself all over the world in the suggested manner. On a side note, this line of reasoning in favour of the practically boundaryless character of law is just another argument in favour of Tardean MON's inadequacy to law, because, as mentioned in the previous chapter, Tarde assumes that entities have their respective outsides.

Returning to the main thread here, let us take another look at Figure 3.1. It represents in a simplified way the ordinary actor-network in the sense of having an outside or Latourian plasma. Such a general shape of an actor-network is explicitly admitted by Latour; however, in light of the above, law does not fit it. Law seems to fit a hypothetical actor-network that is without plasma, due to its all-embracing character, which is visualised in Figure 3.2, consistent with the previous scheme. The problem here is that actor-networks without an outside to themselves are excluded from ANT in accordance with the thesis about plasma as a feature of actor-networks.

If the above line of reasoning is well-grounded, then even though many other specifics of actor-network fit law, ANT's adequacy to it can be regarded as already falsified. Law does not realise one of the defining traits of actor-network. However, for the sake of intellectual integrity, let us address some doubts with respect to the presented diagnosis. There is of course the issue of possible different views among legal scholars relevant to the issue of law's limited or limitless character, which may support the idea that the actor-network of law has its plasma and thus ANT is not falsified here, at least in this aspect and with respect to law.

When it comes to ANT-related doubts more directly, let us notice that the all-embracing character of law can be said to be merely potential in the sense criticised by Latour and covered earlier. In the end, one can say that all that is not explicitly regulated by law, but is still specifically grasped by it by merely being permitted by implication, is not actually within law. Instead, it is just an analogous situation to some entity claiming to have some others or being able to do something, while it does not have or cannot – an epitome of potentiality in Latourian sense. Notice, however, that law is quite different from another

Figure 3.2 Actor-network (without plasma).

figure of potentiality – train – and claiming that it can go anywhere, even if there is not yet the necessary infrastructure (tracks) to reach a myriad of destinations. From this perspective, one can say that law most definitely has the necessary infrastructure to embrace everything. For law to do that, it needs people thinking in line with "what is not prohibited, is permitted". Of course, this does not imply that the infrastructure for law – among other things, specific ways of thinking and all that is necessary for them – is easier to construct than the infrastructure for trains – tracks and all that is required to lay them effectively. Nevertheless, one can say that when the commented way of thinking about law is present, law becomes all-embracing, unfit for Latourian actor-network, and the counterargument from potentiality is undermined.

Such reasoning is ultimately conditional though. In a situation where the way of thinking in question is not present, one can be much more confident about the existence of law's outside; thus, it will fit the vision of the actor-network with plasma. In this light, Latourian ANT's adequacy or inadequacy to law in connection with the plasma issue becomes rather inconclusive, as it ultimately depends on the adopted standpoint concerning how to treat that what is not explicitly regulated – still within law or beyond it.

What Latour himself says about law in the closing part of his *The Making of Law: An Ethnography of the Conseil d'État* not only does not help to move beyond the uncertainty of this inconclusiveness in either direction, but it may also be regarded as creating even more uncertainty. Namely, he says that "[l]aw plunges into everything" (Latour 2010: 263), "it holds everything, in its own way" and "[i]f it holds everything, if it makes it possible to link all people and all acts, if by way of a continuous route it authorizes the Constitution to be linked to a tiny case, it is also because it extracts only a tiny part of their essence from all situations" (Latour 2010: 264). Notice that it appears as ultimately an admittance that, for him, law is all-embracing after all. Moreover, one can add that, in accordance with the basic sentiments of ANT – that to exist is to act, but to act, one must have many allies, as only through associating, one's strength grows – such character of law is perfectly understandable. One of the ways law can become stronger is by attaching itself to everything, either through explicit regulations or through rendering the regulationless areas as still with its grasp, as permitted. On this reading, then, law would be just one of the few most successful actor-networks. We can even say that if ANT basically stresses expansiveness, then the idea of plasma is somewhat inconsistent with it, and all-embracing law is perfectly in line with it.

Notice also that in the quotes above, Latour can be said to be consistent with another classical theme from his ANT. He argues that law reaches only the surface of things it embraces. Indeed, even when law regulates something clearly and explicitly, for instance, in the form of prohibition, it embraces the object of its regulation very superficially. It takes interest only in aspects that are directly relevant to the regulation in question. Even then, one can still say that it formats them for its own needs rather than taking them into account as they are as such. All the rest is, on the one hand, omitted and, on the other hand, permitted. Either way, law addresses such rest in an even shallower manner than the regulation's direct object. Such superficiality of law's embrace is coherent with the translatory character of any relation covered earlier. To put it differently, one should not be surprised that law tackles only the small part of that what it regulates, because every entity does it when relating to others – everything translates.

Nevertheless, although both arguments of Latour from the quotes above – on law's all-embracing character and its superficiality – can be considered convincing and correct, the controversies they cause for what was said earlier are not unnoticeable. On the first possible reading, we can say that he simply contradicts himself. On the one hand, he says that actor-networks have plasma, an outside of them. On the other hand, he argues that there is one thing – law – that is boundaryless. When we add to this some earlier remarks of Latour that also suggest some limitless entities, our confidence in the role and importance of plasma in ANT may dwindle even more.

On the second reading, at first glance, we may say that Latour does not contradict himself after all. Law embraces everything, but its embrace is shallow – it leaves many issues unaddressed, which is consistent with Latourian idea of translation. That what is lost in translation, left beyond after it, constitutes plasma. However, as mentioned earlier, there are some arguments to say that law specifically addresses what it does not explicitly address. Of course, there is also a possible opposite standpoint. If that is the case, then the already presented tension between law and ANT's idea of plasma returns, and with it, the problem of inconclusiveness when it comes to the adequacy question.

Interestingly, on the third reading, some may say that we, in fact, should not address the quotes above on the account that, in them, Latour is already thinking about law as a specific mode of existence. Ultimately, notice that when he (Latour 2010: 264) says about linking "all people and all acts", he actually anticipates what he considers to be the law in AIME – connector of actions with their actors. However, as we argued in the first section of this chapter, and as Latour himself admits, there is a difference between what he names law in AIME and what law can generally be said to be in the Western or Global Northern context, as we adopted for the sake of our investigations here. In short, if we want to engage ANT, and not AIME, we should not focus on Latour's study, which is quite close to AIME. In response to such a possible argument, we must stress that the two issues raised in the quotes above – limitlessness of law and the superficiality of its embrace – also make sense beyond the discourse in AIME's terms. More importantly, the second issue can be read as a specific argument that law has plasma and, as such, must be presented and addressed in the present discussion.

Nevertheless, the problem of how law's limits or limitlessness fits the various works of Latour remains. For instance, the thesis about law's all-embracing character can also be somewhat problematic for the ideas proposed in *Politics of Nature* (2004). In the end, Latour talks about the specific procedure of including various entities in the collective, which implies the inside and outside of it. Law, with its specific recognition of various entities by, for instance, starting to regulate them explicitly or taking them into account in the legal decisions of courts and administrative offices, most definitely can be said to be partaking in constituting the collective (Latour 2005: 254). As such, law can also be regarded as one of the components of the collective. However, its all-embracing character, depending on the interpretation, is either incoherent with the idea of the collective (how something can embrace anything there is, if the collective – the presumably largest entity in Latourian theory – to which it belongs still has some boundaries?) or they can actually be combined. For instance, the mere fact that law regulates something does not entail that the object of regulation is allowed in the collective. Just think about legal prohibitions. Some object may be legally recognised simply by being forbidden, which can also be read in terms of that object being unacceptable by the collective and pushed back at the margins of the common world agreed upon. In such an interpretation, boundaryless law is in line with the collective and its inside and outside. Of course, due to the variety of Latourian studies, of differing degrees of closeness to what can be considered ANT, we could continue similar problematisations for a considerable time and space of printed pages.

3.4.2 Is There Anything Beyond Law that Law Can Act Upon?

However, the more important thing here is to provide a summary of what we said so far, but also take a note of an issue closely connected to the problem of plasma, which so far we did not address for the sake of not throwing everything relevant to the adequacy issue at once and overloading the discussion more than necessary.

Depending on the standpoint of how to consider that what can be said to be left unregulated by law, law embraces everything or not. The latter makes law unproblematic for ANT, at least with respect to plasma, because law proves to have some limits to itself and thus there is something that lies beyond them. The former position renders law unfit because it becomes a plasmaless entity, something practically not allowed in ANT. The counterargument to law's all-embracing character grounded in Latour's critique of potentiality can be quite easily refuted. Another counterargument, that law has plasma due to the superficiality of its embrace, still largely depends on how to understand that what is not explicitly regulated. As a result, then, it does not allow us to move past the inconclusiveness, dependence on the standpoint concerning lack of explicit regulation.

Although heretofore we discussed law's boundarylessness only in connection with the plasma, what is at stake here is an even more fundamental issue for ANT. Namely, in consequence of such law's character, there is also no entity that would be different from law, beyond it, that law could act upon and thus prove its existence, in accordance with the basic principle of ANT – to exist means to act on others. Limitless law would then act only upon itself or, to be more precise, on its various parts. Any change it would provoke would concern not others but ultimately itself.

If such self-containment is not in line with the basic sentiments of ANT, then Latour's idea of plasma is perfectly understandable, despite what we said about it earlier – that the competitiveness and expansiveness in ANT can be read as actually arguments against the plasma. Perhaps, we reach here just another instance of what we call abinarism in Latour. On the one hand, the way he imagines existence and the strength of entities – based on associating with others – make the idea of plasma somewhat inappropriate for an ontology with such commitments. On the other hand, if the measure of one's existence is its influence on others, then the concept of one's outside is just necessary, for there must be some others to act upon, if anything can exist. Of course, Latour himself appears to ultimately solve it in favour of plasma and external entities to act upon by an actor under consideration, but still, the figure of limitlessness is not that distant from the general competitiveness in his ontology.

Law appears to be caught in this tension. There are some reasons to treat law as an all-embracing entity. However, as a result, it becomes problematic for ANT to be adequate to law because of its commitments to the idea of plasma and acting upon other entities as a criterion of existence. These are consistent with each other to the extent that they both may be said to imply each other. Something that lies beyond a given entity can become the object of its influence, which will prove the existence of the actor. That which can be acted upon by some actor as something different from it means that the actor has boundaries, and there is something outside of it. Against such a background, law may be said to embrace everything and thus have no plasma, but also nothing else than itself to act upon. As such, this proves problematic for ANT. However, notice the reservation in the form of "may". Law's all-embracing status can be debated, and, consequently, the inadequacy of ANT in this aspect is not certain and thus inconclusive.

3.4.3 Law's Functioning (But Not by Itself)

Notice that such diagnosis concerns two tightly connected tenets of ANT considered in the very specific context of law's boundaries or boundarylessness. Then, what about the other elements of the framework under scrutiny? Interestingly, beyond what is argued here to be the main challenge to its adequacy to law, ANT appears to be a good fit to grasp it, proving its far-reaching value for inquiries about law and practical engagement with it. To recognise this, consider the following.

Given the very broad sense of action – which is the measure of existence – we can say that law passes ANT's test for being in various ways. Through its recognition, it endows different entities with specific statuses and competences. Its regulations, if adhered to by their addressees, make them engaged in certain activities that move even further entities. In turn, if regulations are transgressed, then law still acts through various agencies that react to illegal activities. Notice that even in the more ordinary thinking about law, we can find sentiments similar to Latour's action-orientedness – just consider the already mentioned *desuetudo* principle. With respect to law, it also assumes that only that which acts, is in actual use, exists, is valid.

Of course, in accordance with ANT's principles, it is already an exaggeration and simplification to say that law does something. Its power to act, just like anything else's, comes not from within but from a myriad of other entities. For instance, the fact that some law can be considered stable, common or actually securing equality of its subjects can be said to come from actors such as pieces of paper, efficient printing presses, digital media, education system and, finally, electric power and internet connections. Obviously, it is just the tip of the iceberg, but the suggested way of thinking already allows us to say that law fits the idea of actor-network. Law acts; however, its actions are not exclusively its own but of an entire network of other entities, many of which may not be immediately and commonly associated with law. As Latour (1988: 204, §3.4.3) himself says, "[t]he strength of the law comes not from within it but from a poor despised rabble which gives it the force of fact: morals, words, truncheons, hopes, administrations, walls, telexes, files, finances, ulcers".

3.4.4 Sources of Law's Strength (and Weakness)

If law is an extremely heterogeneous and numerous association, then, in line with Latour's thinking, it is a strong actor-network. However, it also illustrates the strength-weakness dialectics identified earlier. Law's functioning and existence can start to tremble if one of the actors co-constituting its network somehow malfunctions, not to mention, breaks down.

Just imagine a lawyer in a modern highly complex and vast legal order who cannot get to the legal library or information database to consult what they have memorised from the legal acts relevant to the case under consideration. Their professional activities may even be stopped, which in turn may not be irrelevant for the workings of certain legal institutions and law as such. The writing down of legal acts to some easily accessible form, whether a printed document, pocketbook edition or screen display from governmental sites, allows lawyers not to have the entirety of law in their minds and law to become extremely numerous. If, for whatever concrete reason, such access becomes impossible, lawyers urged by deadlines of already ongoing procedures may make flawed decisions (with respect to what is in legal acts, which they do not have memorised and which cannot be consulted at the moment). Such flaws may then cause the involved parties to return to their cases and undermine the decisions unfavourable to them based on these flaws. Of course, such an extreme situation may never actually happen. Nevertheless, it is worth imagining these and other similar instances to recognise that ANT's idea of strength coming from heterogeneity, even impurity, can be actually seen in the example of law, perhaps to some confusion and even outrage of some people, who like to see law and its power in the profound of values and meanings from which they scrub off the mundane of cables and bricks.

Continuing the thread of law's strength and, at the same, its weakness, notice that ANT's ways to gain strength, to make alliances considered in the previous section, fit law well. Obviously, law commands and makes threats, but it also buys alliances (for instance, promises securing some important values, but to do this, everyone has to play their legally specified parts) and variously convinces other actors to itself (for example, to gain some status and attractive competences connected with it, one must realise some procedures). Notice that here ANT specifically reminds that even if one is the most ordinary person, not connected in any professional way with any legal agency, by following law, for whatever reason, they partake in its subsistence.

Interestingly, law appears to be an actor-network that realises the strategy considered by Latour – to expand as far and strongly as possible, which is visible already in the scope of contemporary overregulation. As mentioned earlier, such a strategy risks some inconsistencies and dissidents. However, law makes even those who ultimately do not follow it still a part of itself. In the end, even the most hardened criminals, corrupted politicians or incompetent officials are not excluded from law but are within it and drive it. This is just another reason why the all-embracing character of law should be treated as a serious proposition.

Besides law also gaining strength through its appearance as a powerful entity, when, in fact, it may be deemed as quite weak, without any inherent strength – in reference to the potentiality-based alliance-making addressed above and the previous subsection – law appears to fall under the monopoly figure considered earlier. It is increasingly difficult to find anything that would not somehow be addressed by law. If one adds to that the issue of no legal decision still being a legal decision – of course, debatable – this impression of law as a monopoly just solidifies. Such an achievement of law may be associated with its subject-creating function. It can be explained with reference to Latour's (2004: 273, note 15, 276, note 45) diagnosis that law is a project that is weakly modern. As suggested earlier, for Latour, modernity is assumed to be based on clear and ready-made differentiations, according to which what is a subject and what is an object are not debatable but simply obvious. However, let us notice that law and lawyers only apparently follow some clear-cut distinctions, but through their constantly changing practice, they define subjects and objects. Just consider some more or less recent cases of or (for now) mere discussions about endowing nonhuman actors with specific legal subjectivity, from various animals (e.g. Pietrzykowski 2018), through rivers (e.g. Tănăsescu 2022), to robots (e.g. Chopra and White 2011). In a way, then, law can be said to make its own allies. In the face of this, its monopolistic status should not be surprising.

This impression is even more justified when one recognises that Latour's idea of gaining strength by translating the needs of others into one's own terms is also noticeable in law. Various entities engage in the realisation of their respective interests, but very often, if not always in the contemporary Western or Global Northern context, they do it in accordance with legal terms. In the end, one cannot simply build one's house. To realise this and many other goals, one must follow some more or less complex regulations. Taking this opportunity, notice that it becomes increasingly debatable whether somewhat comparable to law morality, religion, custom – in the sense of kinds of social normative orders, not in their understanding in AIME – and perhaps even economy achieve this reach.

3.4.5 Law as a Chain of Mediations and Delegations

In reference to the translation mentioned a moment earlier, this specific concept appears adequate for what law does, how it relates to various entities and how entities that create its network relate to each other. The other basic relational categories of ANT fit law as well. Let us first consider the mediator-intermediary distinction.

Obviously, one can try to account for law by treating its various elements as mere intermediaries, which just pass on something without any alteration or distortion. However, not only is such an approach against ANT's principle to multiply mediators – to identify as much as possible how the entities involved in the researched subject transform what they transport – but it also can be regarded as a largely counterfactual projection on law that just does not do justice to all relevant details. Just consider what may be regarded as fundamental to law – legal acts. There is some narrative, even quite popular, that their contents are expressions of political will. Such wording suggests that there is some prior will that is losslessly expressed, put in legal acts, and thus that there is a practical identity between the two – political will and legal acts. To recognise how naive it is to render legal acts as mere intermediaries for some political agenda, notice how different from each other they most often are: the early draft of a legal act before the legislative procedures begin and the legal act that actually passed through them, with all various commissions and voting, and entered the entire system of valid law.

Of course, after this crucial moment, the law in question is subjected to even further mediations. Just think of an actual legal decision on its basis that, due to considering many other regulations and various possible ways of working with relevant textual material, still may alter it, with varying degrees of subtlety. Similar is the case with informing about the contents of the legal act in question by mass media and with ordinary interactions among citizenry, especially when people express in their own words what the new law is about. In the end, as Latour (1993: 137) says, human beings are most definitely mediators. What about, then, some clearly nonhuman elements in law?

There is quite an understandable desire to see among some broadly understood information technologies that allow the dissemination of legal texts mere intermediaries, not mediators. However, when we try to be as meticulous as ANT advises, we may start to notice among official legal journals with legal acts (whether printed or digital), their book editions by some commercial publishers and various digital legal information databases some mediation after all. As mentioned earlier, even the mere act of writing down what one has in mind alters it. Moreover, there are various processes of mass-producing the copies of some original document. At least since Walter Benjamin (2006), we may be suspicious whether even a literal copy of some original passes it on in its entirety, without any, even the slightest distortion. The mediatory character in the relevant context reveals itself more visibly when commercial book editions or various digital databases are considered. On the one hand, they still appear to merely reproduce some texts. On the other hand, they all are not neutral with respect to the source material and alter it, for instance, by more readable layouts, some convenient additional headings to provisions or clear indications on what important other legal provisions should be considered when dealing with a specific provision. From such a perspective, law proves to be a good object to realise the idea of mediators multiplication.

Nonhuman mediators are, of course, easier to identify when we move past the text-oriented elements of law, like the ones just considered. In the end, traffic signs communicate what is expressed textually in some legal act. Obviously, the move from text to some nontextual, visual, ideo- and pictogrammic modes of communication is a significant alteration of the source material. Finally, consider a practically classical Latourian example of a speed bump (Latour 1992: 244; 1999b: 186–190; 2005: 77–78). It can be said to communicate, very specifically, some prohibition, whose roots reach back to some legal texts. However, the fact that some speed limit is passed on by the speed bump is far from being neutral to it. It gains some features, it would not gain if communicated exclusively by some text or traffic sign.

Just as law is full of mediations, so it is full of delegations – making others do some activity, so the actor who delegates does not have to do it itself in a relevant place. ANT's concept of delegation is especially useful in the legal context, commonly associated with text. First, notice that the already introduced idea of programmes of actions fits law. Law can be said to be composed (but not exclusively) of a myriad of such programmes. They are delegated to the often very concise form of legal provisions, which also, as suggested earlier, mediate these programmes. However, as also addressed above, texts and words alone cannot do much. They must associate themselves with something more durable, which may and often actually takes the form of further delegations. The task of bringing to life some programme of action, mediated by some legal act, is delegated to a plethora of other entities, like law-applying and law-enforcing agencies and personnel, as well as traffic signs, speed bumps or sleep-prevention benches from the previously mentioned highly legal example. What should be clearly added to this is that even ordinary citizens who, for instance, are not indifferent to some visible transgressions of legal rules and instruct others on how to act to be in line with law can be regarded as delegates. Obviously, they often may not be aware that they are involved in such a process (like judges or police officers).

Nevertheless, if Latour (1992: 244) himself speaks of the entire chain of delegations, for instance, from some sign or textual delegates to explicitly tangible three-dimensional objects, then we can say that law is such a chain that includes all different kinds of delegates, which are also mediators. Namely, involved entities can be said to be doing someone else's job (delegation), but they also always add some new quality to it (mediation), not merely losslessly transferring some effort (intermediation).

In consequence, ANT most definitely renders law a very big, even enormous, entity. Of course, it may be debatable whether such rendition is, for some, not too far-fetched. Nevertheless, what can be said here more confidently is that ANT, its unit of actor-network with its most fundamental tenets, analysed above, would be an adequate match for law if not for the inconclusive (because it is largely dependent on opinions and the adopted way of thinking) problem of how to treat that what is not explicitly regulated. Ultimately, if law has an all-embracing character, then already its existence in Latourian terms – acting upon, influencing others – becomes questionable. To put it somewhat differently, yes, ANT, even in its very basic reconstruction proposed here, provides a considerably valuable conceptual apparatus largely adequate to law but with the reservation connected with the problem of plasma and acting on others as a measure of existence.

References

Akrich, Madeleine, Michel Callon and Bruno Latour. 2006. *Sociologie de la traduction: Textes foundateurs* [*Sociology of Translation: Founding Texts*]. Paris: Presses des Mines.

Benjamin, Walter. 2006. The Work of Art in the Age of Its Technological Reproducibility: Second Version. In Walter Benjamin, *Selected Writings. Volume 3: 1935–1938*. Eds.: Howard Eiland and Michael W. Jennings. Trans.: Edmund Jephcott, Howard Eiland *et al.*, 101–133. Cambridge, MA: Harvard University Press.

Blok, Anders, Ignacio Farias and Celia Roberts (eds). 2020. *The Routledge Companion to Actor-Network Theory*. Abingdon: Routledge.

Blok, Anders, and Torben Elgaard Jensen. 2011. *Bruno Latour: Hybrid Thoughts in a Hybrid World*. Abingdon: Routledge.

Callon, Michel. 1986. Some Elements of a Sociology of Translation: Domestication of the Scallops and the Fishermen of St. Brieuc Bay. In *Power, Action, and Belief: A New Sociology of Knowledge?*, John Law (ed.), 196–223. New York: Routledge.

Callon, Michel. 1987. Society in the Making: The Study of Technology as a Tool for Sociological Analysis. In *The Social Construction of Technological Systems: New Directions in the Sociology and History of Technology*, Wiebe E. Bijker, Thomas P. Hughes and Trevor Pinch (eds), 83–103. Cambridge, MA: The MIT Press.

Chopra, Samir, and Laurence F. White. 2011. *A Legal Theory for Autonomous Artificial Agents*. Ann Arbor: University of Michigan Press.

Cloatre, Emilie. 2018. Law and ANT (and its Kin): Possibilities, Challenges, and Ways Forward. *Journal of Law and Society* 45 (4): 646–663.

Deleuze, Gilles, and Félix Guattari. 1987. *A Thousand Plateaus: Capitalism and Schizophrenia*. Trans.: Brian Massumi. Minneapolis: University of Minnesota Press.

De Vries, Gerard. 2016. *Bruno Latour*. Cambridge: Polity Press.

Gabel, Peter. 1980. Reification in Legal Reasoning. *Research in Law and Sociology* 3: 25–51.

Habermas, Jürgen. 1987. *The Theory of Communicative Action. Volume 2: Lifeworld and System: A Critique of Functionalist Reason*. Trans.: Thomas McCarthy. Boston: Beacon Press.

Harman. Graham. 2009. *Prince of Networks: Bruno Latour and Metaphysics*. Melbourne: re.press.

Hertogh, Marc. 2004. A "European" Conception of Legal Consciousness: Rediscovering Eugen Ehrlich. *Journal of Law and Society* 31 (4): 457–481.

James, William. 1912. *The Will to Believe and Other Essays in Popular Philosophy*. London: Longmans, Green, and Co.

Jones, Brandon. 2014. Alfred North Whitehead's Flat Ontology: Casting the Bifurcation of Nature as the Other Hard Problem of Consciousness. *Journal of Consciousness Studies* 21 (5–6): 174–195.

Kanger, Laur. 2017. Mapping "the ANT Multiple": A Comparative, Critical and Reflexive Analysis. *Journal for The Theory of Social Behaviour* 47 (4): 435–462.

Latour, Bruno. 1983. Give Me a Laboratory and I Will Raise the World. In *Science Observed: Perspectives on the Social Study of Science*, Karin Knorr-Cetina and Michael Mulkay (eds), 141–170. London: Sage.

Latour, Bruno. 1988. *The Pasteurization of France*. Trans.: Alan Sheridan and John Law. Cambridge: Harvard University Press.

Latour, Bruno. 1991. Technology is Society Made Durable. In *A Sociology of Monsters: Essays on Power, Technology and Domination*, John Law (ed.), 103–131. London: Routledge.

Latour, Bruno. 1992. Where Are the Missing Masses? The Sociology of a Few Mundane Artifacts. In *Shaping Technology/Building Society. Studies in Sociotechnical Change*, Wiebe E. Bijker and John Law (eds), 225–258. Cambridge, MA: The MIT Press.

Latour, Bruno. 1993. *We Have Never Been Modern*. Trans: Catherine Porter. Cambridge: Harvard University Press.

Latour, Bruno. 1996a. *Aramis, or the Love of Technology*. Trans: Catherine Porter. Cambridge: Harvard University Press.

Latour, Bruno. 1996b. On Actor-Network Theory: A Few Clarifications. *Soziale Welt* 47 (4): 369–381.

Latour, Bruno. 1999a. On Recalling ANT. In *Actor-Network Theory and After*, John Law (ed.), 15–25. Oxford: Blackwell Publishers.

Latour, Bruno. 1999b. *Pandora's Hope: Essays on the Reality of Science Studies*. Cambridge: Harvard University Press.

Latour, Bruno. 2002. Gabriel Tarde and the End of the Social. In *The Social in Question: New Bearings in History and the Social Sciences*, Patrick Joyce (ed.), 117–132. London: Routledge.

Latour, Bruno. 2004. *Politics of Nature: How to Bring the Sciences into Democracy*. Trans: Catherine Porter. Cambridge: Harvard University Press.

Latour, Bruno. 2005. *Reassembling the Social: An Introduction to Actor-Network Theory*. Oxford: Oxford University Press.

Latour, Bruno. 2010. *The Making of Law: An Ethnography of the Conseil d'État*. Trans.: Marina Brilman and Alain Pottage. Rev.: Author. Cambridge: Polity Press.

Latour, Bruno. 2011. Networks, Societies, Spheres: Reflections of an Actor-Network Theorist. *International Journal of Communication* 5: 796–810.

Latour, Bruno. 2013. *An Inquiry into Modes of Existence: An Anthropology of the Moderns*. Trans.: Catherine Porter. Cambridge: Harvard University Press.

Latour, Bruno. 2015. The Strange Entanglement of Jurimorphs. In *Latour and the Passage of Law*, Kyle McGee (ed.), 331–353. Edinburgh: Edinburgh University Press.

Latour, Bruno. 2017. *Facing Gaia: Eight Lectures on the New Climatic Regime*. Trans.: Catherine Porter. Cambridge: Polity Press.

Latour, Bruno, and Steve Woolgar. 1986. *Laboratory Life: The Construction of Scientific Facts*. Princeton: Princeton University Press.

Latour, Bruno, Graham Harman and Peter Erdélyi. 2011. *The Prince and the Wolf: Latour and Harman at the LSE*. Winchester: Zero Books.

McGee, Kyle. 2014. *Bruno Latour: The Normativity of Networks*. Abingdon: Routledge.

McGee, Kyle (ed.). 2015. *Latour and the Passage of Law*. Edinburgh: Edinburgh University Press.

Michael, Mike. 2017. *Actor-Network Theory: Trials, Trails and Translations*. Los Angeles: Sage.

Miller, Adam S. 2013. *Speculative Grace: Bruno Latour and Object-Oriented Theology*. New York: Fordham University Press.

Opałek, Kazimierz, and Jan Woleński. 1991. Normative Systems, Permission and Deontic Logic. *Ratio Juris* 4 (3): 334–348.

Pietrzykowski, Tomasz. 2018. *Personhood Beyond Humanism: Animals, Chimeras, Autonomous Agents and the Law*. Trans.: Krystyna Warchal. Cham: Springer.

Rosenberger, Robert. 2017. *Callous Objects: Designs against the Homeless*. Minneapolis: University of Minnesota Press.

Sarat, Austin. 1990. "... The Law Is All Over": Power, Resistance and the Legal Consciousness of the Welfare Poor. *Yale Journal of Law and Humanities* 2 (2): 343–379.

Sartre, Jean-Paul. 2007. *Existentialism Is a Humanism*. Trans.: Carol Macomber. Ed.: John Kulka. New Haven: Yale University Press.

Schmidgen, Henning. 2015. *Bruno Latour in Pieces: An Intellectual Biography*. Trans.: Gloria Custance. New York: Fordham University Press.

Searle, John R. 2014. Interview: It Upsets Me When I Read the Nonsense Written by my Contemporaries. *New Philosopher* January 25, www.newphilosopher.com/articles/john-searle-it-upsets-me-when-i-read-the-nonsense-written-by-my-contemporaries (accessed 20 October 2023).

Sismondo, Sergio. 2010. *An Introduction to Science and Technology Studies*. Second Edition. Chichester: Wiley-Blackwell.

Spinoza, Benedict de. 2018. *Ethics, Proved in Geometrical Order*. Ed.: Matthew J. Kisner. Trans.: Michael Silverthorne and Matthew J. Kisner. New York: Cambridge University Press.

Sutter, Laurent de. 2015. Plasma! Notes on Bruno Latour's Metaphysics of Law. In *Latour and the Passage of Law*, Kyle McGee (ed.), 197–208. Edinburgh: Edinburgh University Press.

Tamanaha, Brian Z. 2001. *A General Jurisprudence of Law and Society*. Oxford: Oxford University Press.

Tampio, Nicholas. 2015. *Deleuze's Political Vision*. Lanham: Rowman & Littlefield.

Tănăsescu, Mihnea. 2022. *Understanding the Rights of Nature: A Critical Introduction*. Bielefeld: transcript.

Tresch, John. 2013. Another Turn after ANT: An Interview with Bruno Latour. *Social Studies of Science* 43 (2): 302–313.

Tournier, Michel. 1969. *Friday*. Trans.: Norman Denny. New York: Doubleday & Co.

Whitehead, Alfred North. 1978. *Process and Reality: An Essay in Cosmology*. Corrected Edition. Ed.: David Ray Griffin and Donald W. Sherburne. New York: The Free Press.

Wittgenstein, Ludwig. 2001. *Tractatus Logico-Philosophicus*. Trans.: D. F. Pears and B. F. McGuinness. London: Routledge.

Ziembiński, Zygmunt. 1976. *Practical Logic*. Trans.: Leon Ter-Oganian. Dordrecht: D. Reidel.

Zirk-Sadowski, Marek. 1985. Permission and Pragmatic Approach. *Studies in the Theory and Philosophy of Law* 1: 109–120.

Chapter 4

Manuel DeLanda's Assemblage Theory (of Law); or, Can Law's Components Exist Outside Law?

4.1 Not … a Filmmaker (Anymore)

4.1.1 Snapshot of DeLanda's Work

Despite having some more or less explicit anticipations, not only in Tarde but also in Whitehead and Deleuze (restricting ourselves here to the period from the turn of the nineteenth and twentieth centuries onwards), flat ontologies became much more visible and recognisable (though the word "popular" may be still far-fetched) only at the turn of the millennia. Of course, one of the main reasons for this is ANT – not only its Latourian version – and the lessons learned from it by various disciplines. Indeed, the point of reference in this chapter – DeLanda and his AST – expresses some critical comments about Latour's project (DeLanda in DeLanda and Harman 2017: 137–138). Nevertheless, despite the differences between them – some more evident, some more subtle and requiring certain uncovering effort – they can still be associated with the idea of a flat ontology and its basic sentiments. In the end, it is DeLanda who came up with the contemporary sense of a flat ontology, as said in the Introduction. In addition to the various manners in which DeLanda realises some fundamental flat ontological sentiments and his own AST's characteristic tenets, his path towards the commented way of thinking and his entire intellectual output also make him stand out.

While this Mexican-American, New York-resident scholar is contemporarily most well known from his various significantly interdisciplinary works, he actually started as a visual experimental artist. The short films he made at the turn of seventies and eighties show his deep engagement in various, mostly continental, intellectual currents. Soon though he abandoned the filmmaker path and entered the scholarly path. Restricting ourselves here only to his main, book-length studies, at the beginning of the nineties, DeLanda (1991) took up the issue of modern (for those times) warfare and analysed the role of various technologies developed for it, but he did this with a meticulous attention to how military functioned in the past.

DOI: 10.4324/9781003440963-4

However, it is rather safe to say that his second book proved to be a specific breakthrough for him. *A Thousand Years of Nonlinear History* (2000) is a work that largely defies the usual distinctions of reality into domains such as nonorganic, organic (genetic and somatic) and social (human) in that DeLanda subjects them and their representatives to the very same logic or principles. This book does not only anticipate some universal ambitions, said to be typical for flat ontologies, which can be found later in his realisation of this idea – AST. In the mentioned book, DeLanda's wide intellectual horizons and competences (from natural sciences, physics, chemistry, biology to history, linguistics, social theory), as well as his interest and specific debt to the work of Deleuze (also with Félix Guattari), manifest themselves clearly. The latter is already seen in the first major contribution, but it comes to the fore in the subsequent works. In the end, DeLanda's (2002) third major study, recalled in the Introduction, is a book-length exposition of Deleuzean ontology, with heavy reliance on a myriad of threads from formal and natural sciences.

However, one would be under a false impression to imagine DeLanda as a pure theoretician. His interest and admiration for chemistry – which he (in DeLanda and Harman 2017: 8, 42) interestingly considers as philosophically more engaging than physics, because chemistry tackles entities that can be completely new and inexistent prior to their synthesis, while physics grapples with beings that are much more ready-made – motivate him (DeLanda 2015) to analyse chemistry textbooks from different time periods, much in the vein of more empirically oriented science studies. This also is perfectly consistent with the amount of attention he (DeLanda 2011) devotes to tracing in various, both human and nonhuman, contexts the emergence of new entities with features that cannot be accounted for with reference to some other beings, whose interactions give rise to those emergent ones. Most recently (at least at the time of writing this book), DeLanda (2022) proposes his original theory of perception, already anticipated in between the lines of his earlier work (in DeLanda and Harman 2017: 94).

Although there are certain threads that run throughout the majority of DeLanda's oeuvre – Deleuze (and Guattari), the idea of virtuality, emergence and other regularities that he considers to cut through diverse domains, from natural to human social – his exposition of AST is, in fact, much more condensed than in the case of Latour and his ANT (DeLanda 2006; 2011: 184–203; DeLanda 2016). Obviously, it is quite convenient for our purposes here. Though, most definitely, it is nothing like Tarde's MON when focusing just on his *Monadology and Sociology* was perfectly justified. Indeed, AST can be said to be expressed not through one but few works largely devoted to this ontological proposition of DeLanda. Although he returns to it on few occasions, he proves to be rather consistent in his conceptual choices, and his theoretical vocabulary does not fluctuate as much as Latour's. Of course, some of the issues in AST are somewhat anticipated in his earlier interpretation of Deleuze's philosophy – especially the ideas of the virtual – but we may safely restrict ourselves here to his works explicitly devoted to AST.

4.1.2 Drawing from Many Sources (Not without Controversy)

Before we address AST's basic sentiments and commitments, there are some reservations to make. First, with reference to Deleuze (and Guattari), the concept denoting what can be said to be the basic unit for ontological inquiries in AST – assemblage – comes directly from the works of the famous French duo. DeLanda draws from *A Thousand Plateaus* (1987), but he also admits that he uses Deleuzean–Guattarian thought more as a basis and point of reference for his own proposition, rather than reconstructing their original position (DeLanda 2006: 4). This is worth pointing out, given some important interventions by prominent scholars such as Ian Buchanan (2021) and Thomas Nail (2017) – known, among others, for their engagement in Deleuze and Guattari's philosophy – who expose a different sense of assemblage than DeLanda by sticking much more to the source material of the authors of *Anti-Oedipus* (1983).

Although such discussions, and even disagreements, are highly valuable, we do not address to what extent DeLanda is true or fair to the other works he uses, in accordance to what we said in the Introduction. Just like we did not assess whether Latour's approach to, for instance, Pierre Bourdieu (e.g. Latour 2005) is justified, here we do not enter the discussion on how just or unjust DeLanda is with respect to his inspirations or negative points of reference (in a sense of other authors). Such an analysis is not only outside the agenda set for this book but would also require much space to be conducted thoroughly. Ultimately, DeLanda does not only draw from Deleuze (and Guattari). Just like the list of disciplines he draws from is eclectic, to say the least, his references include Fernand Braudel, David Hume or the already mentioned Weber and Durkheim, who should also be accounted for when analysing DeLanda from the perspective of his inspirations.

4.1.3 Some Deviations from DeLanda (In What is to Follow)

With respect to another crucial reservation, when we move to address the law from the perspective of AST, we do not entirely follow the methodological principle DeLanda (2006: 32) proposes in his framework, namely to start the analysis of the phenomenon of interest with what can be considered at the bottom of its emergence and then move up to reach its very top. In particular, consider one of the favourite motifs in DeLandaean AST's writings (DeLanda 2006: 17–18; 2016: 14–15) – how individual, often quite modest marketplaces create a much broader economic organisation by establishing relations between them. When addressing the question whether law can be grasped by DeLanda's concept of assemblage (which would mean that AST proves its adequacy), we adopt a somewhat different approach. Having presented the specifics DeLanda assumes in assemblages, we will just consider them with respect to law, as we have done in previous chapters.

Moreover, in the last subsection of this chapter we engage in a rather simple intellectual exercise, much in the spirit of the test of removal, which can be classified as an instance of a thought experiment. DeLanda (in DeLanda and Harman 2017: 15–16) himself admits his dislike for this method on the account of its vagueness, being insufficiently specified. We leave the assessment of what we propose at the end of this chapter to all those concerned, but the scenarios we consider there are sufficient to put into doubt AST's adequacy for law in connection with one characteristic and crucial feature DeLanda assumes in assemblages.

4.1.4 Reservation Concerning Virtuality and the Diagram

Finally, we have to say outright that AST, despite its development, is, to a certain extent, still an unfinished project according to the words of DeLanda himself (in DeLanda and Harman 2017: 69, 72). Namely, it is not only an ontology concerned with what is, but interestingly AST addresses the ontology of what can be. This is the point where DeLanda (2006: 31–32; 2011: 188–189; 2016: 5–6, 108–136) adapts Deleuzean notion of virtuality and elaborates on his sense of the so-called diagram. Trying not to leave anyone in confusion here, let us just present the following basic information on DeLanda's sense of virtuality and diagram.

That what is virtual for a specific entity is all the broadly understood states in which that entity can exist but which are not yet actualised. Think, for instance, of something so mundane as a crystal of salt, the very same we use to season different food items. Now think of all possible interactions, such as mechanical and chemical, in which this salt can partake. Practically, all of them will allow us to notice some broadly understood features or traits of salt, which it does not reveal at the time of observation, when the number of relations with other entities it is currently in is quite limited. In short, then, DeLanda wants to consider both that what is actualised in a given entity (what it actually proves to be and what it does given all its current relations) and that what is not actualised at the moment but merely virtual.

The specific map of the latter, the traits of a given entity that will reveal themselves only when it engages with some other entities (with which it does not interact at the moment) is called a diagram. Think once again of kitchen salt. Under usual household conditions, such as room temperature, humidity and being kept away from liquid water or other substances, salt proves to have some rather stable traits, like shape, most clearly visible to the human eye in its rock form. At the moment of observation, we are dealing with its actualisation. However, it also has some virtuality. It will dissolve in water, and with a proper device and force, it can be ground into dust – some previously unobserved, not actualised, virtual features will reveal themselves when submitting it to a different set of relations than the current ones. Of course, the comprehensive diagram of its virtuality would contain many more scenarios than the two considered examples.

The ideas of virtuality and diagram, though definitely the most abstract in AST – in the end, they tackle what can be not what is at the moment – are, as such, perfectly understandable. DeLanda expresses some doubts not with respect to them but the concepts he proposes to denote the traits of entities that reveal themselves only by relating to others, and thus, are either virtual or actualised in the current set of interactions. Given these self-doubts and admittance that, in this specific respect, AST is still a project under construction (DeLanda in DeLanda and Harman 2017: 69, 72), below, when dealing with assemblage itself, we will limit ourselves to the very basics of these issues. Such a move is even more justified, given that the crux of the issue of adequacy for law in AST lies elsewhere, in its part that deals much more with what actually is than with what can be.

4.2 Stepping into ... DeLandaean Assemblage Theory

4.2.1 One Plane, Many Scales, No Essences and No Transcendence

Having said that, we may talk more directly on the basic sentiments and assumptions of AST. Largely unlike the cases of Tarde and Latour, their exposition does not necessitate any far-reaching anticipation of information on assemblage itself in the penultimate section of this chapter.

When it comes to some initial, without focus on its basic unit for ontological inquiries, exposition of ideas driving AST, we may begin by bringing up once again the figure of flatness. DeLanda (2006: 28; 2016: 12; in DeLanda and Harman 2017: 84) argues that his ontology is one-level ontology. According to him, there is just one plane for all entities, which will be characterised in more detail later, no matter whether, for instance, some may be considered as mere components for some whole. Even some large whole is put in AST on the very same plane as its components, even the smallest ones.

Despite this flat one-levelness, DeLanda (2006: 28; 2016: 16–17, 19) also speaks of multiscalarity of his framework. Given the foundational assumption that, of the interactions of some entities, something new can emerge, one is allowed to differentiate various scales of entities, but due to one-levelness, beings out of various scales can influence each other. If everything is said to objectively be on the same plane, the biggest can influence the smallest. However, the reverse is also true, and the relations do not have to follow the scenario that, for instance, small entities can only interact with other small entities.

Speaking of entities, DeLanda (2006: 40; 2016: 12; in DeLanda and Harman 2017: 54–55) is against the approach of characterising that what exists using the idea of some unchangeable, eternal essence. He considers such rather classical understanding of essences as a kind of allowance of transcendence. The idea that there is some other level of reality that imposes itself, with varying degree of exactness, on the level of reality in reach of senses (not only human) or a very broad understanding of experience is in strict contradiction to one-levelness. To put it differently, AST explicitly adheres to the idea of immanence (e.g. DeLanda 2016: 139). Instead of looking for or assuming some otherworldly principles accounting for this world, for DeLanda, all that happens in it is explainable with reference to it as well. No wonder, then, DeLanda also admits his affiliation to the broadly understood materialism, which he also tends to equate with realism and only relatively recently reflects upon and announces to stop synonymising them in practice in his investigations (in DeLanda and Harman 2017: 4–5).

4.2.2 Realism

Before we expand the crucial thread of AST's focus on immanence, let us address its realist commitment, which may seem as especially intriguing in the context of ontology, which is said to be so general to also account for human social entities. Ultimately, as long as one tackles some nonhuman natural phenomena, the adoption of the mind independence standpoint may not provoke many doubts. However, the situation changes when the realist standpoint is to be applied to what can be considered the human social realm. Namely, once humans and their minds somehow vanish, entities such as languages, various institutions, economical organisations and political parties will also cease to exist.

In light of this, DeLanda (2006: 1–3; 2016: 138–139) attempts to better explain his realist position in that part of his ontology that takes interest in human social beings, by stating that his realism in that context is not entirely mind independence but conception or contents-of-mind independence. He illustrates this with a figure of a person who may have wrong ideas about some social phenomenon, but they do not have an influence on their referent.

On the one hand, such an approach is rather commonsensical and reflects well the actual experience. In the end, it is not that uncommon that we think about certain social entity in this or other way – whether good or bad, with varying degrees of how much we are mistaken about, for instance, public administration institutions, banks or insurance companies – but our conceptions of them leave them rather completely unaltered. On the other hand, DeLanda here does not qualify his idea of conception independence in a quantitative way. Namely, if all people would think about certain social beings in a specific way, then we can reasonably expect that some change will occur after all.

There is obviously another reservation to make, but this time it is largely anticipated by DeLanda. Namely, DeLanda (2006: 1–2) admits that there are some cases in which the way people think about something in the human realm appears to have a significant influence on it. Nevertheless, as DeLanda notices, largely correctly, the referents of some ideas or propositions of humans can be altered by them not exclusively because of them but also because of a myriad of other co-contributing factors, many of which can be conception- or even mind-independent. To acknowledge this, think about the refugee example DeLanda considers at the very beginning of his first book-length exposition of AST. It is not uncommon to see this and other social classifications regarded purely as results of how people think. In turn, DeLanda invites us to recognise how much they also depend on various entities that are not reducible to meanings and conventions only, but, in fact, are much more heterogeneous. Indeed, classifying someone as a refugee will bring some change in that person, but not only because they have been named in such a manner. To exert influence on its referent, this classification must be made in a very broad context involving states, borders between them, various legal regulations, institutions and their decisions. Though they will cease to exist if humans and their minds disappear, when people and their thinking are still present, these entities can remain unchanged by their conceptions. However, the quantitative problem stated earlier – that there perhaps is some critical number of people who, holding some conception about an entity, may ultimately alter it, rendering it conception-dependent – remains in AST, largely due to DeLanda devoting more attention to other threads in this framework.

4.2.3 Immanence, Historicity and Contingency

After this detour, showing also how far DeLanda (e.g. 2006: 134, note 8) situates himself from idealism and social constructivism, let us return to the immanence issue. For instance, if classically understood essences are treated as a case of transcendence, then how does DeLanda want to account for the entities of durable identities? DeLanda advises to focus on entities' historicity, how they came to be (their genesis) and how they subsist (their maintenance) (e.g. DeLanda 2006: 38–39; 2016: 140). In other words, there is always something in the world that can explain some other entity's existence, both its very emergence and how the object of interest manages to survive, keep up in its own being. There is nothing otherworldly towering over (or lying beneath) that what we and other beings can somehow experience that would explain it. To put it differently, DeLanda shows that identification and differentiation of entities can be achieved by tracing their historical trajectories, from something's very inception, through maintained existence, up to ceasing from it, which, although being rarely focused on by DeLanda, can be accounted for in his AST.

Fully in line with his anti-transcendence approach with an emphasis on historicity is the assumption of contingency (e.g. DeLanda 2016: 19). The fact that there are entities as they are is nothing that some necessary regularities could be responsible for. Beings of the world are the way they are because some entities started interacting with each other at some more or less distant moment in time from the one considered. Out of the specific set of interacting entities, a new object emerges, whose continuing existence depends on maintaining underlying relations that originally gave rise to it. If such is the case, and DeLanda thinks so, then notice how little necessity his AST allows. Given the contingency, the degree to which various things in the world could have been very different than they actually came to be is very high. To recognise this, it suffices to imagine how many diverse objects had to meet and somehow remain in contact so that some other entity, emergent with respect to them, could exist and function. If their meeting did not take place or if even after upholding some initial connection, they ultimately dispersed, the entity emerging out of their interactions would either never start to exist or vanish rather quickly. To better understand the issues of historicity and contingency, not very often brought to the fore in DeLanda's relevant writings, we should focus on one of the crucial and most explicitly presented tenets of AST – emergence.

4.2.4 Emergence, Properties, Tendencies and Capacities

So far, this thread was in between the lines above, and this is the appropriate moment to clarify DeLanda's take on this issue. Even though in his AST, he addresses, mostly negatively, various other kinds of entities, he is perfectly clear as to how he proposes to see that which exists. DeLanda (2006: 4, 10; 2011: 184–185; 2016: 9–10) focuses on emergent beings. Of course, emergence is only one of the few basic features in DeLandaean ontology. For the sake of not overloading our discussion, for now, let us focus here exclusively on emergence.

Basically, DeLanda argues that existing entities, out of all domains usually distinguished (for instance, nonorganic natural, nonorganic artificial, organic nonhuman, organic human, social nonhuman and social human), are emergent wholes – in relation to entities that, through interactions with each other, gave rise to them – of irreducible traits – they have features not found among their co-composing elements. Consider, for instance, oxygen and hydrogen (e.g. DeLanda in DeLanda and Harman 2017: 8). Each is a very good fuel for fire, but out of their relation, dihydrogen monoxide can emerge, commonly known as water, which works well in extinguishing fire.

However, this is only the tip of the iceberg of DeLandaean description of emergent entities, known in his framework as assemblages and characterised by some other features. Namely, next to what DeLanda calls properties – stable and actualised features of an emergent entity that are not found among its respective co-constituting elements, there are also traits that reveal themselves only when the object in question is in a specific situation or interacts with others (e.g. DeLanda 2006: 10; 2011: 185–186; 2016: 12). To put it differently, as long as an analysed entity does not engage with some other being, some of its qualities will not actualise themselves and remain in effect only virtual. As anticipated earlier, this is exactly the point where DeLanda admits that some elements of his AST are not finished in his opinion. Nevertheless, note that, despite some varying accents in his AST writings, DeLanda speaks of the virtual, not yet actualised, features of entities that are relational; they reveal themselves only in some engagement with others – as dispositions. Moreover, he distinguishes two of their general categories.

First, the so-called tendencies are said to be the simplest virtual dispositions (DeLanda 2016: 185). Consider here the example DeLanda (in DeLanda and

Harman 2017: 64–65) himself proposes – heating up liquid water under standard pressure and at the sea level up to, to be exact, 100° Celsius (212° Fahrenheit) changes its state of matter from liquid to gas. Second, in addition to such more standard tendencies that can be said to be strongly dependent on environmental conditions, there are also more complex virtual dispositions, called capacities. Consider another DeLandaean example, also from one of his favourite domains, but this time not from chemistry but relating strongly to his interest in military (DeLanda 2016: 73; in DeLanda and Harman 2017: 68). Think about the blade in a knife, a bayonet or any other melee weapon. Given the materials from which it is made, the utilised metal alloys, employed thermal treatment and the process through which it was sharpened and ground, the blade has some properties that are emergent and non-reducible to those of its co-composing elements. Its properties can be said to be a foundation for its capacities, which actualise themselves only in some engagement with other entities. As DeLanda himself explains, our chosen object here can be proven to have the capacity to cut into slices, but such virtual trait actualises itself only in relation with entities that can be cut in such a way, for instance, some cheese (but not overly creamy) or a sausage (but not overly soft). A blade – in relation to something else, like a block of some metal – may not actualise the cutting but, at best, the scratching capacity.

With respect to what we just said, we should make some additional comments. First, notice that even the most mundane objects may have significantly vast virtuality characteristic to themselves and, as a result, diagrams mapping their non-actualised dispositions would also be extremely broad. In consequence, although diagram preparation is a highly valuable and useful activity, it may also be in many instances practically impossible to finish. From a different angle, when it comes to its more practical, epistemic implications, AST calls to engage the objects of inquiry as much as possible, because only by being related to others, they reveal what they may be hiding – their virtual traits will be actualised. In addition to such call to testing objects by making them interact with others, AST somewhat provokes to reflect on the sheer amount of what we do not know about practically all objects in the world due to a simple fact that they happen to be or enter in a very limited number of interactions.

Second, leaving aside similar, more epistemic issues of AST, let us notice that DeLandaean sense of virtuality can be read in such a way that contradicts and undermines the one-levelness commitment we began this section with. In the end, if DeLanda speaks about actuality and virtuality, one can get the impression that, despite his declared anti-transcendence standpoint, he falls into transcendence as virtuality can be said to be something over and ultimately different than actuality. Moreover, one can even say that actuality is merely a derivative of virtuality, which is the one true and real level of reality (Kleinherenbrink 2020). However, such readings do not only go against DeLanda's significant emphasis on concreteness, on the "here and now" of various entities with followable history since their emergence. They also contradict quite literally what DeLanda says about the status of virtuality. Namely, he (in DeLanda and Harman 2017: 85) states that the virtual is merely the part of the actual. Virtuality is not "a transcendent ontological plane, hovering above that of actual objects" – it "can be embedded into a flat ontology of individual entities".

Third, and finally in this line of additional comments, one can have some doubts with respect to DeLandaean triad of properties and two kinds of dispositions: tendencies and capacities. Of course, one can wonder about DeLanda's dissociating his AST from essentialism in the face of how he understands properties. In the end, they can be likened to a given entity's essence, but not in the sense of something unchangeable and eternal, given the commitment to contingency. However, this is not what can be regarded as most important here.

Namely, it is quite unclear how to exactly distinguish properties and dispositions (tendencies and capacities) from each other. Indeed, the former are actualised, while the latter are virtual but can be actualised in some situations. However, if properties are to be traits of the entity as such (in comparison to dispositions which are said to actualise themselves relationally), then what are they in reality? In the end, one can say that even the features of an entity that are specific proof of its status of emergent being – are not found among its co-composing elements – are not always present and noticeable but reveal themselves relationally. Just think again about the dihydrogen monoxide example above. Some water just standing in a container does not extinguish fire because it has not been poured on the fire source. Obviously, dihydrogen monoxide has some features that are possessed by neither hydrogen nor oxygen, but which of them are to be deemed as "always its own" properties and which as virtual dispositions that remain unmanifested until interactions with other specific entities?

Perhaps, to address this, properties should be considered as very thin and rudimentary, for instance, as quantifiable qualities like volume or weight. However, these qualities can be seen as human constructs in a sense that it is us humans who consider things in such categories. Of course, given DeLanda's realist affiliation, one can propose to distinguish features that are measured or observed by human beings and those that prove themselves in relation to other entities, even when no human is present at the scene, nor observes it. Nevertheless, even if we focus on the latter option, the raised problem seems to remain: What should be qualified as properties and what as dispositions?

In the end, despite DeLanda's (2011: 4) assurance that "properties can be specified without reference to anything else" (which would differ them from circumstantially and relationally dependent actualisation of tendencies and capacities), properties also need some point of reference to reveal themselves. Think of what DeLanda considers to be a blade's property – its sharpness (the basis for the cutting capacity), and notice that "without reference to anything else", neither we nor anyone and anything can recognise this, nonetheless, good instance of emergent quality. We are raising this issue here not for the mere critical exposition of major tenets of AST but because it will prove highly important when addressing the adequacy for law.

4.2.5 *Against Micro- and Macroreductionism*

Before we do that, with special emphasis on DeLandaean characterisation of assemblage, let us bring some closure to this reconstruction by returning to emergence. DeLanda's strong commitment to it has quite obvious consequence of adopting a standpoint critical to what can be named microreductionism. By this, DeLanda (2006: 5; 2016: 9; in DeLanda and Harman 2017: 82) means all approaches that explain the chosen objects of inquiry referring to the elements they are composed of. As a result, microreductionist positions do not consider their object of reference as a being in its own right with some existence specific to itself but render it a mere aggregate of some components. While the emergentist position, such as DeLanda's, when dealing with some object would, or at least attempt to, prove that it has properties not found among its components, whose interactions are said to give rise to it, the aggregationist, microreductionist standpoint works differently. The chosen object of inquiry is ultimately regarded as nothing more than the mere grouping of its elements. In other words, microreductionism diffuses its object into more or less numerous and heterogeneous components, in consequence of which the entity under scrutiny is denied any independent existence but is rendered as nothing more than impression, because, after all, there are only parts, no bigger whole emerging out of them. Even though DeLanda does not address Tarde, it is rather safe to assume that the already commented version of MON is close to the idea of microreductionism, which is strongly against emergence, especially in the spirit of Durkheim.

The latter's position and other similar positions that assume some grand extrapersonal entities, like the entire society, and state that all individuals are nothing more than epiphenomena of these big beings are referred to as macroreductionism by DeLanda (2006: 5; 2016: 9–10; in DeLanda and Harman 2017: 82). Here the problem is not so much about denying emergence. In the end, macroreductionism works well with the idea of some being emerging out of interactions between its relatively smaller elements. DeLanda is against the commented standpoint as it denies the autonomy of these smaller components. They are deemed as nothing else than the (by)products of the macroscale entity towering over them in a practically transcendent manner. In DeLandaean rendition, macroreductionism is so extreme that the entities that can be said to compose the big object cannot exist beyond it – their subsistence is dependent on remaining within their respective whole, upholding the relations with its other co-composing entities.

Just as microreductionism is associable with the figure of aggregate, macroreductionism can be understood with reference to Hegelian idea of totality, "in which the very identity of the parts is constituted by their relations in the whole" (DeLanda 2016: 73; see also DeLanda 2006: 4, 9–10; 2011: 184). While microreductionism denies wholes, macroreductionism denies parts, or, to be more precise, their independent existence. DeLanda envisages his AST as a specific middle road, because in this framework, there are autonomous entities whose interactions may give rise to some relatively bigger objects of irreducible qualities. These bigger entities may, in turn, relate to other beings which may cause the emergence of an even bigger object, even up to the point of reaching the grandiosity of society, culture, science, state or capitalism. DeLanda (2006: 26, 32, 34, 40, 85; 2016: 14, 16, 48, 72, 88; in DeLanda and Harman 2017: 55, 142) does not deny the existence of such vast objects but warns against treating them as some overly convenient ready-made reified generalities that even play the role of transcendent beings (in relation to the phenomena under consideration) and advises to consider them just as (DeLanda 2016: 37, 102) "assemblage of assemblages" (of assemblages, one might add). This indicates the need to account for them in a detailed manner, just like the already mentioned example of national and even international markets having their roots in individual marketplaces that started to relate to each other in the far past and the subsequent years only intensified these interactions. Obviously, this particular thread in Delanda's AST brings him quite close to Latour, as one might recall the previous chapter. This similarity is not the most crucial here though.

In the end, notice that Delanda's critique of both micro- and macroreductionism already tells a lot in terms of the ontological unit of his framework. He is against mere aggregates; however, he also disagrees with totalities, which, as the very name suggests, utterly submit the parts to the whole. His way out of these two extremes is assemblages. Let us now take a more focused look at them. In some contrast to previous chapters, we do not end this section with considering AST through the lenses of our adopted sense of the idea of a flat ontology. This is because, in order to do that, we still need to have a fuller account of DeLandaean ontology, which we get only when considering its basic unit in detail.

4.3 Focusing on ... Assemblages

4.3.1 Emergent Whole

In a rather clear contrast to the previously considered Latour and Tarde, DeLanda's idea of the basic unit for ontological inquiries can be expressed quite concisely in one sentence. Assemblage is an emergent whole, coming out of interactions of its heterogeneous, material and expressive components (assemblages that may co-compose other assemblages than the one considered at the moment), which remain in relations of exteriority. As usually is with similarly packed propositions, it can and should be expanded for better understanding.

First, when it comes to the trait of being an emergent whole, as already said, assemblages come out of interactions of other entities (their elements) and are irreducible to them, have properties not found among objects that co-compose them, which proves that they are something more than a mere aggregate of their parts. Properties, characterised as finite features of an assemblage, are relatively stable and actual. However, in addition to what is actual in an assemblage, there is also its virtuality – dispositions.

Their first kind, tendencies, are deemed as simplest virtual traits that are real but remain unmanifested until actualised in some situations. The second kind, capacities, are treated as much more complex and, in fact, infinite – they reveal themselves only in some interactions with other entities, and as long as a specific interaction does not take place, they are virtual, non-noticeable.

As their very name suggests, capacities are about what can be done and, thus, do not have to be "there", actualised all the time. If they are actualised, then one can speak of them as a specific event, which, it should be stressed, is of, at least, dual character – it involves an object actualising its capacity to influence something, which can be influenced by that object in a specific way (DeLanda 2016: 73). Just think again of the blade example and notice that its capacity to cut into slices is correlated with the capacity to be cut into slices of some other entity.

As mentioned earlier, mapping virtuality, understood in such a way, into a diagram of a given assemblage can be an enormous task to undertake, if not even actually impossible. Given we addressed these fundamentals above, at this point, it is more important to bring to the fore some parts-whole relations considered by Delanda in his AST.

4.3.2 Bottom-Up, Top-Down and Exteriority Relations

Of course, given its emergent status, the whole is basically dependent on its parts, or, to be more precise, on their interactions. In the end, out of these, the whole emerges with its specific properties. Obviously then, if all relations between components are somehow severed, the assemblage will cease to exist (DeLanda 2016: 12). It appears that only when dealing with a specific assemblage, and not considering this unit in abstraction, one can assess the impact of the situation when only some parts of the whole stop relating to others. However, given the fact that DeLanda (2006: 39; 2016: 21) considers explicitly a city as an assemblage whose parts came to existence after its own emergence – just think of a modern public transportation infrastructure implemented in already existing cities – it is rather safe to assume that the partial severance of interactions among components may not be completely destructive for the assemblage.

In addition to the bottom-up direction of relations between parts and whole, DeLanda (2016: 18) addresses explicitly what he names downward causation – top-down influence of the assemblage upon its components, which themselves are assemblages. Although being or not being a part of some assemblage is said to be completely irrelevant for the properties of the considered object – as properties come out of interactions that bring the object into existence in the first place and, thus, are not something that can be altered once the object emerged – it is highly relevant for other, virtual but actualisable, traits. Just think of some large consortium grouping several once completely independent companies but now realising some common business goals. Their participation in the consortium – bigger assemblage than themselves – endows them with some new broadly understood possibilities, which will cease to exist once moving on. However, even if such exit from the consortium happens, the withdrawing company will remain itself, as long as what can be considered its own parts maintain the necessary relations between themselves.

Having considered such an example, it is the right moment to address the mentioned relations of exteriority, perhaps the most characteristic accent in DeLandaean AST (DeLanda 2006: 10–11; 2016: 10). Namely, assemblages, as entities emerging out of interactions among other entities, themselves said to realise the conditions of assemblages (DeLanda 2016: 3), are obviously composed by something, have some parts or elements. Although they contribute to the whole, which also has some influence on them, in reference to the mentioned downward causation, to say that they remain in relations of exteriority simply means that they still have their autonomy. In other words, parts of an assemblage do not derive their identity from being parts of an assemblage. They remain themselves even if they somehow exit the assemblage considered at the moment and can enter into another one. This is the commitment to autonomy, which clearly distinguishes DeLandaean assemblage from the concept of totality referred to earlier. The latter is characterised by relations of interiority – the part somehow severed from the larger whole it co-constitutes may be said to lose itself, as its very identity utterly depends on remaining in interactions with the other parts of the whole in question. This is why DeLanda (2006; 2011: 184; 2016: 10–13) uses the word "seamless" to describe totalities – relations of interiority-based entities he is strongly against.

To illustrate the assemblage-totality opposition, consider the examples DeLanda (2016: 2, 70) uses – military alliance and some familial relations, like brotherhood. The former can be regarded as one of the more archetypical instances of DeLandaean assemblage. Namely, all parties to an alliance (for instance, entire national armies or some more concrete military troops, depending on the exact scale of alliance considered) can be regarded as assemblages themselves out of a myriad of entities, like some even smaller troops, individual soldiers, their equipment and weapons. When an alliance is formed out of parties to it, it can be said to be emerging out of their relations, also with properties not possessed by its components. When in alliance, its parties gain some new opportunities, but, if they decide to leave, they remain themselves – their own properties do not come from this or other assemblage they can co-create, but from their own prior genesis, and thus remain unaltered by their movement into or beyond some assemblage. For DeLanda, the situation looks quite different in the case brotherhood, treated by him as an instance of totality, with other familial relations. Namely, one can say that parties to a brotherhood – brothers – derive their sense of self, or, at least, that part of it directly related to familial relation considered, from being in it. In other words, while party to an alliance may enter and leave it and still remain itself, one cannot be and remain to be a brother beyond someone who is a brother as well to a considered person.

4.3.3 Materiality and Expressivity of Components

Having brought to the fore the emergence and bottom-up, top-down and exteriority relations – whose basic sense can also be grasped with some easy visualisation in Figure 4.1 (though DeLanda appears to avoid such means in his own publications), let us now address the third main tenet of an assemblage – the heterogeneity of its components. As already suggested in the above examples, consortium, when considered in detail, emerges out of a plethora of varied entities, which themselves have a complex composition. Just think of each company that enters it; similar is the case with military alliance. It emerges out

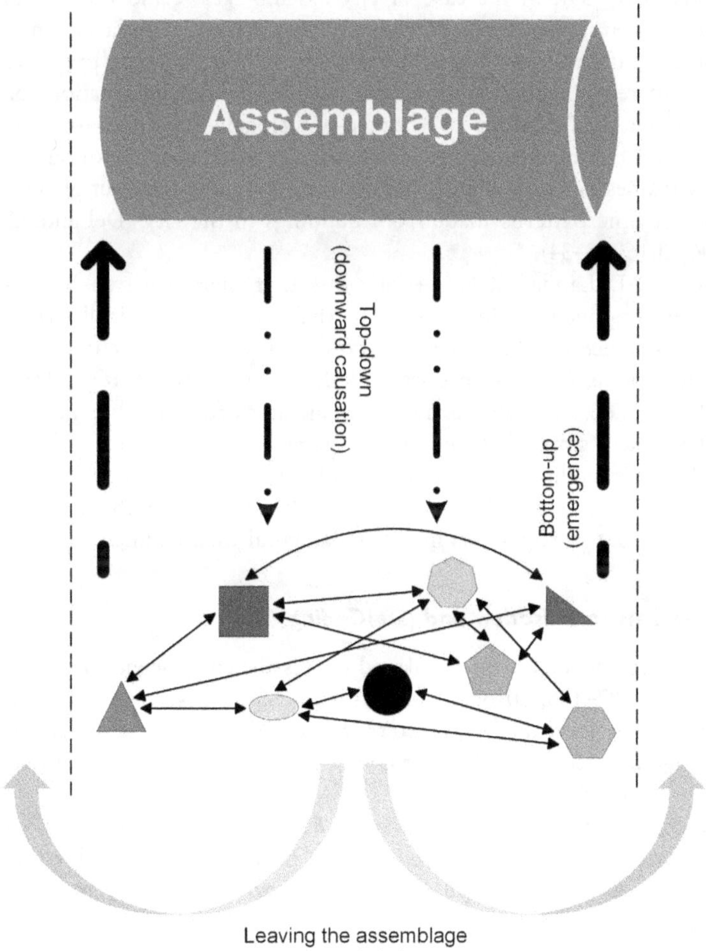

Figure 4.1 Assemblage and its parts.

of, to name just a few, various troops, military technologies and some tactical decisions. Obviously, given the formal character of DeLanda's assemblage – it is a concept that is meant to grasp with it a plethora of entities out of many usually considered domains, like natural or cultural – so typical for flat ontologies, in order to somehow address the heterogeneity, DeLanda (2006: 12; 2011: 200; 2016: 20) comes up with quite straightforward distinction between material and expressive components and allows specific mixtures of these two basic characteristics in that what composes certain assemblages.

The materiality of an assemblage's components encompasses in AST both literally physical objects and technologies – for instance, "water and sewage pipes, conduits for the gas [...], and [...] electricity cables and telephone wires" (DeLanda 2016: 33), in the case of city assemblages – and humans and their activities. When it comes to expressive components, DeLanda has in mind not only broadly understood linguistic elements – some content presented in the form of differently mediated utterances, such as written instructions of a manager in some organisations or shouted-out slogans at some anti-government protest. The expressivity of an assemblage's parts is understood way more broadly. It does not only include all non-verbal expressions but also the fingerprints or skyline patterns made from buildings in the city (DeLanda 2006: 14, 105–106; 2016: 33–34).

Moreover, DeLanda (2006: 14) suggests that there are two basic kinds of expressive components: non-functional – those that are practically irrelevant for the very existence of that what they co-compose – and functional, which are crucial for the assemblage in question. DeLanda (2006: 14–16; 2011: 187–188; 2016: 22) considers two expressive components as functional: genetic code and language. Their somewhat special character is tightly connected with what DeLanda names coding of an assemblage. However, given that there is a specific sequence assumed, we will address it only after we deal with the parameter of assemblages that is deemed as more fundamental than coding.

4.3.4 (De)Territorialisation and (De)Coding

In addition to the axis of material and expressive components, DeLanda (2006: 12–16; 2011: 187–188; 2016: 22) proposes to characterise assemblages with two similar oppositions, called parameters: territorialisation and deterritorialisation and coding and decoding. When it comes to the first, (de)territorialisation concerns two somewhat different issues: to what extent the given assemblage has well-defined boundaries – understood quite literally, in spatial terms – and how much its components are homogenised. To make this concept clearer, think of two companies – one is a purely local enterprise, while the other is a truly transnational corporation. Then, we can say that in the first, spatial sense of (de)territorialisation, the former is more territorialised, while the latter is largely deterritorialised. What about then the second, homogenisation sense, especially given the fact that heterogeneity is considered as a basic tenet of assemblages? This apparent tension is easy to resolve if one considers that even very different objects can be rendered quite alike and that assemblages as wholes can exert their downward causation influence on their parts. In consequence, for instance, objectively different elements once within certain assemblage can be homogenised by it, like different recruits moulded into soldiers by using various training methods and something so seemingly trivial like cutting their hair short. Moreover, the very fact that various elements interacting with each other lead to the emergence of a new entity – and that, from this moment, they become its parts – is already homogenising. Such an approach to the discussed matter is justified given the fact that for DeLanda (2006: 14), territorialisation is a synthetic process from which a new whole – assemblage – emerges.

However, DeLanda (2006: 15–16) also talks about another process that is said to supplement territorialisation – coding, which is understood as producing and maintaining the identity of an assemblage. As suggested earlier, coding cannot be undertaken by any kind of assemblage's components but by functional expressive ones – genetic code (obviously, with respect to organic entities) and language (in reference to the human domain, under the assumption that only we have developed it). High genetic coding would manifest itself in not moving beyond what follows from genetic makeup itself but merely expressing it in one's various activities, with no flexibility, which very strongly consolidates the identity of such highly coded being. High linguistic coding, in turn, would be exemplified in very rigid conventions or rules in, for instance, some subculture. Of course, given their very specifics, one can venture to say that genetic coders are stronger than linguistic ones.

More important to note here, in the prospect of trying to engage law through AST's lenses, is that the broadly understood linguistic entities can be said to take part not only in coding-decoding dynamics but also in territorialisation-deterritorialisation, especially when we consider it in the mentioned homogenisation terms. Although not directly, this apparent ambivalence when it comes to locating language within assemblages – is it only a coder or something else? – is addressed by DeLanda (2016: 51–52; see also DeLanda 2011: 197). He explicitly says that language is simultaneously the assemblage itself, the component of some assemblage and the coder for it. If this is the case, then it is rather safe to say that linguistic entities are not only involved in coding but also in (de)territorialisation dynamics. In the end, various linguistic means may not only take part in upholding this whole's identity but also in homogenising the components of an assemblage, even in demarcating its boundaries.

4.3.5 DeLandaean Assemblage Theory as Flat Ontology

Given the above presented information, a concise summary is rather in place and in no need of any further comment. For Delanda, assemblages are emergent, irreducible wholes (in contrast to aggregates) of properties not found among their components. Their components are themselves assemblages. The components of an assemblage relate to each other in terms of exteriority – even when beyond the assemblage they co-composed, they retain their identity due to their very own properties. The assemblage's parts are then independent of an entire assemblage they give rise to – can exist beyond it (in contrast to totalities). Given their emergent status, assemblages are dependent on their parts. Nevertheless, assemblages still influence their parts in a downward causation. Assemblages can be characterised not only by the actual properties – traits not found among their components, but coming out of their interactions, just like the entire assemblage – but also by virtual, yet actualisable dispositions – tendencies (rather simple and countable) and capacities (more complex and infinite, given the number of other objects any assemblage can interact with). Moreover, assemblages can be described using two parameters, two axes: (de) territorialisation, concerning the spatial boundaries and components' homogenisation, and (de)coding, related to the consolidation of the assemblage's identity. In turn, the mere components of assemblages are material, expressive or somehow combine these two basic characteristics. When it comes to the expressive components, two of them – language and genetic code – are given the status of coders. Nevertheless, linguistic entities, while realising this particular function are also components of assemblages and assemblages themselves, so all the traits we addressed above should be related to them as well, taking part in the (de)territorialisation included.

After such focused look at an assemblage itself, we may look at AST through the very idea of flat ontology. Despite DeLandaean AST's self-description as flat ontology (DeLanda 2006: 28), we should address whether such classification is correct, especially given the fact that we proposed our own reconstruction of its very idea. AST's ambitions are so universal in terms of the kinds of entities that are supposed to be grasped by it that we can safely say that it adheres to the pluralism tenet proposed in the Introduction.

When it comes to nonhierarchy, the situation may seem more complicated. On the one hand, DeLanda's objective one-levelness and only relative multiscalarity and that entities that can be said to belong to different scales can still interact with each other appear as the epitome of nonhierarchy. On the other hand, when changing the perspective from relations between entities to relations between an entity and its co-composing elements, one can get the impression that DeLanda from the very outset prioritises the broadly understood language, as it, in his rendition, besides being a component in some assemblage and an assemblage itself, also plays the role of a coder. Coding is one of the parameters of assemblages that is about stabilising their identities. This could be read as a specific prioritisation of one kind of element over others within some assemblage, which is rather in tension with nonhierarchy. However, coding is regarded by DeLanda (2006: 14) as a somewhat subsequent parameter, when he says that coding is, in fact, a process that supplements a more fundamental process of territorialisation. If that is the case, then coding by linguistic expressions is not prioritised from the very outset but merely something that may only prove to have special, assemblage's identity-centred role. In the end, in addition to coding (which may turn out to be even low in the case of a specific assemblage), language is said to be a component of the assemblage (so it may take part in (de)territorialisation) and an assemblage itself (in line with the idea that assemblages' components are themselves assemblages). With such reservation, we may say that AST ultimately falls under the idea of a flat ontology, as adopted earlier.

4.4 Law and … DeLanda's Assemblages

4.4.1 Law as an Emergent Whole

Having introduced ourselves to the way of thinking developed by DeLanda through the name of AST, we may address whether it is adequate for law. DeLanda (2016: 7) says that "assemblages are everywhere", but does the law fit the description? In a way quite similarly to previously considered cases of Tarde and Latour, AST also proves in some of its most characteristic and defining details to be problematic for law, which of course can be read somewhat differently, that law, due to its specifics, slips away from just another ontological framework that practically announces itself to be universal.

When one looks at the very concise and packed one-sentence definition of DeLanda's assemblage from the beginning of the previous section, one can see basically three main tenets: (1) being an emergent whole out of (2) heterogeneous, material and expressive components (assemblages themselves) in (3) relations of exteriority. Let us begin, then, with emergence. For DeLanda, it means two tightly connected things – that an assemblage emerges out of interactions between that what can be named its components and that it has properties not found among them and thus is actually some new entity.

In terms of the former aspect, on the one hand, one can say that the thesis that law is a separate and somewhat greater entity than all that gives rise to it should not cause too much controversy, already given the fact that functionalistic thinking was highly influential for the large part of the twentieth century, also with respect to the reflection dedicated explicitly to law (e.g. Milovanovic 2003: 155–170; Deflem 2008: 108–116; Treviño 2017: 311–347). Moreover, notice that speaking of law as a single entity, even when it consists of a plethora of relatively smaller entities, is so widespread that it can even be regarded as a commonsensical view. On the other hand, we already know, due to Tarde, that even the apparently big entities can be nothing more than the simplifying average of their smaller parts and that the big does not need to have any new irreducible qualities. Such a standpoint is obviously in strict opposition to DeLanda's emergentism and still can be regarded as rather far from being common in thinking about law.

Having reached the point that necessitates addressing the second aspect of emergence – having properties not found among components – let us notice the following. It can be said that proving specific irreducible properties of law considered as a whole is, in the end, more difficult than proving some emergent qualities among some of the components of such broad sense of law.

Consider, for instance, a purely textual aspect of law – all the texts of legal acts in a given jurisdiction. Such interrelated documents and their contents can be said to create new quality, even an entire system that has properties not found among its components. In the end, with respect to single legal provision – definitely a component of an entire legal system – it is rather unfounded to consider it in terms such as hierarchical relations or some interprovision coherence. Hierarchy and varying degrees of coherence, in the legal context, can and do emerge only when one moves beyond a single legal provision and considers a myriad of these. In other words, out of the mere quantity of what can be considered single units of legal text, something new can emerge, which is not merely an aggregate of its parts but has some properties which make practically no sense when one would like to refer them to parts themselves. Moreover, the system of texts of law with its hierarchy and coherence also acts on its very parts. For instance, some legal provision may need to undergo various changes or even be derogated if it disturbs the system's hierarchy and coherence and all that they entail, especially some division of competences.

From such a perspective, one can say that emergence in Delanda's AST does not prove to be much problematic for law. However, note that there is still the Tardean controversy, according to which whether any emergent wholes which are more than mere sums of their parts should be admitted at all, and the fact that heretofore we exclusively refer to the textual sense of law.

In accordance, then, to what we said in the Introduction and in line with AST, which, not only due to its focus on heterogeneity, is far from adhering to some idea of ontological purity, let us now consider the suggested very broad sense of law, which consists of much more than just texts. Think again of the understanding of law proposed in the Introduction as the main point of reference in our investigations in this book. As mentioned earlier, the identification of a quality in law rendered so complex, which can be deemed irreducible to this whole's diverse parts appears more difficult than in the just considered case of exclusively textually understood law. For the sake of consistency between the chapters here, we may return to what we thought about in the concluding section of the chapter on Tarde and consider law's autocreativity as an instance of its emergent property, which, if correct, would bring us closer to be able to say that law realises the first tenet of DeLanda's assemblage. Moreover, even though DeLanda himself seems to avoid talking in terms of autopoiesis, perhaps given his dislike for macroreductionism he would most likely accuse Luhmann of (who is interestingly absent in Delandaean AST's writings), he actually is very close to explicitly allowing autocreativity in his own theory. Just recall the city example mentioned earlier, where the city – assemblage – is also composed of entities that emerged themselves way after the city itself. Moreover, DeLanda (2006: 39) says that "while some parts must pre-exist the whole others may be generated by the maintenance processes of an already existing whole". Most definitely, then, autocreation is allowed in AST, but the exact way in which it is admitted may still raise some doubts from the perspective of assessing this framework's adequacy for law.

First, note that the quote above is somewhat unclear – is autocreation one of the defining traits of assemblages, in general, or is it perhaps a property only some assemblages have? It appears that only the latter is correct, because one can easily find examples of entities that realise the assemblage conditions but are not autocreative themselves. Just think of the blade example. It is an emergent whole with very specific properties, but it just cannot self-multiply itself. However, even if autocreativity can be regarded as an irreducible property of at least some assemblages and not one of their general traits, the quote above gives another reason to be uncertain about AST's adequacy for law with respect to its first main tenet. Namely, DeLanda says in the quote about generating parts of the whole during its maintenance process. This incentivises us to wonder whether the fact that law can be said to make its own parts using its own parts (for example, it regulates how its regulations should be created or legal institutions grant permissions to do something, like building a house, and once it is done, some other regulations acquire a new object for their influence, like how to manage one's newly built immovable property) is for that very purpose. If yes, then law fits the first tenet of DeLandaean assemblage, and if not, then AST's inadequacy reveals itself, at least partially.

No matter which option will be argued in favour of, we reach here some inconclusiveness: instead of one statement, positive or negative about AST's adequacy, we get two possibilities. The problem here lies not only in the difficulty in assessing whether law's autocreativity is for the sake of maintenance but also due to lack of any more precise idea on how to identify assemblage's properties that are not found among its parts. Think of a more clear, typically social examples considered by DeLanda (2016: 10) himself: "tightly knit communities that inhabit small towns, or neighbourhoods with an ethnic composition in large cities". While the density of such human groups is definitely their irreducible quality, one may seriously doubt whether storing the reputation of and opinion about their members and enforcing some rules among them is really something not found in their components (DeLanda 2006: 56; 2011: 112, 124, 125; 2016: 10–11). In the end, individual people can, and actually do, remember what others did and can even engage in some informal enforcement of norms. In this light, human communities are not that different from humans themselves.

To put it differently, while emergence in the nonhuman domain is more clear and convincing in AST – especially given its not uncommon references to chemistry – it may raise some crucial doubts in what can be named the human social domain, obviously highly relevant for our engagement in law here. Moreover, even if we would stick to the idea that law is indeed an emergent whole with at least one property not found among its highly heterogeneous components – autocreativity for its maintenance purposes – then there is still that what we said on the occasion of Tarde's MON. Recall that there we considered a possibility that what rather can be most easily associated with the idea of law's emergent being status – autocreativity – can be, in fact, accounted for in a vehemently anti-emergentist framework. If that is the case, then AST's adequacy in relation to its tenet of emergence can be said to be even more undermined, as here the property deemed irreducible is put in a completely different light and rendered as something that does not need a figure of the emergent whole. However, to be fair, perhaps there are some other properties of law that would prove not to be graspable by an anti-holistic approach, such as Tarde's, and, consequently, the issue of AST's adequacy would still be in play.

Nevertheless, at this point, we can say that it is inconclusive whether the first main tenet of an assemblage – emergence – fits law in its sense that moves way beyond the focus on textuality. It is because the uncertainty whether such law actually constitutes the whole with properties not found among its components and those not possible to address in anti-emergentist terms that would undermine AST in a relevant aspect. Of course, this uncertainty is, to a certain extent, due to the vastness and complexity of law itself but also due to some vagueness when it comes do DeLandaean sense of emergence, especially in the social human domain.

Having said that, DeLanda's other concepts related to the emergence issue are at least interesting for purposes of investigations about law. With all the reservations we made about emergence in this section and even earlier about the relevant tripartite distinction, DeLanda's actual properties and virtual, yet actualisable dispositions – tendencies and capacities – are not only an intriguing yet challenging framework to use when dealing with law. In the end, it shares and even enhances the intuition that what law can do or what can be done with law will reveal itself only in practical interactions between law and some other elements of the world. If there perhaps are still objects free of law's influence or given a quite justified prediction that some new entities will emerge, then it means that what we know about law is far from being complete and that we will never obtain comprehensive knowledge about it. There will always be some new objects emerging, with respect to which law may reveal something previously not seen. Such sentiments bring us close to the idea of the diagram of virtuality. If such a diagram can be enormous even with respect to some relatively simple chemical substance, then its scale in relation to law can be practically beyond human comprehension.

Of course, assemblages are grasped in AST not only with properties and dispositions but also with the parameters of (de)territorialisation and (de)coding performed by their material and expressive components. We will address law from their perspective below, when dealing with the second main tenet of assemblage – heterogeneity.

4.4.2 Material and Expressive Components of Law

As already mentioned, the entirety of DeLanda's AST largely supports the vision that law is and should be considered not as some ontologically pure and homogeneous entity made of just one kind of entities, though DeLanda himself avoids referring to law directly. It is interesting especially given the fact that entities that are relevant to law, like various organisations, or even entire states and beings that can be compared with law, like economic markets or science, are addressed explicitly by DeLanda. Nevertheless, what is most important here is that the heterogeneity of assemblage's components – their materiality and expressivity – seems a good fit for law (of course, with reservation concerning positions in ontology of law that argue in favour of a much more modest composition and character of law).

When it comes to expressive components of law, one can obviously refer to legal provisions themselves, their various interpretations, decisions based on them and uttered or written arguments in favour of or against decisions and interpretations. In order to exist and realise their functions, they need to be put in some media, whether analogue, like print; digital, like text display and, finally, sound waves passing through the air. Having said that, one can venture to say that what may appear for some as a purely expressive component is also, to a certain extent, material. Obviously, material components of law are much more than printed documents, files or computer hardware and software allowing access to some digital content. One can also classify in such a way so diverse entities like teleinformatic networks, buildings, specific outfits and poles for traffic signs. In short, in AST, the heterogeneity tenet is itself capacious enough to be adequate for law.

The same can be said in relation to the already anticipated thread of an assemblage's parameters realised by material and expressive components. In terms of the first parameter – (de)territorialisation – one can venture to say that law is more deterritorialised than territorialised. Such a diagnosis appears to hold in the case of both senses of territorialisation – literal, spatial boundaries-centred and its homogenisation-oriented sense. With respect to the former, there are state boundaries, but national law in certain situations can extend beyond them and be also applied to citizens when they move past the border. Moreover, law appears weakly territorialised in the latter relevant sense. As mentioned earlier, much in line with the heterogeneity tenet as such, it is rather made from highly heterogeneous components, which can be said to be under some homogenising influence of law given that they are rendered by it as, for instance, addressees of law or its subjects and objects of regulations. Nevertheless, their more objective diversity remains. Individual people become addressees of law, but they still are individuals. This is why one can say of the relatively weak territorialisation of law. In comparison, when it comes to the second parameter, one can rather safely say that law is strongly coded by its characteristic expressive and linguistic components – texts of legal acts and their contents. Indeed, they also seem to take part in territorialisation's setting the boundaries and homogenisation by specifying law's reach and by imposing their categorisations and definitions on a myriad of referents. However, they can also be deemed responsible for the identity of the law they co-compose.

In light of the above, law appears as a weakly territorialised and strongly coded entity. DeLanda (2016: 3) himself, when dealing with the two parameters of assemblage, says that this is "a concept with knobs", in a sense that the parameters for a concrete assemblage may be very different from each other (for instance, the combination of strong territorialisation with weak coding is possible). In consequence, one can say that such a diagnosis of law is definitely within AST and does not disturb its propositions and general idea.

Nevertheless, the fact that law fits the heterogeneity tenet is ultimately not that important, given the most significant problems for AST's adequacy for law connected with the third main tenet – relations of exteriority. In the end, an assemblage's defining traits are presented in a conjunction. If even only one of them can be clearly put into doubt, then DeLanda's assemblage turns out to be problematic, at best, or simply unfit, at worst, for law despite the universal ambitions of the commented framework and some other traits proving adequate. However, to show that the adequacy problem is much more nuanced than the simple binary "either some flat ontology fits the law or not", we consider an assemblage's crucial specifics in some analytical isolation, also for the sake of addressing the value question. While heterogeneity itself is rather the least controversial issue here and the emergence issue is somewhat problematic due to its inconclusiveness, the relations of exteriority – arguably the most characteristic part of AST (still only generally commented in the literature, e.g. Müller 2015; Müller and Schurr 2016; Rutzou and Elder-Vass 2019; Spies and Alff 2020; but see Savage 2020) – can be regarded as the most crucial here as there are serious doubts concerning the extent to which law realises this particular condition of an assemblage.

4.4.3 Law's Components in Relations of Exteriority

Just recall that, in strong opposition to the figure of seamless totality, whose parts derive their identity from remaining in relations with other parts of the totality in question, DeLanda's assemblage is meant to respect the autonomy of beings. Namely, that what composes an assemblage is not in relations of interiority (like in the case of totality's parts) but in exteriority – it may withdraw itself from the relations with other components and remain itself. This is because the defining properties of such a withdrawing element (said, by DeLanda, to be assemblage itself) come from the relations of its own interacting components, out of which it itself emerged. The assemblage's parts are then free to stay within it or move on.

Additionally, such autonomy takes the form of the possibility that an entity that co-constitutes one assemblage simultaneously takes part in another assemblage. When it comes to law, this specific point should not raise any doubts. In the end, individual people who are also more or less important legal officials definitely take part in what can be named other assemblages, such as local communities near their place of residence or sports clubs. Similarly, various examples of the broadly understood material infrastructure for law, from entire buildings to simple office writing utensils, are not only of law but also of the economy, as each can be, and actually is, endowed with some economic value.

Crucial doubts with respect to law in the context of DeLandaean exteriority reveal themselves not when considering the simultaneous participation in various assemblages but what can be named their parts' detachability. In the end, even though an assemblage's parts can gain from assemblage's downward causation various capacities, they can still detach from it without harming their identity and properties. For AST to be adequate for law, law should be made from components that realise the exteriority condition – will remain themselves even if somehow withdrawn from the law. "Somehow" is used here completely deliberately, because DeLanda does not always clarify how exactly such detachment unfolds. We may say here that the specifics of the detachment depend largely on the assemblage and its concrete part considered.

There is, however, an even more fundamental issue: the difference between a part detaching from the assemblage and not entering any other and a part that detaches but then joins a different set of relations with other entities which constitute another assemblage or just remains in the rest of assemblages it partakes in (except for the one from which it has withdrawn itself). DeLanda does not seem to consider the former scenario, which entails some rather utter isolation of such entity detached from its (only) assemblage and not entering any other. This is why we focus here on the latter scenario and consider a few examples of entities that can be said to be parts of law and try to answer whether they can retain their identity if detached from law, or, to put it differently, what will remain of them after the detachment.

Let us begin with some personal human component of law – a person who, because of their work for some public institution, like legislature or adjudication, can be deemed as part of law. Their potential detachment from it may be realised in different ways, for instance, by simply resigning from their current legal job or by moving abroad and thus removing themselves from the current national jurisdiction, which can even be connected with the renunciation of citizenship. Even if such scenarios actually occur, one can say that the person in question remains themselves. Indeed, after the job resignation, travelling abroad or even renouncing the previous citizenship, that person will most likely have their set of relationally dependent traits changed but not their properties. For instance, once a judge, now this person does not have the same competences as before, when within law, but still can be said to be the very same person. In short, if this reasoning is correct, the human components of law seem to realise the exteriority condition.

Let us now then consider what can be regarded as much more than a single person-type component of law and think about an entire legal institution, such as the Police. Its detachment – besides being rather difficult to imagine, perhaps beyond the scenario of derogating the legal regulations specifying it and privatising the mentioned institution – would be rather much more significant for its identity than leaving some legal profession or national jurisdiction for individual persons. In the end, what would be left after such detachment? On the one hand, one can say that quite a lot – various buildings; vehicles; databases; enforcement gear, like batons and firearms; and, of course, people working for the institution in question. On the other hand, although so much is left, it is rather not an exaggeration to say that the Police outside or beyond law just stops being itself, loses its very identity. In particular, this is because, for the Police or any other legal institution to be itself, it must have a proper legitimacy for itself, which is gained by being and remaining legal – having legal regulations that ground this institution and its competences, regulations made in specific procedures (one of the more important sources of legitimacy themselves), by people who may participate in them because of being elected (an even more fundamental legitimacy source).

Of course, one can say that legitimacy is a trait that is in no way inherent to the object with it and that it just comes from relations with other beings. From such a perspective, legitimacy can be likened to a disposition, in a specific DeLandaean sense, which comes from remaining within some larger whole – assemblage – which, through its downward causation, grants its parts some new traits. From such a standpoint, the legitimacy of a legal institution is not regarded as its property – a quality which comes directly from its emergence – but is merely something subsequent and, in fact, unnecessary for the object in question. In the end, properties are much more fundamental to entities and their identity in AST than both types of virtual yet actualisable dispositions. If that would be the case, then the Police's or any other legal institution's detachment from law would cause losing their legitimacy. However, given that legitimacy is rendered in the discussed standpoint as something secondary, the identity of the objects in question can remain intact. As a result, the Police's and other legal institutions' status of law's parts remaining in relations of exteriority would not be undermined. However, it would also mean that to be a legal institution, legal legitimacy is not necessary.

Thus, it is justified to consider legitimacy as a property which comes directly from the emergence process – elements interacting with each other and thus giving rise to the entity in question (see also DeLanda 2016: 11). In the end, one can say that the Police and other legal institutions emerge out of heterogeneous beings relating to each other in a specific way. Law and concrete legal regulations can be said to be one of such beings. Recall the one-levelness of AST and that even the seemingly biggest entities can interact with the smallest ones. From such a perspective, it is justified to say that law can be just one of the many other elements, often from clearly different scales than that of law, that, through interacting with each other, generate something else. Law's influence on a legal institution in terms of its legitimacy would be then bottom-up – from the very emergence of a legal institution – and not top-down – when the institution is somewhat already created and is legitimised only subsequently. Such a standpoint not only corresponds better with the rather common intuition to regard the legitimacy of institutions not as something secondary to their identity. More important, in the current engagement with the tenet of relations of exteriority, is to notice that, in the considered scenario, potential detachment from the law of Police or any other legal institution would significantly alter their identities – they would not remain themselves. In consequence, relations of exteriority of what can be said to be one of the more important law's components are undermined here.

Notice also that the two scenarios we analyse here – one where legitimacy is considered as a property coming directly out of the very emergence of a legal institution and the other where legitimacy is something similar to disposition – can be read in light of the previously regarded problem in clearly distinguishing DeLandaean properties from tendencies and capacities. Basically, if some trait is considered the property of an object, then its detachment from some larger assemblage is indifferent to that property. In turn, if a quality of the entity in question is disposition, which actually comes from co-constituting some assemblage and being within the range of its downward causation influence, then abandoning it will also annul that quality. As long as we do not have a very specific way to actually distinguish properties and dispositions in concrete cases, we will often find ourselves involved in such duality and examples as clear as the legal officials case considered earlier will be a rarity. This problem will manifest itself also in the last, third instance of what can be considered as parts of law – legal provisions in legal acts – which should be analysed here.

Do legal provisions realise the relations of exteriority? Again, already their very detachment from the law they currently co-compose and plugging them into other assemblage or just considering them in relation to assemblages they remain in even after the detachment is difficult to envisage. In the end, if the given legal provision is derogated, then it stops being part of the current valid legal system. Of course, it does not have to vanish completely. It may remain in the form of a mere piece of written text. Someone with a competence in the ethnic language in which it is written can read it, but its original meaning may be lost, because the provision's ties with other legal regulations can be said to be specifically severed, and they significantly contributed to its very sense. The legal provision after detachment from law can be considered as a piece of text from some general linguistic or even literary perspective. However, through such sensitivities, it will become something else rather than remaining still itself as when within law.

In such a case, legal provisions cannot be said to be law's parts in relations of exteriority. Obviously, one can argue that, after the detachment, there is still some string of letters of some alphabet, but the question is whether the identity of linguistic units of legal provisions can be reduced to just that. If one would be inclined to answer affirmatively, perhaps due to the inspiration from the interwar approach to legal interpretation proposed by Polish scholar Sawa Frydman (1936: 173; see also Moś 1991), then, in DeLandaean terms, it would mean that the emergence of legal provision amounts just to positioning various letters in a specific pattern, for instance, on a piece of paper, and its characteristic irreducible properties have nothing to do with meaning or sense as they are something much more subsequent. Of course, the meanings of various linguistic messages can change after they have been created, which also applies to legal provisions.

However, their very original creation is more than just preparing some visual patterns out of letters and punctuation marks but expressing and giving form to some sense. In DeLandaean terms, such a standpoint indicates that the meaning of a legal provision is, in fact, something much more intimately related to its very creation, emergence, even up to the point of considering it the property of a provision. Given the specifics of law creation in the contemporary context, especially the obvious fact that all newly created regulations are plugged into a plethora of others already valid, with which consistency is very important, one can say that the already existing legal system, or at least some of its provisions, take part in the emergence of another provision. This is similar to the previously considered case of the Police or other legal institutions whose emergence involves law. If law can be said to not only influence some of its part in a top-down fashion of downward causation but also participate in its original emergence, then one cannot say that the element in question has the degree of autonomy suggested by DeLanda's exteriority. In this light, the legal provision's hypothetical detachment from the law that co-created it cannot be said to be completely neutral with respect to this provision's identity. Given the fact that what AST provokes us here to consider appears to be even more complex, we will return in a moment to the issue of legal provisions and exteriority.

Nevertheless, even that what we considered thus far seems to allow us to say that AST's adequacy for law is put in serious doubt due to its characteristic insistence on the relations of exteriority, while law can be said to be composed of very diversified, in the commented aspect, parts. Namely, some of them seem to realise the relations of exteriority – in the hypothetical scenario of detachment, they retain their identity, while the identity of others appears to be threatened to such an extent that one can say that they are rather in relations of interiority with other components of law. Perhaps the closer a given element of law is to that what can be considered stereotypically legal, or the more law participates in the emergence of some object, the more its very identity depends on remaining within law. In turn, if the given element is far from such a stereotypical "core", or emerges largely independently of law, then its hypothetical detachment from law would do very little to its identity. For instance, think of, on the one hand, legal texts and institutions, and on the other hand, computers and specific dresses. The former examples are difficult to imagine as remaining themselves after the detachment from law. In turn, the identities of the latter appear to be able to remain completely unaltered and perfectly well in such a scenario. However, one can say that all the mentioned objects are parts (with others not mentioned here clearly) of law.

On a side note, if this is the case, then Tardean MON is weakened even more when confronted with law. Namely, while Tarde was also eager to endow what can be named parts of the big entities with far-reaching independence of what they can be said to co-create, our discussion above shows that law, to a certain yet significant extent, undermines such idea.

Returning to AST, one can venture to say in a similarly falsificationist way that law is not an assemblage in the entirety but rather has some traits of assemblage and totality. Such a conclusion is in very clear tension with DeLandaean vision, which explicitly opposes assemblages and totalities. This is rather interesting to notice, because while DeLanda (2016: 3; see also 2011: 187) likes to speak of an assemblage as "a concept with knobs" – due to (de)territorialisation and (de)coding – he appears to treat the exteriority tenet in very binary terms. For Delanda, either something is in relations of exteriority or not, while law appears to show that just as gradual (de)territorialisation and (de)coding are, so should in-/exteriority be treated. DeLanda does not appear to even consider such possibility. Such insistence can perhaps explain why he (DeLanda 2011: 184) is ready to say in one of his expositions of exteriority that "pulling a live animal's heart out will surely kill it but the heart itself can be implanted into another animal and resume its regular function". However, notice that some animal's heart can only be transplanted into another animal that is a compatible recipient (for instance, belongs to the same species as the donor). In other words, the idea of detachability and implementation, derived from the exteriority tenet, is much more complex and in need of a more nuanced approach than what often appears to be suggested by DeLanda himself.

To recognise this, consider what can come out of trying to follow the general idea from the quote above in the case of a legal provision. Let us imagine any legal provision, for instance, out of my home country's – Poland's – legal order. If it would actually realise the autonomy implied by DeLanda's relations of exteriority, we could hypothetically detach it from its original system and implement it into another without any change or harm to its identity. Given the fact that Polish language is used for legal regulations only in Poland and European Union, there is a very high chance that, after detachment from Poland's law, it would be implemented into a legal system based on a different ethnic language. To complete the implementation, it would then need to be translated. Even if, after such translation, it would prove to be coherent with the rest of the receiving legal system, it would be rather unfounded to say that it has remained itself if written differently. Of course, one can argue that a legal provision's identity is not about the mere visual look of words and punctuation marks but its sense. However, such a standpoint would bring us back to the issue we considered earlier – that the sense of a provision is due to its relations to other similar linguistic units; thus, its potential detachment from them would be far from being irrelevant to its identity.

In the end, legal provisions within an entire legal system are not similar to words in a sentence. Indeed, "the relations between words in a sentence must be conceived as relations of exteriority" (DeLanda 2016: 62), but DeLanda does not say it explicitly that the words detached from some sentence retain their identity when they are still within some much larger entity – an entire language they co-compose. When plugged into another language without adequate translation, they get, in fact, reduced to some string of visual signs. In turn, when translated, they can be said to be changed to something else – a word in the other language – so their identity practically vanishes.

In the face of this, if someone would still like to prove the exteriority of a legal provision, they can consider once again the idea that the legal provision's identity is very slimmed-down to just a string of some signs. However, then our scenario about detaching a legal provision from one legal system and ethnic language and implementing into another makes the exteriority idea in relation to law even more questionable. Notice that Polish language uses Latin alphabet as well as characteristic diacritics. While their absence in the language of the recipient legal system, if it is also based on the same alphabet, may be less problematic, consider the hypothetical scenario of plugging a legal provision into a system using alphabet other than Latin. In consequence, it can be said that the identity of a legal provision whose peculiar journey we have been considering here, even if understood as a mere string of letters, is threatened even more than in previous scenarios. Namely, looking at some written message in foreign alphabets, one cannot even correctly distinguish the letters used. The legal provision we tracked – at the very beginning, when still within its "home" assemblage, it is full of complex and significant meaning – ends up being something practically undecipherable after the detachment and implementation considered here. Arguing that the provision in question before and after the detachment has maintained its identity, retained itself, is peculiar, to say the least.

Obviously, what we have done above with respect to the exteriority condition can be thought of in terms of a very thickly drawn intellectual experiment. Although it is a method disliked by DeLanda, its use here is actually required to carefully think about law in terms of relations of exteriority. This highly important and characteristic part of AST proves to be problematic for law and puts the adequacy of the commented framework into doubt.

Of course, one can correctly say that the identified problem is tightly connected to an even more general issue of AST – distinguishing properties and dispositions. The former are said to be untouched by the detachment of the part from an assemblage, while the latter, when coming from the assemblage's downward causation, are dependent on remaining within the assemblage. Law appears to have different elements that can be said to be its parts. We have considered only few of them and only few of their traits, which can be seen in terms of properties or dispositions. However, our confrontation of law with exteriority already justifies the serious doubts with respect to this tenet of AST and its adequacy for law. Interestingly, many other parts of this framework, which is the closest to some of the most classical approaches in social theory out of all considered in this book, can be said to be unproblematic (heterogeneity), somewhat less controversial (emergence) or even intriguing (like considering law's virtuality or characterising law using two DeLandaean parameters).

Speaking of being intrigued, notice that even the most controversial issue of exteriority can and should be read in more affirmative, not exclusively critical, terms as an invitation to seriously consider how much law's elements are dependent on law. Just as anticipated in the Introduction – even if some framework's adequacy proves to be clearly questionable, it still may have some value for investigations about law. Having addressed DeLandaean AST, let us now move to analysing and assessing the penultimate framework.

References

Buchanan, Ian. 2021. *Assemblage Theory and Method*. London: Bloomsbury Academic.

Deflem, Mathieu. 2008. *Sociology of Law: Visions of a Scholarly Tradition*. Cambridge: Cambridge University Press.

DeLanda, Manuel. 1991. *War in the Age of Intelligent Machines*. New York: Zone Books.

DeLanda, Manuel. 2000. *A Thousand Years of Nonlinear History*. New York: Swerve Editions.

DeLanda, Manuel. 2002. *Intensive Science and Virtual Philosophy*. London: Continuum.

DeLanda, Manuel. 2006. *A New Philosophy of Society: Assemblage Theory and Social Complexity*. London: Continuum.

DeLanda, Manuel. 2011. *Philosophy and Simulation: The Emergence of Synthetic Reason*. London: Continuum.

DeLanda, Manuel. 2015. *Philosophical Chemistry: Genealogy of a Scientific Field*. London: Bloomsbury.

DeLanda, Manuel. 2016. *Assemblage Theory*. Edinburgh: Edinburgh University Press.

DeLanda, Manuel. 2022. *Materialist Phenomenology: A Philosophy of Perception*. London: Bloomsbury Academic.

DeLanda, Manuel, and Graham Harman. 2017. *The Rise of Realism*. Cambridge: Polity Press.

Deleuze, Gilles, and Félix Guattari. 1983. *Anti-Oedipus: Capitalism and Schizofrenia*. Trans.: Robert Hurley, Mark Seem and Helen R. Lane. Minneapolis: University of Minnesota Press.

Deleuze, Gilles, and Félix Guattari. 1987. *A Thousand Plateaus: Capitalism and Schizofrenia*. Trans.: Brian Massumi. Minneapolis: University of Minnesota Press.

Frydman, Sawa. 1936. Dogmatyka prawa w świetle socjologii [Legal Dogmatics in the Light of Sociology]. In *Ogólna nauka o prawie: Tom I* [*General Science of Law: Volume I*], Bronisław Wróblewski (ed.), 141–316. Wilno: Koło Filozoficzne Studentów Uniwersytetu Stefana Batorego w Wilnie.

Kleinherenbrink, Arjen. 2020. Metaphysical Primitives: Machines and Assemblages in Deleuze, DeLanda, and Bryant. *Open Philosophy* 3 (1): 283–297.

Latour, Bruno. 2005. *Reassembling the Social: An Introduction to Actor-Network Theory*. Oxford: Oxford University Press.

Milovanovic, Dragan. 2003. *An Introduction to the Sociology of Law*. Third Edition. Monsey: Criminal Justice Press.

Moś, Urszula. 1991. Sawa Frydman: A Polish Legal Realist. *Ratio Juris* 4 (1): 72–78.

Müller, Martin. 2015. Assemblages and Actor-Networks: Rethinking Socio-Material Power, Politics and Space. *Geography Compass* 9 (1): 27–41.

Müller, Martin, and Carolin Schurr. 2016. Assemblage Thinking and Actor-Network Theory: Conjunctions, Disjunctions, Cross-Fertilisations. *Transactions of the Institute of British Geographers* 41 (3): 217–229.

Nail, Thomas. 2017. What is an Assemblage?. *SubStance* 46 (1): 21–37.

Rutzou, Timothy, and Dave Elder-Vass. 2019. On Assemblages and Things: Fluidity, Stability, Causation Stories, and Formation Stories. *Sociological Theory* 37 (4): 401–424.

Savage, Glenn C. 2020. What is Policy Assemblage?. *Territory, Politics, Governance* 8 (3): 319–335.

Spies, Michael, and Henryk Alff. 2020. Assemblages and Complex Adaptive Systems: A Conceptual Crossroads for Integrative Research?. *Geography Compass* 14 (10): e12534.

Treviño, A. Javier. 2017. *The Sociology of Law: Classical and Contemporary Perspectives*. London: Routledge.

Chapter 5

Karen Barad's Agential Realism (of Law); or, Does Law Fit the Binary or Non-binary Model of Intra-Action?

5.1 Not … an "Ordinary" Physicist (Anymore)

5.1.1 Note on New Materialism(s)

In the nineties, even way before DeLanda's AST took the form we addressed in the previous chapter, DeLanda and Rosi Braidotti, independently of each other, used the phrase of *new materialism* or *neo-materialism* (Dolphijn and van der Tuin 2012: 93). Interestingly, while DeLanda practically does not refer to it in the works relevant to our investigations in the previous chapter, Braidotti's use of the phrase has been somewhat fluctuating, at some time, almost completely avoiding it only to clearly return to it just a few years later (compare Braidotti 2013, 2019, 2022). However, despite their approach to the term in question, which may be deemed as somewhat uncertain about it, the name of new materialism gained huge popularity in the first decades of the third millennium. Behind it, there is no single concrete theoretical proposal. New materialism should be rather understood as an umbrella term that groups underneath it various individual frameworks or more general research sensitivities, classifiable as flat ontologies in many cases. Of course, the exposition of what new materialism is about, due to how broad the use of the term often becomes, can be said to depend on who is answering a question about it.

For our purposes (compare Fox and Alldred 2017: 4), it is justified to say that new materialism denotes frameworks that ultimately stress the relationality of that what exists, various entities' entanglements with each other, which also leads to stressing the dynamism of being instead of stability. This becomes, through new materialist lenses, something to be explained, because the more default state of the world is change. This certain fluidity of reality that new materialism raises awareness about or merely projects – in dependence on the employed interpretation of its theses – also leads to a strong disagreement with dichotomies, most importantly, nature and culture. At this point, in the face of all that we considered thus far in this book, it should be obvious that such anti-dichotomy stance of new materialism practically necessitates to specifically make humans and nonhumans more alike than so distant from each other as in

DOI: 10.4324/9781003440963-5

more classical approaches. However, against the background that such post-anthropocentric equalisation or flattening can be realised in different ways – as already shown in previous chapters, with more to follow below – new materialism can be said to be focused on the agentification of matter. While it is largely us, humans, who are most usually endowed with agency by us, humans, new materialism also distributes the activity and agency among the most seemingly passive nonhuman entities.

Despite some clear resonance with the idea of a flat ontology, thus far, we did not, and in fact will not, in the rest to follow engage new materialism as such. First, given it is an umbrella term grouping various more concrete proposals, it seems much more reasonable to focus on a specific framework than on some general trend that may or may not be coherently inferable and reconstructable from diverse grouped ideas. Just recall our back-to-basics agenda, a more patient focus on some theoretical details and a strong conviction that doing justice to them is much needed. Second, the idea of new materialism appears to be even undermined by the very people who happen to be associated with it. Consider the comment made by Elizabeth Grosz (in Cielemęcka and Rogowska-Stangret 2018: 285) in an interesting series of short interviews conducted by Olga Cielemęcka and Monika Rogowska-Stangret with scholars associated with new materialism: "I do not think of myself as a 'new materialist,' although I am commonly included in this category. It is a misleading category, in my opinion." Third, indeed, one cannot help but notice that, sometimes, new materialism's capaciousness as a term is expanded way too broadly. In the end, one can seriously wonder whether including under the term in question the theoretical proposals developed much earlier and with a very rich conceptual apparatus, like ANT (e.g. Boysen and Rasmussen 2023), is a justified move. In addition, one can come across such expositions of new materialism that also include a theoretical proposal that is explicitly meant by its main developer as being against basic new materialist sensitivities, like Harman's project (compare Harman 2016b and Lemke 2021) we will address in the next chapter.

Having said all that, it should not be understood as disregard for those grouped, whether justifiably or not, under this category. On the contrary, each theoretical proposal associated with new materialism deserves careful consideration as very often an original and intriguing set of ideas. What can raise doubts is the mere general banner.

5.1.2 Why Barad?

Given the fact that, behind this banner, there are often placed proposals other than the ones investigated in this book, the following question arises: What do we choose for this chapter and why? Recall that we investigate in this book frameworks that can be deemed flat ontologies and which have explicitly presented and discussed their assumed basic units for ontological inquiries.

Especially this criterion provokes us to engage in Barad's AGR, which is undoubtedly one of the most prominent representatives of new materialism. Of course, under this banner as well, the already mentioned Braidotti, Haraway and Bennett are grouped. Why then are we not addressing their or, in fact, other new materialist thinkers' proposals here?

As already mentioned, AGR is the most clear when it comes to its assumed most basic unit of ontological investigations, in comparison to, for instance, Braidotti or Haraway (e.g. Braidotti 2013; Haraway 2016), who appear to ultimately focus much more on the issues of subjectivity rather than on ontology in the spirit of the investigated flat ontologies. We do not consider Bennett's (2010) work in detail either, because vital materialism draws heavily on Latour's and DeLanda's projects, so they can be regarded as much more fundamental and as such a better fit for the back-to-basics agenda we set for this book. In turn, AGR is most definitely comparable in its intended scope, generality and even certain abstractness to other considered flat ontologies in this book, despite some often crucial differences between them. Before they can be brought to the fore, we must deal with AGR itself.

5.1.3 From Lattice Gauge Theory to ...

This intellectual project's path to certain prominence, visible by the mere amount of book-length publications dealing with AGR or even more specific ideas of Barad (e.g. Kaiser and Thiele 2018; Harris 2021; Juelskjær et al. 2021; Merten 2021; Murris and Bozalek 2023), has been rather winding (Hollin et al. 2017: 920). Barad began their academic work not as a philosopher, social theorist, anthropologist or cultural studies scholar but as a physicist. Barad obtained a PhD in physics and, at the very beginning of the intellectual work, published some research in lattice gauge theory. However, soon after this particular output, Barad became somewhat silent (academic publications-wise) as they decided to pursue a different intellectual path of engaging in continental philosophy, feminist theory or science and technology studies. Although such direction can be deemed as very far from the original discipline Barad chose, they came to be known for still drawing heavily from physics, especially the broadly understood quantum theory, with special emphasis on Bohr's work. In the end, he himself is often regarded as one of the most philosophically inclined major physicists of the twentieth century.

Barad's intellectual project of AGR can be ultimately regarded as a result of a strong background but also ongoing interest in physics (e.g. Barad 2022), intense reading of Bohrian writings and sensitivity close to and, in fact, driven by the likes of Foucault, Judith Butler (e.g. Butler 1990) or Haraway. Although throughout Baradian relevant writings, one can notice some changes in where Barad puts the intellectual emphasis on or engages some other (than usually) thinkers (such as Jacques Derrida or Benjamin; Barad 2010, 2017) and expands the use of conceptual resources from physics (like with quantum field theory;

Barad 2012b), they can still be regarded as a more consistent thinker – in terms of methodology, concepts and objects of interest – than the previously considered authors. Before we engage in some fundamental assumptions and sentiments for AGR, there is still some proverbial ground to prepare here.

5.1.4 Baggage of Physics, Ethico-Onto-Epistemology and Addressing the Unaddressed Issue (Just Another One)

As in previous chapters, we will not address the correctness of Barad's interpretation of their intellectual inspirations and sources. This is obviously in line with our general approach in every chapter devoted to specific flat ontology, but we still recall it here, because especially drawing inspiration from quantum physics provokes us to wonder about the appropriateness of AGR given the problem of scale. Namely, the following question arises: Is it justified to consider some regularities observed or merely hypothesised at the micro or quantum level as taking place at the macro level, social human included? While some commentators have argued that such a move is unjustified (e.g. Everth and Gurney 2022, but see also Jaksland 2023), Barad clearly expresses the underlying idea for AGR that what can be drawn from quantum physics is not as such limited to the micro world only (Barad 2007: 85, 110, 457, note 41; but also 70). In what follows, we attempt to avoid such discussions because this book is not devoted to them, but to assess, from a legal perspective, the analysed frameworks.

Of course, as Barad likes to stress, AGR is not and should not be regarded just as an ontological project, because they actually promote the view that epistemological, ontological and ethical issues are inseparable (e.g. Barad 2007: 409, note 10). In the face of this, AGR is explicitly meant as a framework that is simultaneously about cognition, the is and the ought. Indeed, these threads are tightly connected by Barad, but below, we still devote the majority of attention and focus to the ontological part of AGR. On the one hand, it can be then regarded by some as a specific deviation from Barad's intentions. On the other hand, the epistemological and ethical sensitivities are brought to the fore in the last section of this chapter, so it would be rather unjustified to say that we strayed far from the path proposed explicitly by Barad.

Moreover, just as our previous analyses that tackled the crucial yet rarely carefully reflected upon, within or outside the context of law, details for Tarde's MON, Latour's ANT and DeLanda's AST – anti-emergence, utter fragility of things, the existence of boundaries and acting upon others as proof of existence and relations of exteriority and parts' autonomy from the whole – our take on Barad's AGR is also original. Interestingly, although Barad practically constantly refers to what is assumed to be the basic unit for ontological inquiries in their framework, in a burgeoning secondary literature on it, so little is devoted to the very structure of this unit (e.g. Bryant 2016: 4; Berg 2019: 80, footnote 4). Below, we not only bring this neglected issue to the fore but also relate it to the law, which has not been done so far. However, before we delve into some rather technical yet relevant details of AGR's basic unit in relation to law, we must introduce this framework.

5.2 Stepping Into ... Baradian Agential Realism

5.2.1 Anti-individualism and Priority of Relations

Although Barad's manner of writing sometimes turns out be rather dense and far from some always welcome user-friendliness, AGR's fundamental assumptions and sentiments can be quite clearly reconstructed, as seen in some quotes from Barad's (2007) main work to date, *Meeting the Universe Halfway: Quantum Physics and the Entanglement of Matter and Meaning*. As one can see even in a relatively short proposition – "Existence is not an individual affair. Individuals do not preexist their interactions; rather, individuals emerge through and as part of their entangled intra-relating" (Barad 2007: ix) – AGR is a strongly anti-individualistic framework, not in a socio-political sense but in a metaphysical or ontological sense. It basically argues that there are no autonomous individual beings, at whatever scale, which even if somehow isolated from others, would remain themselves. On the contrary, but perfectly in line with the general commitments of new materialism, AGR argues that everything that exists is not due to some self-confinement or self-sufficiency but due to relations with others.

The other side of anti-individualism is very strong relationality, so strong that Barad argues that relations are prior to relata (e.g. Barad 2007: 136–137, 139). To put it differently, the disagreement with the idea of existence of some ready-made largely autonomous beings is so insistent that the entities are said to emerge out of relations in which they partake. Instead of usual interactions – where parties can be said to already exist before the specific analysed interaction – Barad introduces the crucial concept of intra-action, which is meant to reverse this usually held idea. In accordance with that concept, parties to some relation emerge out of it, and are not prior to it. Where does this idea come from and how can it be illustrated is addressed below, because we will largely focus on it later.

5.2.2 Dynamism, Anti-essentialism and Against (Presupposed) Domains

At this point, we should rather acknowledge some further implications of such strong anti-individualism and relationality. First, notice that such sentiments entail far-reaching dynamism and even fragility of that what can be said to exist. In the end, it appears that, as soon as some entity's relations change, it will be changed as well.

Moreover, in AGR, there is a considerable emphasis on anti-essentialism (e.g. Barad 2007: 106). Indeed, it is explicitly against the idea of some ready-made objects of well-defined properties. Instead, all is said to be intra-actively constituted and the characteristics of an object are considered as dependent on how it is measured or, more generally, in what relations it remains. Needless to say, it undermines the idea of essence as some defining core of an entity that is in it from its very inception and, thus, any measurement, observation or relation can reveal what is already in that object.

In line with such commitments, Barad is also against thinking in terms of ready-made distinctions into various domains of reality with presupposed clear-cut boundaries (e.g. Barad 2007: 93). Domains with some lines dividing them from each other are still possible in AGR but only in the course of dynamic intra-actions that establish and maintain some boundaries and differences. In the end, these are not prior to some relation but actually come out of one. Consistently with that, Barad often talks about "naturalcultural" practices, much in the spirit of Haraway, instead of assuming some entity or situation to belong to either reified nature or culture (e.g. Barad 2007: 32).

5.2.3 Post-anthropocentrism (and a Short Remark on Baradian Agential Realism as Flat Ontology)

This string of anti-individualism, relationality, dynamism, fragility, anti-essentialism and disagreement with thinking in terms of some well-defined and ready-made distinctions into different domains brings us to clear anti-anthropocentrism. Indeed, in the face of statements such as "nonhumans play an important role in naturalcultural practices, including everyday social practices, scientific practices, and practices that do not include humans", a call to refuse "to take the distinction between 'human' and 'nonhuman' for granted" (Barad 2007: 32), and concrete analyses carried out by Barad and various applicators of the commented framework (e.g. Harris 2021: 45–96), it is justified to name AGR a posthumanist theory. Moreover, despite some criticism accusing Barad of basically sliding back into some kind of idealism – where human's relating to some entity endows it with existence (Harman 2016a: 1; 2016b: 14; in DeLanda and Harman 2017: 3–4, 9) – they (e.g. 2007: 32) on more than just one occasion correctly stress that the intra-active vision of reality holds also with respect to relations between nonhumans, even when no human is present at the scene. Barad (2007: 66) actually subordinates everything there is to the single intra-active "logic" and calls AGR "a unified theory of cultural and natural forces".

In light of this, we already may deem it as realising the mere idea of a flat ontology, with its pluralism and nonhierarchy, proposed in the Introduction. AGR's clear closeness and adherence to the idea of ontological flattening or equalisation is seen on the occasion of just another crucial general tenet of this framework – anti-representationalism. There it becomes clear that Barad treats the broadly understood language as just another entity subordinated to the same intra-active regularities like everything else there is. Taking this opportunity, notice that, in the case of DeLandaean AST, we had to take a much closer look at the characteristics of an assemblage itself and the roles of language in it to become more confident in classifying it as an instance of a flat ontology. In Baradian AGR, it suffices to consider its fundamental sentiments and tenets, such as those of anti-representationalism.

5.2.4 Anti-representationalism and Moving Past the Divide of Realism and Social Constructivism

Let us begin with some basic exposition of representationalism itself. In Barad's (2007: 28) own words, it is "the idea that representations and the objects (subjects, events, or states of affairs) they purport to represent are independent of one another". Disagreement with representationalism comes not only from its underlying assumption that the knower or the object that experiences something is beyond or outside the world whose part is under scrutiny at the moment (Barad 2007: 88). Perhaps the most crucial problem with representationalism is that it assumes metaphysical individualism – the existence of autonomous entities, ready-made, well-defined and fully endowed with their specific properties even before partaking in any relation with others (Barad 2007: 46, 55).

Notice that, as a relation, one can also classify any instance of relation between some entity and its linguistic description. In turn, if relations in AGR are not supposed to be among perfectly autonomous and complete beings but, in fact, relata are said to emerge out of relations, do not occur prior to them, then the mere relation between something linguistically described and that description itself is far from neutral with respect to its elements. One can even say that the intra-active emphasis of AGR goes hand in hand with anti-representationalism – that objects and their representations (for instance, concepts in some language that denote them) are not independent of each other but can be said to be mutually constituted by relating to each other (Barad 2007: 28). In short, in AGR, words and things are not independent of each other (Barad 2007: 107) but actually make each other.

In consequence, language, meanings, semanticity are no more treated as something towering over the rest of the being and the broadly understood materiality is no more rendered as only a perfectly passive, inert matrix to human senses, with no agency of its own and with no influence over linguistic entities (Barad 2007: 60, 65). In the end, notice that representationalism makes the words and things significantly unequal. If the access to, cognition of things is mediated by words and concepts – broadly understood representations of objects, said to be mutually independent with respect to represented things – then the following question may arise: Why the access to the very representations is not problematised in a similar manner (Barad 2007: 87)? In representationalism, the objects of representations are independent of them, but still need them, if they are to be in any way grasped. In turn, representations themselves, also not experiencing any influence from their referents, do not need any mediation to reach them and use them. Then, anti-representationalism not only aims to end with the idea of mutual influence immunity of both objects and their representations but also problematises the idea of representations as some resources just being there to be used whenever suitable. Rather, it reminds the well-known idea that each use of some concept is far from being neutral to it.

Before moving on to the presentation of the already announced main source of inspiration for AGR, which also helps better understand the abstractness of this framework reconstructed thus far, let us just attempt to position it somewhat better against some popular theoretical directions. Obviously, the anti-representationalist stance of Barad (2007: 48, 55–56) stresses that their framework is against the usually understood realism, which assumes the objective existence of reality and that human knowledge, or in fact any observation, is supposed to just represent it, create its images and not alter it during the cognitive processes.

Interestingly, Barad (2007: 48, 86), with their anti-representationalism, is also against social constructivism, because, on their account, it entails addressing the world with some human cultural concepts, which themselves are practically ready-made and remain unaltered during the process of signifying the reality with them. Additionally, both realism and social constructivism play a significant part in maintaining clear dichotomy in our thinking – emphasising the nature and culture, respectively.

5.2.5 Interpreting Bohr Extendingly

As mentioned earlier, AGR is a project that draws heavily from Bohrian reading of certain classical problem in broadly understood quantum physics. Note here that Barad (2007: 123) admits that their project is not meant as a "true" interpretation of what Bohr himself had in mind while engaging in physics and his specific philosophy-physics. Barad rather uses Bohr's writings and their specific reading as a foundation for their own agenda. Having said that, we may argue that AGR rests upon extending, ontological approach to Bohr's work. To recognise this, let us consider here a longer quote from Barad and then succinctly bring to the fore some crucial threads out of it.

When raising the well-known problem of measuring two specific properties of particles – position and momentum – and that when the measurement apparatus is set for the sake of the former quality, the latter cannot be determined at the same time (this is because determining the position requires a stable setup, while momentum needs a setup with moveable parts) and vice versa, Barad (2007: 19) says the following:

> For Bohr, what is at issue is *not* that we cannot *know* both the position and momentum of a particle simultaneously (as [Werner] Heisenberg initially argued), but rather that particles do not *have* determinate values of position and momentum simultaneously. While Heisenberg's point that in measuring any of the characteristics of a particle, we necessarily disturb its premeasurement values, so that the more we know about a particle's position, the less we will know about its momentum (and vice versa) seems at least believable, Bohr's point is utterly counterintuitive and unfamiliar. In

> essence, Bohr is making a point about the nature of reality, not merely our knowledge of it. The lesson that Bohr takes from quantum physics is very deep and profound: there aren't little things wandering aimlessly in the void that possess the complete set of properties that Newtonian physics assumes (e.g., position and momentum); rather, there is something fundamental about the nature of measurement interactions such that, given a particular measuring apparatus, certain properties become determinate, while others are specifically excluded. Which properties *become determinate* is not governed by the desires or will of the experimenter but rather by the specificity of the experimental apparatus.

Some commentary is in place here. First, notice that while Bohr can be seen as addressing the issue of determination of properties of some being in a very specific relation – being measured by some human-made scientific apparatus, Barad wants to extend such relationality onto the very existence of entities. In the end, AGR's motto is not that the properties of relata are not prior to relations but that relata as such do not pre-exist their relations. Second, while Bohr refers to the context of physics, which is also very close to Barad themself, Barad regards AGR as a universal framework, of what seems to be a much more clearly ontological character than Bohrian relevant investigations. Third, in the quote above, we already see the source and sense of practically all previously reconstructed tenets of AGR: anti-individualism and its reverse – relationality (there are no autonomous things, things as such, but only within specific relations), anti-essentialism (there is no thing with ready-made set of qualities – these emerge only when relating to others) and anti-representationalism and mutual dependence of concepts and things, even the agency of the latter (think of the suggested Bohrian idea that abstract concepts, such as momentum and position, are very concrete, even embodied, because to measure momentum or position, one has to arrange the measurement apparatus differently, and without such physical, tangible setup, the relevant concepts become practically meaningless [Barad 2007: 109]). With respect to the last point here, recall the title of Barad's main work and its last part – matter and meaning are thought to be inseparably entangled with each other. Having reached this particular point and with just another reminder that Barad, in fact, announces the universal ambitions of their framework – reaching way beyond the context of physics – we may move on to an even more technical issue – AGR's basic unit for ontological inquiries.

5.3 Focusing on … Intra-Actions

5.3.1 Neither Kantian Noumenon nor Phenomenon, but Close to Bohrian Phenomenon

To make an as clear as possible argument, let us begin with a statement, that Baradian (e.g. Barad 2007: 128–129) reality, irrespective of whether its parts can be deemed natural, cultural or artificial, does not consist of things, noumenal or phenomenal in the Kantian sense (Kant 1998: 354–365). As should be obvious by now, things-in-themselves do not make any sense in the light of AGR's commitments, which basically stress that there is no and cannot be any "in-itself" of anything. In order to be, to subsist, one must be relationally constituted and remain in certain relations. In turn, when it comes to the Kantian phenomenon, it is also rejected by Barad, given its quite clear anthropocentrism.

For Barad, reality can be said to consist of things-within-phenomena; however, note that the last word should be understood in accordance with Baradian reading of Bohr. Let us then have a look at this telling fragment of Barad's (2007: 33) main work:

> the primary ontological unit is not independent objects with independently determinate boundaries and properties but rather what Bohr terms "phenomena." In [...] agential realist elaboration, phenomena do not merely mark the epistemological inseparability of observer and observed, or the results of measurements; rather, *phenomena* are the *ontological* inseparability of agentially intra-acting components. (The notion of intra-actions figures centrally here [...]) Significantly, phenomena are not mere laboratory creations but basic units of reality [...] The notion of intra-action is a key element of [...] agential realist framework. The neologism "intra-action" *signifies the mutual constitution of entangled agencies*. That is, in contrast to the usual "interaction," which assumes that there are separate individual agencies that precede their interaction, the notion of intra-action recognizes that distinct agencies do not precede, but rather emerge through, their intra-action. It is important to note that the "distinct" agencies are only distinct in a relational, not an absolute, sense, that is, *agencies are only distinct in relation to their mutual entanglement; they don't exist as individual elements*.

Perhaps the clearest example of such sensitivities and intra-active constitution of things-within-phenomenon, in addition to the already mentioned case of position and momentum, is the similarly famous case of the wave-particle paradox (e.g. Barad 2007: 103), which illustrates how matter (like electrons) can act like waves – more specifically, create diffraction patterns – depending on the experimental setup. However, there is something more important here than referring to just another illustration or recognising once again the universal ambitions of the commented framework, the fact that it draws from what it may appear as ideas dealing with rather narrow methodological issues in physics, but it expands them to everything there is, which also connects well with post-anthropocentrism.

Namely, notice that in the quote above, Barad speaks explicitly about the primary ontological unit. Although the specifically understood phenomenon in the cited fragment is deemed as one, one can say that this issue is more complicated. Perhaps due to the already mentioned dense prose or the fact that

AGR is still considered "an ongoing project" by Barad themself (in Juelskjær et al. 2021: 133), there are moments in which Barad can come across as somewhat uncertain regarding what is, in their opinion, the most fundamental ingredient of the world. In the end, Barad (2007: 72) even suggests, in the specific context of dealing with the opposition of reflection and diffraction, that diffraction patterns play this role. In addition to such suggestions, Barad also quite often treats phenomena and intra-actions – both referred to in the cited fragment – as practically synonymous (e.g. Barad 2000: 232; 2007: 128; 2012a: 32; see also Harris 2021: 147–148). However, the quote above alone can make one wonder, whether ultimately the more basic and fundamental are not phenomena, within which partaking objects can be differentiated, but intra-actions – Baradian "substitutes" for interactions, mere relations, from which relata are supposed to be just emerging. Of course, one can also say that in AGR, phenomena already imply intra-actions. Indeed, the already mentioned characteristic concepts of Barad and other relevant concepts to follow are tightly connected to each other. However, one can still reconstruct some sequence among them. Such an approach allows for much greater clarity not only for the sake of mere exposition of the structure of the crucial part of AGR, but, even more importantly, in discussing it from the perspective of law.

5.3.2 Bohrian Model (In Baradian Interpretation)

First, on the pages of their mentioned *magnum opus*, Barad presents more than one model of the basic unit for ontological inquiries. Not only for the sake of brevity but also because, as said earlier, an intra-action is arguably the most fundamental element in AGR, which also implies many other notions relevant here, we will be talking about intra-action models. In Barad's main work, on the one hand, there is an elaboration of Bohrian ontology, and on the other hand, it is treated as a foundation for Barad's (2007: 33) own proposal. In the face of this, let us begin with the Baradian account of the Bohrian ontological unit (Barad 2007: 128).

To a certain extent, one can say that it involves two beings – measured object and measuring apparatus. The former, only by intra-acting with the latter, can be said to "mature" ontologically, become endowed with some concrete properties, not had prior to the intra-action in question. Just think once again of the wave-particle paradox. Some particles may actually manifest properties of matter or waves depending on how the measuring apparatus is arranged for the sake of their specific relation. Beyond this, the properties may be very different. However, the measured object intra-acting with the measuring apparatus is not the entire picture relevant here.

Of course, there is the already introduced, specifically understood notion of phenomenon that can be interpreted as denoting a product of intra-action within which the involved elements remain as long as they maintain intra-acting. However, in accordance with Baradian interpretation of Bohr, one should also take into account what Barad names an agential cut (e.g. Barad 2007: 140). For Barad, it takes place during the intra-action and is basically the process of clearly differentiating the involved entities from each other. To put it differently, for both Barad and Bohr in Baradian reading, as long as there is no intra-action, one cannot be confident about the boundaries of some entity – where something begins and where it ends. Such boundaries, obviously crucial to what can be named identities of given beings, emerge only during the intra-actions.

In this light, as Barad argues, intra-action actually involves two tightly connected processes – bringing entities together while they intra-act and remain within the phenomenon they specifically co-created and, at the same time, separating the involved objects by establishing a boundary between them. "Cutting together-apart" (Barad 2014). Of course, this difference is not absolute or objective; it holds only in the case of the very specific intra-action considered. Having said all that, although Barad's narrative is not so easy to visualise like it was in the case of Tarde, Latour or even DeLanda, we may venture to create some visual aid to better understand the issue at hand (Figure 5.1).

5.3.3 Baradian Model

Although many points out of such Baradian interpretation of Bohrian ideas prove to be still valid in what can be named Barad's own model of intra-action, they ultimately part ways with their reading of Bohr's ideas for practically one

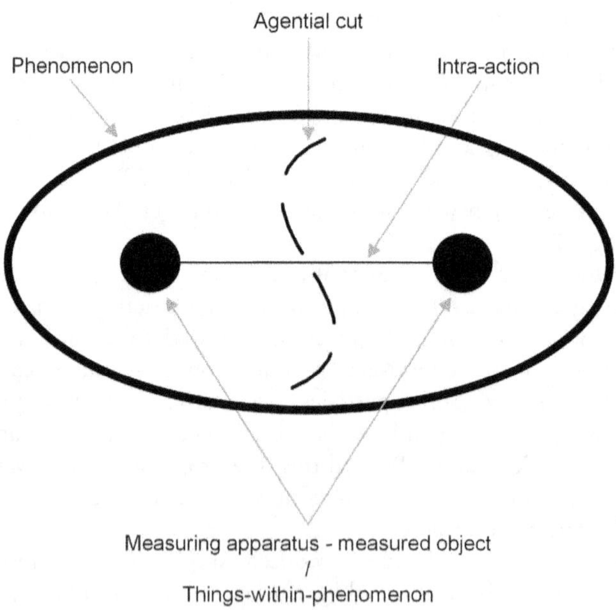

Figure 5.1 Bohrian and Baradian basic (binary) model.

specific reason. Namely, Barad (2007: 144–145) argues that Bohr treats the measuring apparatus as a ready-made, finished, well-defined entity even before taking part in a specific intra-action, through which the properties of the measured object are determined and, thus, that entire object can be said to become ontologically "mature". To put it differently, Barad sees in Bohr a specific inequality between those involved, thus creating the phenomenon. The measuring apparatus is thought to be already there and the intra-action practically does not make any difference for it, of course, with an exception of recording the measurement, while the impact on the measured object is much greater.

Barad (2007: 161–168) refers to just another famous case in physics, the experiment of Otto Stern and Walther Gerlach. Not going into the technical details of it, it suffices to say that, ultimately, their original experiment succeeded, but not only due to what can be named most usually understood experimental setup consisting of objects under consideration and a measuring apparatus that is easily identifiable and confined in time and space. Namely, it turned out that one of the experimenter's habit of smoking cheap cigars with fumes containing relatively high levels of sulphur was a practically indispensable part of the experiment, also for the sake of its reproducibility. The sulphuric fumes interacted with the silver used in the experiment, and their absence in any iteration would simply not lead to the confirmation of the original outcome.

Barad interprets this case in the following terms – even that what appears as the most stable and well-defined element of some research intra-action – measuring apparatus – is itself dynamic and changing in relevant relations. Of course, this clear difference in relation to Bohr (or, at least, his reading by Barad) is not the only one relevant here (see also Barad 2007: 146). As said earlier, Barad expands the intra-active "logic" to everything and thus does not confine it only to the scientific context, which nevertheless is the most significant source of inspiration. Finally, in accordance with AGR's motto – relata do not pre-exist relations – Barad ultimately stresses the emergence of the very elements of relation out of the relation in question, not only their specific qualities.

In consequence, one can safely say that upon Baradian reconstruction of Bohrian phenomenon, Barad proposes and focuses their attention on the much more general vision of intra-action. It also involves an agential cut and leads to a phenomenon, but, in place of measuring apparatus and measured object, there are just its "components", things-within-phenomenon. Of course, their intra-action is equally ontologically important to them, as they both can be said to emerge out of it, not only their properties. In general, then, the diagram from Figure 5.1 holds, but the dots stop standing for the apparatus and measured entity and symbolise things-within-phenomenon. In this way, we come to what can be named a basic, binary – structured around two "components" – model of Baradian intra-action (see also Barad 2011: 453, note 13; Bryant 2016: 4; Juelskjær et al. 2021: 16).

However, one cannot say that, in AGR, it is structured exclusively in such a binary way. In their later works – post-*Meeting the Universe Halfway* – where Barad aims at drawing from quantum field theory (see Barad and Gandorfer 2021: 34), their theoretical resources are expanded by Derrida or Benjamin, and the used narrative moves even more into a register that can be named poetic; there is admittance that an entity can intra-act with itself. To be more precise, Barad proposes the idea that some being can be considered as intra-acting with its very own virtual versions (e.g, Barad 2012b: 14–15) – that which it is not at the moment but potentially could be. Obviously, such an expansion can be read as a deviation from the mentioned binarism, but it can be also regarded as ultimately in line with it. Binary intra-action holds, but only one of its participants can be deemed as existing in the most usual sense of the word. Although such self-referentiality in AGR can be read as an interesting counterpoint to Latourian ANT, where existence is dependent on acting on others (not itself) – which proves to be important from the legal perspective – we will not focus on this particular issue, in order to remain consistent with our decision in the previous chapter. In the end, just recall that when dealing with DeLanda's AST, we did not delve into the somewhat similar issue of what can be and not what actually is – virtuality.

5.3.4 Problems with Binarism

From the perspective of trying to engage law with the help of the main AGR's conceptual device, we should recognise some problems in connection to Baradian basic, binary model of intra-action. Let us begin with what can be named the additivity controversy and can be explained as follows.

For an ontology that stresses relationality to such an extent as AGR, it should be able to address the obvious and common fact that objects in the world rarely remain in relation with just one other object. Rather much more universal is the situation in which the thing within one particular phenomenon (intra-acting with the other thing within it) is simultaneously within another phenomenon (and intra-acts with a different entity within that second phenomenon). To make this abstractness somewhat more digestible, consider an illustration of such a situation (Figure 5.2).

The following question arises: Does the particular "component" taking part in two ultimately different intra-actions/phenomena constitute itself simultaneously in them, or perhaps that what it becomes in those two relations is not additive? To put it differently, is X in AX intra-action (simultaneous to XC intra-action) ultimately different from X in XC intra-action? Affirmative would mean that additivity is not allowed in AGR, while negative would mean that it is. Looking carefully at Baradian main exposition of AGR, one can conclude that additivity is allowed in this theory. Just consider the following fragment of Barad's (2007: 203–204) investigation of the piezoelectric crystal and ultrasound technology:

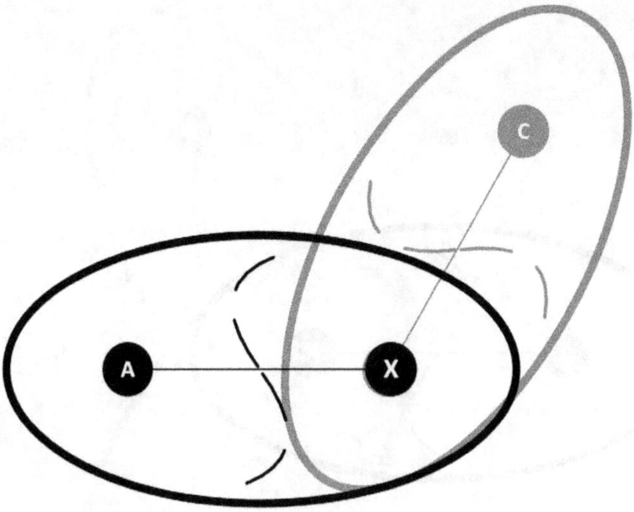

Figure 5.2 One element in two (binary) intra-actions.

> piezoelectric transducers materialize (and are iteratively rematerialized) in intra-action with a multitude of practices, including those that involve medical needs; design constraints (including legal, economic, biomedical, physics, and engineering ones); market factors; political issues; other R & D [research and development] projects using similar materials; the educational background of the engineers and scientists designing the crystals and the workplace environment of the engineering firm or lab; particular hospital or clinic environments where the technology is used; receptivity of the medical community and the patient community to the technology; legal, economic, cultural, religious, political, and spatial constraints on its uses; positioning of patients during examination; and the nature of training of technicians and physicians who use the technology.

In other words, the object being the centre of attention here – piezoelectric transducers – is the way it is, emerges to its current form out of its relations with a myriad of other beings, for instance, both clearly tangible and easily localisable in time and space, such as human operators, and much more difficult to localise, like culture.

Obviously, given the intended universal reach of AGR, it can be said that the model underlying Barad's above-cited account can also be used with respect to other entities. Some given X is the way it is at some moment of its analysis, because it intra-acts with a plethora of other objects: A, B, C, D, etc. (Figure 5.3). Of course, given the strong relationality and disagreement with any "in-itself" of anything, we should take into account that it is still a certain simplification. In the end, there is no X as such. We should then avoid thinking in terms of the following pattern: X as such in some intra-action with, for example, A.

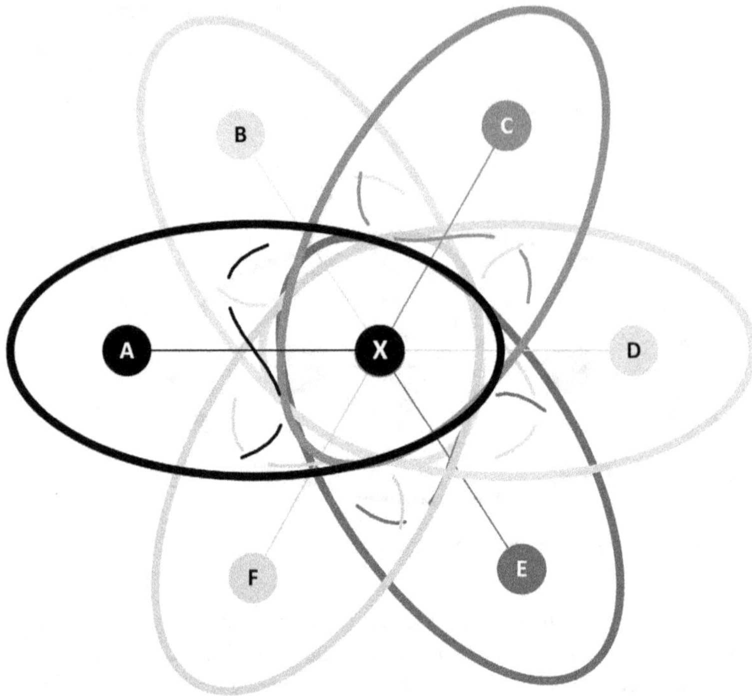

Figure 5.3 One element in multiple (binary) intra-actions.

Instead, given the fact that we are still considering here the binary model of intra-action, we should analyse, for instance, X, as it is in intra-action with A, and how its other intra-action (with some B) unfolds. Just take another look at the quote above. Following Baradian "logic", it is reasonable and justified to say that piezoelectric transducers intra-acting with the educational background of engineers and scientists are already somewhat different than the transducers in intra-action with market forces. Of course, all these intra-actions are practically simultaneous, and here we are just considering them in some analytical isolation. Nevertheless, market forces do not intra-act with transducers as such, but with, for instance, transducers "out of" their intra-action with engineers' and scientists' backgrounds.

Ultimately, in addition to being able to switch our attention and, for instance, consider intra-action of transducers as "out of" relation with legal constraints on their uses with actual practices of medical personnel performing pregnancy ultrasound examinations, we should rather propose the following approach. Given the fact that all intra-actions in which some chosen object of inquiry partakes can be parallel to each other, attention should be given to how some X, as it is in its intra-actions with A, B, C, D, etc., intra-acts with the single remaining other thing out of the entirety with which X actually intra-acts, because these entities – A, B, C, D, etc. – can be said to be already covered. One should then abandon just another thinking pattern: X, as it is "out of" intra-action with A, intra-acting with B. One can venture to say that the most thorough scheme would be the following: X, as it is "out of" intra-actions with A, B, C, D, etc., intra-acting with some "final" Z.

The problem, then, is not so much the mere complexity of some chosen objects of inquiry to be conducted in line with AGR but its quite clear attachment to binarism – conceptualising intra-action as assuming just two things-within-phenomenon. Such visible commitment not only renders the mere analysis of some entity as increasingly complicated, as it was just attempted to be shown. It also provokes us to notice some other issues, which practically rise to the level of other controversies, in the face of not being addressed clearly in Baradian AGR's writings. Just think again about some X that is the way it is due to many simultaneous binary intra-actions with A, B, C, D, etc. The question that can come to mind in the face of it is as follows: Do entities with which X intra-acts intra-act among themselves as well, for instance, B with C? Or perhaps, given the fact that both these entities intra-act with X, does X somehow "mediate" between the relevant two (Figure 5.4)? However, if that

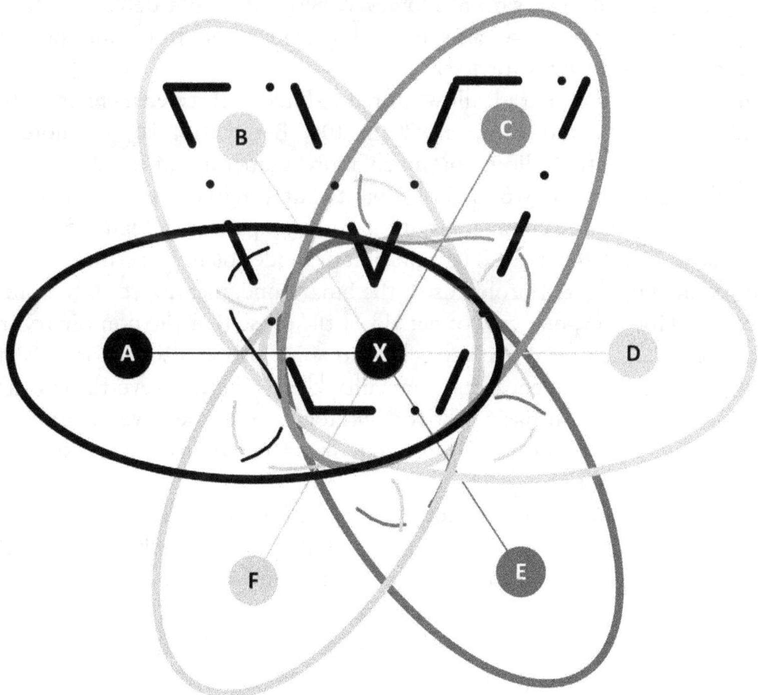

Figure 5.4 One element in multiple (binary) intra-actions "mediating" between other elements.

would be the case, then it would be rather a deviation from the basic, binary structure of intra-action, which assumes just two things-within-phenomenon.

5.3.5 Beyond the Binary Model

Having said that, we reach the already anticipated moment to reveal that, in Baradian AGR's corpus, there are also suggestions of a non-binary structure of intra-action – involving more than just two things-within-phenomenon. Interestingly, these happen not only in what appears to be an exposition of Barad's own take on phenomenon but also when still dealing with Bohrian vision. To recognise this, consider, for instance, the following fragments out of Barad's main work: "the material apparatus that enacts an agential cut between determinately bounded and propertied entities within a phenomenon" (Barad 2007: 176) and "for every given apparatus, there is an unambiguous resolution of the distinction between the object and the agencies of observation" (Barad 2007: 115; see also Barad 2010: 256). Both these quotes suggest a three-element model of intra-action. The former speaks about apparatus and entities between which an agential cut is made. The latter can be said to complicate the issue of Bohrian vision of phenomenon, or its Baradian interpretation, even further, because it speaks not only about the apparatus and the object measured by it but also about the agency of observation. However, here, let us not delve any deeper in that particular controversy and instead consider the following possibility, having quite clear ground for itself.

Namely, as long as Barad allows for non-binary, three-element intra-action (see also Milwertz and Fengxian 2012: 104; Berg 2019: 80, footnote 4), it appears that they also allow for much more numerous phenomenon, within which there are not just two or three objects but a myriad (see Barad 2007: 389, fig. 34 and surrounding commentary to it, and compare with Figure 5.5; see also Barad 2000: 234; 2008: 172). The non-binary model of intra-action can be said to escape the highlighted problems of the binary one, mentioned in the previous subsection. However, one cannot get rid of the sense that the non-binary model brings a crucial part of AGR very close to some other, also historically prior, frameworks; in consequence, its originality clearly fades. Nevertheless, having dealt with the Baradian basic unit for ontological inquiries, we have reached a point where we can address AGR from law's perspective, after some short conclusion of the above.

On the one hand, the binary model of intra-action is perfectly understandable in the context of direct inspiration for AGR and the background of Barad themself. It is also quite convenient for the reasons of mere clear exposition of the fundamental idea of the commented framework. On the other hand, the binary-structured intra-action can be said to be a much more appropriate idea to deal with the relations of entities than their ontology as such. The latter can indeed be conceptualised in Baradian binary terms, as seen earlier when discussing the situation of simultaneous participation of one entity in a myriad of

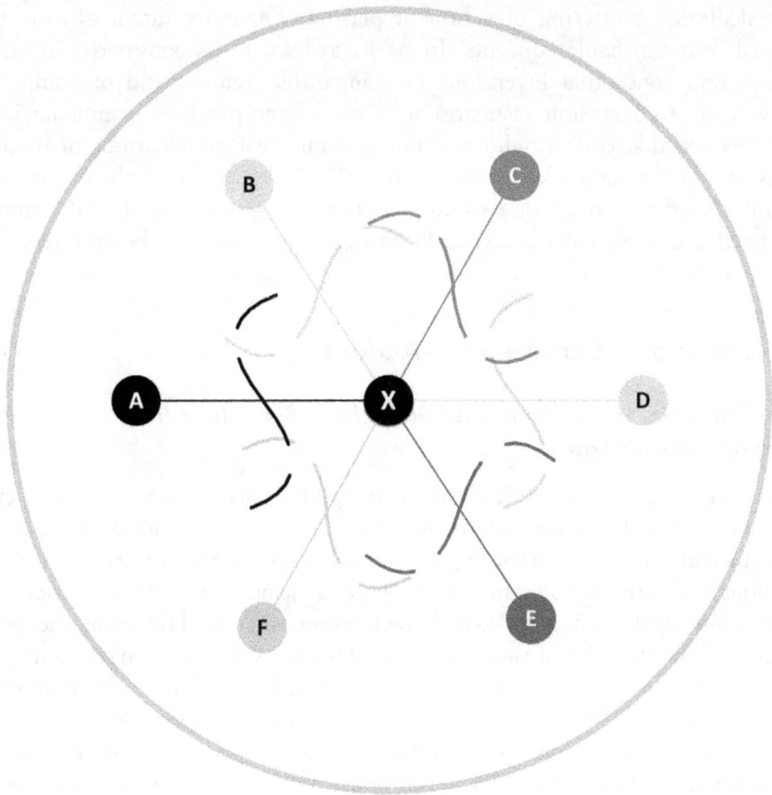

Figure 5.5 Non-binary model.

intra-actions. In the end, AGR, to a certain extent, appears to equalise the entity's constitution or identity with all its relations. However, the basic, binary structure of intra-action makes accounting for the ontology of entities ultimately, from one perspective, quite original, and from the other, very complicated enterprise with some controversies that only increase such complicatedness, as suggested earlier.

The situation specifically changes when one acknowledges that Barad themself does not appear to be entirely limited to the binary model of intra-action. Namely, the complications in analysis due to binarism obviously stop, but the entire non-binary structure of intra-action that can embrace a myriad of entities renders AGR as quite unoriginal. For instance, the mere idea of the importance of relations, often involving a mass of diverse entities, in constituting some being can be easily seen much earlier than in Barad's work – in Latourian ANT (compare also Figure 5.5 with Figure 3.1). However, the latter, when it comes to the broadly understood ontological investigations, can be said to ultimately offer much richer conceptual resources. Just think of translation, mediators and intermediaries, scattering of action or plasma. These are rather already well-defined distinguishable concepts. In AGR, at least in its considered form, one cannot find conceptual inventions in comparable amount and of comparable roles. Such a conclusion resonates well with some previous commentaries on AGR by social scientists, who also notice some clear anticipations of Baradian ideas in other frameworks (Hollin et al. 2017: 933, 936). Nevertheless, it would be unfounded to expect some exclusively negative assessment of AGR from the perspective of law. On the contrary, its assessment needs to be and actually is below much more nuanced.

5.4 Law and … Barad's Intra-Actions

5.4.1 Law from Intra-Action with Something, Something from Intra-Action with Law

When engaging the law-AGR nexus, with special attention paid to intra-action, one can begin with its basic, binary model kept in mind. First, notice that Baradian fundamental sensitivity, according to which things are the way they are due to relations with others, not some innate self-confinement and self-sufficiency, resonates quite well with some well-known approaches to law from the period researched for the sake of this book. Just think of Arthur Kaufmann, among his other achievements, a highly important and original voice in discussions about the ontology of law. Although, in reference to the categories proposed in the Introduction, his ontology of law as correspondence of being and duty, is and ought, in which human person plays a crucial role (e.g. Kaufmann 1966: 372), can be deemed as anthropocentric and distant from any materiality equalisation and other general sentiments of a flat ontology, his famous idea that "the law does not exist before interpretation" (Stelmach and Brożek 2006: 196, referring to Kaufmann 1985: 122) fits well AGR. Just as relata do not pre-exist relations, law can also be argued to be inexistent until it finds itself in some relation, for example, with some concrete instance of the objects of its regulation. Only when such juxtaposition occurs, the regulation in question can be said to emerge completely as especially its sense becomes specified. Obviously, it resonates well with the previously presented idea that abstract physical concepts are meaningless if not for the corresponding material arrangements of specific measurement apparatus.

However, notice that already given the clear mutuality of influence of things-within-phenomenon assumed by Barad – that in AX intra-action, not only A but also X emerges – AGR suggests something more with respect to law than Kaufmann's mentioned motto. The latter focuses on law emerging out of a specific instance of its relations – being confronted with some object of its regulation during the interpretation. In comparison, AGR suggests that not only does law come into existence in intra-action with something else, like the object of its regulation, but other entity in the intra-action in question does the same as well.

Of course, such deep, ontological sense or function of law is not rarely noticed. For instance, consider not only a similar thread in Latourian ANT presented earlier, but rather the common observations about the extent to which law is a crucial "ingredient" in one's subjectivity. Just recall how the criticisms of individual rights and freedoms offered by the Critical Legal Studies movement were countered by the just-emerging Critical Race Theory discourse (Williams 1987: 431). For the representatives of the discriminated groups, but not only for them, the fact of being given some legal rights, competences or more generally understood possibilities impact the very selfhood of those endowed with them and is not some mere addition to their identity, without which it would remain unaltered.

Despite what these or other possible parallels between some threads of a broadly understood reflection about law and utter mutuality of things-within-phenomenon in AGR – law is the way it is due to its relations to others, but various entities are the way they are also due to the law with which they intra-act – may suggest, there is some noticeable, subtle yet practical novelty in AGR that should be of interest among lawyers and legal scholars. It is tightly connected with the ethical part of the commented framework, which thus far we have not brought to the fore of the argument.

5.4.2 Dual Responsibility of Law and Transgressing the Input and Output of Law Distinction

Notice that due to the anti-individualism/relationality of AGR, practically any, even the most subtle form of relating to something has some ontological impact on it. In the end, entities emerge out of the relations they have with others. Having said that, the mere fact of law somehow relating or referring to some entity, even just pointing out at it, for instance, in some prepared legal text, should not be treated as something neutral and unworthy of attention. On the contrary, AGR most definitely can and should be read as an invitation to analyse how the seemingly exclusively formal fact of law somehow relating to something, rendering it its point of reference, impacts that thing.

Of course, at first glance, one can respond to that with some puzzlement, because does the discourse about the effectiveness of law or legal policy, starting from its original Petrażyckian (1955) sense, not provide such analyses and tools for their sake? One can venture to say that, ultimately, the investigations on legal policy and law's effectiveness are much more focused on something clearly subsequent in law's action than what can be read out of AGR. Namely, while the latter can be interpreted as a provocation to wonder how mere law's relation to something impacts that very thing and its identity and boundaries, legal policy and law's effectiveness focus one's attention on specifically further issues – whether the regulation will be complied by its addressee and with what consequences.

In this light then, AGR can further expand some sensitivity to what law does. It does not only make some entities do something, or at least, aims at exerting such influence on their actions but also makes the entities it regulates in the first place. In reference, then, to the ethical aspect of the commented framework, law has a dual responsibility – for its regulations and their consequences, as well as for the makeup of various entities it creates. One can say that this is a rather clear implication of what we addressed earlier – that law participates in intra-actions through which other entities emerge. Given that this intra-active process is mutual, law is as it is due to the very same intra-actions. This leads us to another observation important for AGR's proposed assessment.

Namely, in light of this particular flat ontology, the distinction between the input of law – that what creates the law – and the output of law – that what law, once created, does – is significantly blurred. Namely, in accordance with Barad's framework, one ought to say that any relation law establishes, for instance, through its regulations, with some other objects, feeds back into law itself. That what law does also makes that law. Obviously, the assessment of that very observation driven by AGR depends on one's prior theoretical commitments. For instance, some accustomed to a much more clear-cut differentiation between the creation of law and law's broadly understood activities can deem this noticeable consequence of the commented framework as even iconoclastic.

5.4.3 Law Regulating Only That What is Already Legal

One can venture to say that, with a similar reaction can be met another general implication for the law of AGR, which was already suggested between the lines above, when bringing to fore the issue of law creating its own points of reference while intra-acting with others. Just as Barad (2007: 67) convinces that "we are a part of nature that we seek to understand", one can say that following agential realist sensitivities, law is a part of practices that it seeks to regulate or actually regulates. To put it differently, law does not regulate things as such but refers to that what is already made legal by it. Namely, law intra-acts with various entities, which can be said to be made in their relation to law and thus are already rendered legal entities. They are also subjected to regulations of law. In consequence, one cannot say that law can regulate or even refer in any manner to something that is truly non- or extra-legal. On the contrary, AGR (Barad 2007: 121) suggests quite clearly that law is always a part of that what it regulates. It follows directly from what we considered above – the ontological role or function of the law intra-acting with some entities, which are also objects or addressees of its regulations, expected to comply with them.

To make it somewhat less abstract and more direct – in AGR, law does not address, for instance, textile industry as such, but considers this industry through legal lenses. Such a situation should not be understood as a proof of some deep flaw or imperfection of law that ought to be somehow bypassed but rather as an instance of a perfectly typical thing law does. It relates only to things that are already legal (on the mere account of being in intra-action with law), because there is simply no other way possible, or, to be more precise, at least in accordance to the commented framework.

5.4.4 Rejecting the Classical Distinctions

What we considered thus far in this section proves that one can infer out of AGR at least few rather subtle yet significant points about law, whose originality with respect to other ideas about law from the researched period is varying. Law can be said to be intra-acting with a plethora of entities. In the process, both law and the entities emerge. This means at least two separable things: first, law, in fact, does not refer to various beings as such but always to their legal renditions, and second, even the law that can be deemed as finished and already created is still in the process of its very own creation, because of the mutuality of influence in intra-action. Such observations can be interesting not only for some strictly cognitive needs but also for the sake of practical engagement.

Namely, AGR invites us to think carefully about the consequences of the mere fact that law somehow relates to something, intra-acts with it and, thus, has an impact on that thing's ontology, and not only on the somewhat subsequent issues of regulations' effectiveness. As a result, it can be said to be an incentive to broaden the scope of reflection about what law does practically to the "earliest" moment, like law drafters referring for the first time in the given country's jurisdiction to some object or a type of situation. While Baradian impact on discourse on legal policy and law's effectiveness can be described as provoking some development, as illustrated, AGR's repercussions on other classical threads in a broadly understood reflection on law can deemed as more ambiguous.

Think, for instance, about law and society distinction guiding an uncountable number of research currents, specific theories, concrete studies, academic grants and practical recommendations. AGR rather undermines this differentiation because, as discussed earlier, whenever law relates to something that very thing is already rendered legal as it has found itself in intra-action with law and thus its very specifics depend on it. In consequence, especially when dealing with legal regulations, there is nothing non-legal or extra-legal upon which law imposes its rules or principles. One, then, should not speak of law and society, or actually any another consequent after "and", as if it was something truly external to and not already entangled with law.

A similar case is that of another classic – the is–ought distinction. Baradian anti-representationalism, inspired by Bohrian idea of physical concepts acquiring their meaning and sense only in relation to some tangible research apparatus and experimental setups, can be seen as undermining the concept of rift between facts and obligations, so influential in reflection on law throughout history, on the following ground. Barad argues that all concepts, thus also those meant to express what should be done, make sense only in relation to their referents (which, of course, are also specifically made during such intra-action). In particular, legal texts containing very general images of their regulated objects are tightly, even intimately, related to them, just as these objects are related to the texts. In consequence of this particular point, obviously having some antecedents way before Barad, for instance, in general semiotics on relations between meanings and referents (e.g. Ponzi 1990: 36), ought is so closely connected with is (and vice versa) that their mere differentiation stops making any sense, at worst, or proves to have only exclusively analytical grounds for itself, at best. This implication makes it possible to put AGR next to other instances of getting rid of the distinction in question in investigations about law (e.g. Stelmach 2011). However, more important than multiplying some possible parallels between the heretofore observed AGR's implications for law and some voices in general reflection on law is to notice the following.

So far, we addressed law practically as one of the two things-within-phenomenon. In the end, we consistently oriented our discussion here around what we named a binary model of intra-action. This particular sense of the fundamental Baradian concept has some value for thinking about law, especially about what the law does and how it acts. With full acknowledgment that, in AGR, one's actions – most definitely a type of relation to others – also impact one's very ontology, we still might say that, thus far, we did not address explicitly whether the commented framework can grasp the law as imagined in the Introduction, that is, involving a plethora of diverse entities. As can be seen below, the answer to the adequacy question posed in this book is somewhat different in AGR's case than in the previously considered flat ontologies (with one still to follow in the next chapter).

5.4.5 Adequacy for Law Between the Binary and Non-Binary Intra-Action

Let us recall that AGR's basic unit for ontological inquiries – intra-action – appears to have its two renditions – binary and non-binary versions. When one would like to account for law with the use of the former, one would most definitely face some problems in analysis, which render the commented framework as troublesome for law. The binary model of intra-action, while being a ground for some interesting, yet not without anticipations in relevant literature, observations about what the law generally does, as presented above, seems problematic to address law which can be said to involve a plethora of various elements. Having said that, one can, of course, refer to our earlier discussion on problems with AGR's binarism and recall that, ultimately, even when sticking to binary intra-action, one can still account for entities whose composition or identity can be said to coming from their simultaneous participation in many binary intra-actions with various objects. However, in response to that, one can and should express some puzzlement – exactly why and how law, and in fact any more complex object, should be conceptualised as a series of twos – many binary intra-actions. Of course, the basic model of one of the most crucial conceptual inventions of Barad is useful, also for the sake of law, when not dealing with the entire complex entity, but, for instance, wanting to investigate more carefully some fragment of it. Nevertheless, if one seeks a framework to grasp some complicated entity, a binary intra-action can be deemed as controversial, at least, choice, due to its practical insistence of dual structures. Sticking to them in the case of something that involves a myriad of entities, which rather remain in much more complex relations than dyads, like law, seems simply artificial, even strained, and ultimately overly complicated.

If such reading is justified and convincing, taking the opportunity here, we can also venture the following explanation concerning the commented Baradian binarism. Despite convincing of the wide, even universal, applicability of AGR, it has very strong roots in scientific or technoscientific realm, which is visible in the number of phrases, such as "scientific and other social practices", used throughout the major exposition of the discussed framework (Barad 2007: 26, 42, 67, 70). Obviously, Barad wants to have their framework as far-reaching as possible, but the above shows that what can be regarded as the original point of reference for their work – technoscientific practice – still exerts its significant influence in that the idea of intra-action is largely presented by Barad in its binary version. This fits really well the relation between the measurement of some object and the measured object. However, it is puzzling when referred to any situation or entity that has a more numerous and complex composition. The additivity and the possibility of one entity partaking in many binary intra-actions are rather insufficient or merely an apparent solution to the presented problem. This is not only because of the actually unaddressed issue by Barad of why and how exactly various entities, also of even a highly complex composition involving a plethora of objects, should be grasped with the help of the binary model of intra-action, or whether our particular object of interest – law – "divides into two". In the end, recall that one specific problem with the binary model – whether the object that partakes in all considered intra-actions can be regarded as, in fact, "mediating" between other elements involved in them – ultimately leads to a non-binary model.

In it, there can be ultimately one phenomenon that includes a myriad of intra-acting entities, which is a clear deviation from the original structure, which involves two things-within-phenomenon, patterned on the relation between the measurement and its object. It can be said confidently that law fits the non-binary model of intra-action. However, as suggested earlier, notice that this particular model does not appear to say something clearly different than other frameworks potentially applicable to law, some of which we already considered in this book. In the end, the non-binary model rather just says that law emerges out of a plethora of relations with various entities. While getting rid of restrictive yet somewhat original, binary model, the non-binary one does not offer any far-reaching novelty. Law, as everything, is supposed to emerge fully out of intra-actions, but this turns out to be troublesome to address in accordance with their binary model. In turn, the non-binary one does not pose any similar issues or puzzles, but it is rather unoriginal with respect to other, also earlier, flat ontologies.

Barad (2011: 446), in response to the commentary on their work by Trevor Pinch (2011) – himself holding a degree in physics – admits that AGR may turn out to be flawed or not adequate enough to various intra-actions, but it is said in the context of physics. What we considered above justifies rather to say that AGR is not so much marked with a very specific issue that makes it not a good fit for law, but that there are, in fact, others who appear to speak much more with respect to law, even when the adequacy of some of their theses proves to be questionable. In the end, notice that ultimately Barad can be said to make an argument about the common, universal regularity of entities mutually constituting each other while relating to each other. For instance, in comparison to Latour and DeLanda, who notice many other functions among a heterogeneous myriad of beings they consider, like being translators, mediators, intermediaries or delegates (in the former case) or taking part in (de)territorialisation and (de)coding (in the latter thinker), AGR may indeed be regarded as offering not much. Having said that, it does not mean that legal scholars and all those interested in law cannot find anything valuable in AGR. On the contrary, for instance, the implied provocation to investigate how the mere fact of law somehow relating to something impacts that thing, even before considering the details of such law and its effectiveness, is inspiring, to say the least. Nevertheless, if one would like to have a framework that offers a wide array of conceptual tools to delve deep into the ontology of law, then Baradian AGR will rather not meet such need.

References

Barad, Karen. 2000. Reconceiving Scientific Literacy as Agential Literacy: Or, Learning How to Intra-Act Responsibly within the World. In *Doing Science + Culture*, Roddey Reid and Sharon Traweek (eds), 221–258. New York: Routledge.

Barad, Karen. 2007. *Meeting the Universe Halfway: Quantum Physics and the Entanglement of Matter and Meaning*. Durham: Duke University Press.

Barad, Karen. 2008. Living in a Posthumanist Material World: Lessons from Schrödinger's Cat. In *Bits of Life: Feminism at the Intersections of Media, Bioscience, and Technology*, Anneke Smelik and Nina Lykke (eds), 165–176. Seattle: University of Washington Press.

Barad, Karen. 2010. Quantum Entanglements and Hauntological Relations of Inheritance: Dis/continuities, SpaceTime Enfoldings, and Justice-to-Come. *Derrida Today* 3 (2): 240–268.

Barad, Karen. 2011. Erasers and Erasures: Pinch's Unfortunate "Uncertainty Principle". *Social Studies of Science* 41 (3): 443–454.

Barad, Karen. 2012a. Nature's Queer Performativity. *Kvinder, Køn & Forskning* 1–2: 25–53.

Barad, Karen. 2012b. *What Is the Measure of Nothingness? Infinity, Virtuality, Justice*. Ostfildern: Hatje Cantz Verlag.

Barad, Karen. 2014. Diffracting Diffraction: Cutting Together-Apart. *Parallax* 20 (3): 168–187.

Barad, Karen. 2017. What Flashes Up: Theological-Political-Scientific Fragments. In *Entangled Worlds: Religion, Science, and New Materialisms*, Catherine Keller and Mary-Jane Rubenstein (eds), 21–88. New York: Fordham University Press.

Barad, Karen. 2022. Agential Realism – A Relation Ontology Interpretation of Quantum Physics. In *The Oxford Handbook of the History of Quantum Interpretations*, Olival Freire Jr (ed.), 1031–1054. Oxford: Oxford University Press.

Barad, Karen, and Daniela Gandorfer. 2021. Political Desirings: Yearnings for Mattering(,) Differently. *Theory & Event* 24 (1): 14–66.

Bennett, Jane. 2010. *Vibrant Matter: A Political Ecology of Things*. Durham: Duke University Press.

Berg, Anne-Jorunn. 2019. The Cyborg, Its Friends and Feminist Theories of Materiality. In *Discussing New Materialism: Methodological Implications for the Study of Materialities*, Ulrike Tikvah Kissmann and Joost van Loon (eds), 69–86. Wiesbaden: Springer.

Boysen, Benjamin, and Jesper Lundsfryd Rasmussen (eds). 2023. *Against New Materialisms*. London: Bloomsbury.

Braidotti, Rosi. 2013. *The Posthuman*. Cambridge: Polity Press.

Braidotti, Rosi. 2019. *Posthuman Knowledge*. Cambridge: Polity Press.

Braidotti, Rosi. 2022. *Posthuman Feminism*. Cambridge: Polity Press.

Bryant, Levi R. 2016. Phenomenon and Thing: Barad's Performative Ontology. *Rhizomes: Cultural Studies in Emerging Knowledge* 30.

Butler, Judith. 1990. *Gender Trouble: Feminism and the Subversion of Identity*. New York: Routledge.

Cielemęcka, Olga, and Monika Rogowska-Stangret (eds). 2018. *Feministyczne nowe materializmy: usytuowane kartografie* [*Feminist New Materialisms: Situated Cartographies*]. Lublin: e-naukowiec.

DeLanda, Manuel, and Graham Harman. 2017. *The Rise of Realism*. Cambridge: Polity Press.

Dolphijn, Rick, and Iris van der Tuin. 2012. *New Materialism: Interviews & Cartographies*. Ann Arbor: Open Humanities Press.

Everth, Thomas, and Laura Gurney. 2022. Emergent Realities: Diffracting Barad within a Quantum-Realist Ontology of Matter and Politics. *European Journal for Philosophy of Science* 12 (51): 1–20.

Fox, Nick J., and Pam Alldred. 2017. *Sociology and the New Materialism: Theory, Research, Action*. London: Sage Publications.

Haraway, Donna J. 2016. *Staying with the Trouble: Making Kin in the Chthulucene*. Durham: Duke University Press.

Harman, Graham. 2016a. Agential and Speculative Realism: Remarks on Barad's Ontology. *Rhizomes: Cultural Studies in Emerging Knowledge* 30.

Harman, Graham. 2016b. *Immaterialism: Objects and Social Theory*. Cambridge: Polity Press.

Harris, David. 2021. *Karen Barad's Feminist Materialism: Intra-action and Diffraction*. Newcastle upon Tyne: Cambridge Scholars Publishing.

Hollin, Gregory, Isla Forsyth, Eva Giraud and Tracey Potts. 2017. (Dis)entangling Barad: Materialisms and Ethics. *Social Studies of Science* 47 (6): 918–941.

Jaksland, Rasmus. 2023. Decoherence, Appearance, and Reality in Agential Realism. *European Journal for Philosophy of Science* 13 (24): 1–18.

Juelskjær, Malou, Helle Pauborg and Stine W. Adrian. 2021. *Dialogues on Agential Realism: Engaging in Worldings through Research Practice*. Abingdon: Routledge.

Kaiser, Brigit Mara, and Kathrin Thiele (eds). 2018. *Diffracted Worlds – Diffractive Readings: Onto-Epistemologies and the Critical Humanities*. Abingdon: Routledge.

Kant, Immanuel. 1998. *Critique of Pure Reason*. Trans. and ed.: Paul Guyer and Allen W. Wood. Cambridge: Cambridge University Press.

Kaufmann, Arthur. 1966. Analogy and "The Nature of Things"; A Contribution to the Theory of Types. Trans.: Ilmar Tammelo, Lyndall L. Tammelo, Anthony R. Blackshield and Albert S. Foulkes. *Journal of the Indian Law Institute* 8 (3): 358–401.

Kaufmann, Arthur. 1985. Problemgeschichte der Rechtsphilosophie [Problem History of Legal Philosophy]. In *Einführung in Rechtsphilosophie und Rechtstheorie der Gegenwart* [*Introduction to Contemporary Legal Philosophy and Legal Theory*], Fourth Edition, Arthur Kaufmann and Winfried Hassemer (eds), 23–123. Heidelberg: CF Müller Juristischer Verlag.

Lemke, Thomas. 2021. *The Government of Things: Foucault and the New Materialisms*. New York: New York University Press.

Merten, Kai (ed.). 2021. *Diffractive Reading: New Materialism, Theory, Critique*. Lanham: Rowman & Littlefield.

Milwertz, Cecilia, and Wang Fengxian. 2012. Non-governmental Organizing in the People's Republic of China – a Reading Inspired by Agential Realism. *Kvinder, Køn & Forskning* 1–2: 104–110.

Murris, Karin, and Vivienne Bozalek (eds). 2023. *In Conversation with Karen Barad: Doings of Agential Realism*. Abingdon: Routledge.

Petrażycki, Leon. 1955. *Law and Morality*. Trans: Hugh W. Babb. Cambridge, MA: Harvard University Press.

Pinch, Trevor. 2011. Karen Barad, Quantum Mechanics, and the Paradox of Mutual Exclusivity. *Social Studies of Science* 41 (3): 431–441.

Ponzio, Augusto. 1990. *Man as a Sign: Essays on the Philosophy of Language*. Trans. and ed.: Susan Petrilli. Berlin: Mouton de Gruyter.

Stelmach, Jerzy. 2011. And If There is No "Ought"?. *Studies in the Philosophy of Law* 6: 15–20.

Stelmach, Jerzy, and Bartosz Brożek. 2006. *Methods of Legal Reasoning*. Dordrecht: Springer.

Williams, Patricia. 1987. Alchemical Notes: Reconstructing Ideals from Deconstructed Rights. *Harvard Civil Rights-Civil Liberties Law Review* 22 (2): 401–434.

Chapter 6

Graham Harman's Object-Oriented Ontology (of Law); or, Is Law Exhausted by Under- and Overmining?

6.1 Not ... a Sports Reporter (Anymore)

6.1.1 To Be in Constant Development (and the Downsides of That)

While one cannot say that Barad's AGR is presented in a relatively small writing output – after all, in addition to the main book-length voluminous exposition of that theory, Barad develops and applies their approach in many, often also lengthy, articles and chapters – in comparison to the final flat ontology analysed in this book, its presentation can still be deemed as rather modest. In the end, Harman is not the common case of a contemporary philosopher who consistently, practically throughout his prolific writing, proposes, justifies, corrects, expands and applies his own theoretical proposal. One can safely say that what came to be known as Harmanian OOO – after some fluctuations when it comes to the exact name of the commented proposal (e.g. Harman 2013b: 6–7) – has its very beginning in his PhD studies in philosophy. His specific take on ontology – which, at its very fundamental level, can be branded as a result of blending his (Harman 2002) original, for some even iconoclastic, reading of Martin Heidegger, especially his tool analysis and fourfold, with Husserlian phenomenology – has its roots in that early period, which, interestingly, Harman combined with working as a sports reporter. Ultimately though he stayed on and followed the academic path further.

While on it, as already said, Harman consistently sticks to his original position and, of course, develops it. Such an approach, on the one hand, can be deemed as recognition-worthy already given the level of devotion it requires, but, on the other hand, is connected with some problems. Developing and expanding some initial intellectual project over the years in a plethora of publications renders the entirety of it rather difficult to thoroughly reconstruct, as, when engaging some slow and careful reading of the relevant corpus, one can practically always notice some tensions, often subtle yet important, or even ruptures in continuity of some line of argument. Against such a background, Harman turns out to be sometimes very clear and indicates the precise spots where he ultimately changed or corrected his position (e.g. Harman 2009: 164, footnote 12, 210–211), but, when it comes to some other noticeable instances of

DOI: 10.4324/9781003440963-6

alterations, he remains silent about them and it is up to the readers to notice them (we will see such a case below, when dealing briefly with Harmanian highly specific sense of space).

Obviously this book is not meant to analyse some (dis)continuities in the chosen flat ontologies but to address the issues of their adequacy and value for the law. Nevertheless, given that very goal of the book, below, we will still have some occasion, or even necessity, to bring some relevant tensions within Harmanian oeuvre to the fore. Before we do that, speaking of the oeuvre, we should here, as in the first sections of all previous chapters, somehow explain ourselves about the adopted selection of the source material for the analysis.

6.1.2 Classifying the Works of Harman

It appears that Harmanian main works can be divided in the following way. His early studies (Harman 2002, 2005) devoted to past yet highly important thinkers – such as the already mentioned Heidegger and Husserl, as well as Emmanuel Levinas or Maurice Merleau-Ponty – are in fact also a springboard to his own project, or, to be more precise, its early renditions, not structured as some later works (compare Harman 2002, 2005 with Harman 2009, 2010b, 2011, 2012c, 2013b). However, taking this opportunity, we should stress here that given that the conceptual apparatus of Harmanian OOO, in fact, matures in these later works, we will focus on them.

Harman, in addition to dealing with the various classics, out of the twentieth century, like those mentioned, but also reaching way back to, for instance, Greeks and occasionalists, is known for constantly engaging with contemporary thinkers, also those who may be regarded as flat ontologists. As already stated in the Introduction, it is largely due to Harman engaging in dialogue with Latour (e.g. Harman 2009), DeLanda (e.g. Harman 2010c: 170–198) and Barad (e.g. Harman 2016a) one can say that flat ontologies constitute currently a specific discourse. Having said that, one should also take into account the following reservations.

First, when it comes to flat ontologists, Harman (2012a) even reaches way back to Tardean MON. Second, when dealing with both historical figures and his contemporaries, Harman has a rather unfortunate tendency of trying to impose upon them and their works his own conceptual apparatus and interpretations flowing from it to such an extent that he even appears to ignore some explicit arguments of these figures that clearly contradict or, at best, problematise Harmanian reading. To be more illustrative, recall that we have already shown some of this questionable practice when addressing the accusation of Barad of being ultimately an idealist (Harman 2016a: 1; 2016b: 14; in DeLanda and Harman 2017: 3–4, 9), and that of Latour of arguing that, in any relation between two parties, there has to be a mediator, or that objects are nothing more than their relations and thus they do not have inherent specifics (e.g. Harman 2009). In line with our agenda, we do not assess whether

Harmanian reading of his main historical inspirations is justified or not. Nevertheless, some of his ideas concerning other flat ontologies, especially those analysed in this book, can and should be commented. It is so because some of them distort the discussed frameworks, and by countering them, we additionally clarify their proposed reconstructions.

Of course, the fact that out of the sample of thinkers considered in this book, it is only Harman who also engages all the rest is not the sole reason we consider him as last. Note that the sequence of chapters is largely chronological – it follows the time sequence of the main publications of the investigated thinkers where their respective ontological frameworks get their big expositions. Of course, as said above, Harmanian OOO has its roots already in the nineties and his first two books (Harman 2002, 2005), his highly original interpretation of Heideggerian case of tool analysis included, were published in the first part of the first decade of the third millennium, before book-length expositions of DeLandaean AST and Baradian AGR (DeLanda 2006; Barad 2007). However, given the fact mentioned earlier – rather constant development of Harmanian OOO and that his fundamental conceptual vocabulary somewhat specified, matured and stabilised itself only in some later studies (e.g. Harman 2009, 2010b, 2011, 2012c, 2013b), published after the relevant books of DeLanda and Barad – we deal with Harman only at the end of our series of analyses.

Returning to the issue of classifying his work, in addition to the studies more or less thoroughly focused on works of others, from the past as well as contemporaries, there are also Harman's writings that can be deemed as devoted entirely to his own theoretical proposal (e.g. Harman 2011, 2018). There are still in them references to other thinkers, but their character is not anymore "to discuss others, and, at the same time, to introduce and develop one's own position on the proverbial back of those others", but simply "to give the most up-to-date account of OOO". However, even such works turn out to be not entirely comprehensive and as complete as one would wish, as Harman himself admits (Harman and Roffe 2014: 29, 52). Namely, some parts of the proposed framework and their concepts are rather merely sketched than elaborated to the fullest (Harman 2011: 143). Fortunately, these are the parts that are not crucial to make the assessment of OOO from the perspective of law. To realise this original task – heretofore there were no similar analyses as ours – the core concepts will suffice.

Moreover, at the time of writing these very words, it appears that the situation will not change itself soon and some rather still merely provisional parts of Harmanian OOO will remain so. Namely, it is difficult to get rid of the impression that rather soon after more theoretically oriented works devoted to OOO as such, instead of developing and refining it further, Harman dedicated his attention to more application-centred studies. To put it differently, there is at least one another type of Harman's works that can be deemed as broadly understood applications of OOO to different types of objects – literary works (e.g. Harman 2012c), pieces of art (e.g. Harman 2020a), architecture (e.g. Bedford 2020), archaeological findings (Harman and Witmore 2023) and, last but not the least, in the case of our interests, social entities (Harman 2016b; 2018: 105–146; see also Campbell et al. 2019). Of course, being ultimately interested in law, below we will take into account Harman's work on the latter subject, but we will also not forget about the rest in question. Having already somewhat prepared the ground, there is still one issue to address before moving on to the reconstruction of the basic tenets and sensitivities of Harman's OOO.

6.1.3 Second Wave of Object-Oriented Ontologies and Speculative Realism

Similarly to the case of ANT and that, with this name, one can associate not only Latour but also many other scholars, the name of OOO, while at the time of writing these very words rather most commonly brings to mind Harman, can be also connected to projects of other scholars. Consider the works of already mentioned Bryant (e.g. Bryant 2011), Ian Bogost (2012) or Timothy Morton (e.g. Morton 2013). All of them engage in, to a certain extent comparable with Harman's, ontological projects, which have their specifics, yet express their general closeness to Harmanian version of OOO. Given that, one can ask as to why we are dealing here with Harman and not with some of the other representatives of OOO. We follow here the criteria used earlier while deciding to focus on Latour – just as Latour is for ANT, so Harman is undoubtedly the most prolific and devoted to OOO thinker among others mentioned – and while not choosing Bennett's vital materialism over Baradian AGR out of the rich resources of new materialisms – Harman is chosen here over others conducting similar object-oriented philosophical investigations, because he is much more fundamental to this particular current, and they draw significantly from him. To put it differently, and in reference to Tom Sparrow's (2014: 161) apt idea of the second wave of OOO consisting of Bryant, Bogost and Morton, we focus here on the more fundamental, first wave – Harman.

In addition to the issue of name OOO grouping underneath itself not only Harman, but many others, there is also a problem comparable to that with which we began the previous chapter. Recall that we considered there Baradian AGR in the context of a way broader trend of the new materialism with which it is associated. Harmanian OOO is also connected with an intellectual phenomenon of speculative realism, having its beginning in the philosophical workshop held at Goldsmiths, University of London, on 27 April 2007. That event, entitled "Speculative Realism", consisted of talks by Ray Brassier, Iain Hamilton Grant, Harman and Quentin Meillassoux (Brassier et al. 2007). Soon after the event, the individual intellectual projects of the four came to be associated with the name of speculative realism. While it is indeed much narrower than the umbrella term of new materialisms, the participants of the workshop still turned out not to be attached to the name ascribed to them by some. In consequence, the very identity of speculative realism can be said to be clearly diluted, of course, unlike the specific positions of the Brassierian brand of nihilism (Brassier 2007), Grant's version of vitalism (Grant 2006), Meillassouxian speculative materialism (Meillassoux 2008) and, last but not least, Harmanian OOO. We focus on the latter, not only because of its popularity in comparison to other mentioned "speculative realists" and the scope of OOO's development over the following years, but, even more importantly, given its explicitness about the assumed basic unit for ontological inquiries. In turn, when it comes to speculative realism, given its increasingly problematic character – whether it actually denotes some intellectual position and what is its exact scope (does it embrace a rich catalogue of commitments or ultimately very modest, even narrow) – it will not be referred to below. Harmanian OOO as such, without the recourse to speculative realism, is rich enough. Having said that, let us look at its basic sentiments and commitments.

6.2 Stepping Into ... Harmanian Object-Oriented Ontology

6.2.1 Against Onto-Taxonomy, For Objectifying Everything (Humans Included)

We may begin giving insights into OOO, by bringing to fore one of the relatively more recent (though somewhat anticipated between the lines of earlier works) concepts of Harman – onto-taxonomy (e.g. Harman 2016b: 4; Harman in DeLanda and Harman 2017: 86; see also Harman 2010c: 146–147, 156, 167). It basically denotes rendering the main subject for general, philosophical reflection in terms of opposition between that what is human and quite literally everything else. Obviously, from the perspective of the mere idea of a flat ontology and increasingly common posthumanist sentiments, such division of reality into two utterly uneven parts – after all, at the time of writing this book, there are about 8 billion of us, while one can safely say that all the rest are incomparably much more numerous – is highly controversial as simply upholding stark anthropocentrism in the spirit of Immanuel Kant.

Not only given Harman's critical position with respect to the latter, OOO can be read as a decisive counteroffer to such onto-taxonomy. Already at the level of the main unit for ontological inquiries it uses also with respect to people, it should be clear how much of anti-anthropocentric philosophy Harman proposes. Namely, humans are de-exceptionalised by considering them as just one specific instance of a general category of object (e.g. Harman 2013b: 38–39). Instead of somehow highlighting that humans are ontologically special among the rest of being, by, for instance, calling them subjects or even agents, they are put on the very same plane as, for example, hamsters or desk lamps. This is because, for Harman, in general (because some more detailed reservations are to follow), the world consists of objects, and we are said to be their instance as well.

Having said that, we should stress that Harman is thinking here strictly in ontological categories, and thus, the fact that he "objectifies" humans (with all the rest) does not entail straightforward conversion into an ethical position according to which we are of the same ethical worth as plush toys or tardigrades. Although Harman does not stray from some ethical and even political interventions, we will practically limit ourselves here just to the ontological part of his project.

Before going further, after naming OOO as anti-onto-taxonomist, anti-anthropocentric and "objectifying" humans, we should take the opportunity and notice the following. The anti-anthropocentrism of Harman is not entirely consistently realised by him. For instance, Harman convinces us that the difference between the so-called sensual object and its sensual qualities (for example, consider a particular desk seen by people at a library and how its very appearance for them changes due to light in the room, but the very identity of the desk in question remains unquestionable for all its human perceivers) – more on that below – is common, in a sense it is not restricted only to humans and their cognitive abilities (e.g. Harman 2009: 211–212; 2010c: 204). However, one can seriously doubt whether such phenomenological nuance can be sensed by a myriad of entities other than humans and perhaps some of the more developed nonhuman animals.

Leaving such reservation aside, let us notice that, thus far, OOO is based on sentiments that are not foreign to previously considered flat ontologies. In the end, practically all of them want to subdue also humans to the very same fundamental principles as everything else and thus end with human exceptionalism. However, as seen below, Harman's project is very different from other flat ontologies in its other crucial tenets.

6.2.2 Against (Overestimating) Changes, for (Appreciating) Stability

First, Harman is against what he would consider to be an overly dynamic accounts of reality, which render practically any fluctuation in or directly around some analysed object as so crucial to that very object's identity that any change in any relations changes their elements as well. Instead, OOO is built on the conviction to clearly distinguish from each other an entity as such, its components whose relations allow for the emergence of the entity in question and that what it does or what general influence it exerts on others (e.g. Harman 2009: 112).

To put it differently, Harman wants to appreciate the individual existence of objects as much as possible. These come into existence thanks to the interactions between that what can be said to constitute their components – domestic relations. Once already existing, objects obviously can exert some specific-to-them type of influence on others, group with them and even take part in the emergence of another entity (foreign relations). For Harman (e.g. in Latour et al. 2011: 115; Harman 2009: 135, 188; 2013b: 21; 2014: 43), objects are supposed to be largely independent of both their foreign and domestic relations. While independence of the former may be, at first glance, more easily acceptable, one can wonder how anything can be independent of its composition. Harman addresses this question with reference to emergence (e.g. Harman 2009: 187; 2010b: 12; 2016b: 9, 27–28; 2018: 32, 46; 2020b: 124). It leads to entities that are ultimately irreducible to their components and with properties not found among them. While Harman, of course, admits that going beyond some critical measure of alteration in domestic relations may be even destructive for the emergent being, some fluctuation among them is still possible without entailing a change in that being (e.g. Harman 2009: 188).

In short, Harman strongly wants to differentiate between some changes in or around an object in question, which turn out to be merely superficial for that object, not influencing its very core, and those that actually achieve this level of influence (e.g. Harman 2016b: 104–105). As we will see below, even in relation to this characteristic tenet of OOO, there are some reservations following directly from Harman's analyses, especially the differentiation of the real and sensual objects and the possibility of existence of exclusively sensual objects. For now, we may conclude this thread by saying that OOO is marked with a strong anti-relationism and conviction that the default state of things is stability and not constant dynamism, of which he seems to be accusing thinkers such as Tarde, Latour and Barad.

Taking this opportunity, while Tardeaen MON and Baradian AGR with their focus on possessing others and thus acquiring properties and on relata emerging out of intra-active relations, respectively, can indeed be deemed as ontologies that, by default, assume dynamism and, thus, stability is something for them to be explained, the situation is more complicated in the case of Latour. In the end, as we showed earlier, he (in Latour et al. 2011: 43–44) explicitly countered Harman's reading that, for Latour, everything is supposed to be utterly relational to such an extent that entities are devoid of any singularity. On the contrary, Latourian ANT with its insistence that any relations between entities entail their translation means that there is some specificity to beings, beyond the myriad of relations in which they partake. Interestingly, after such important public self-commentary by Latour, Harman appears not to take it into account in his own writings addressing the Latourian project.

Nevertheless, sticking to the main issue here, notice that the talk of broadly understood anti-relationism, scepticism of constant dynamism and assumption of stability as a much more common state of the world brought us to mentioning the issue of basically what is characteristic and defining for entities. This calls for uncovering another tenet of OOO.

6.2.3 Essentialism

Speaking of some core traits of entities, Harman generally adheres to essentialism, with important reservations to make. His OOO does not assume universal essences, for instance, of cats in general. Instead, his (Harman in DeLanda and Harman 2017: 101; see also Harman 2009: 206) essentialism is individual or singular in a sense that particular objects are said to have their individual essence. While there is no essence common to all actual cats that ever were, are or ever will be, Harman proposes a vision in which a specific cat, for instance, the one that may be around you just as you read these words, in addition to its other feline counterparts, has an essence characteristic to itself only. Because the sense of such essence is tightly connected with the model of the basic unit for ontological analyses, we will address it in more detail below.

It will suffice to say here that what Harman calls essence can be said to concern that what realises the conditions of real object exclusively. In fact, one can venture to say that, in its entirety, OOO is proposed in such a way that reveals a specific focus on or dedication of this framework to real objects. To put it differently, only dealing with that what can be named a real object in Harmanian sense allows one to put into use all of his OOO's main conceptual apparatus. Before providing some basic insight into just another tenet of the commented framework – sensualisation or, as Harman often likes to call it, caricaturisation (e.g. Harman 2007: 177; 2011: 75; 2020b: 92) – we should address here even the more fundamental one.

6.2.4 The Real and the Sensual

In general, Harman proposes to see the world through the distinction of the real and the sensual (e.g. Harman 2011: 123; 2012c: 4; 2018: 9). This, in connection with another fundamental division between the object and the quality, is crucial for the exposition of the Harmanian basic unit for ontological inquiries. For now, let us just say that the real denotes for Harman everything that can and actually does exist perfectly well in itself, autonomously, even beyond anyone's or anything's perception or experience of that thing, or, in fact, even any relation. In turn, the sensual refers to that what is somehow related to by some relating entity, for instance, perceived by any of its senses (no matter how well or poorly developed they are) or, in fact, experienced in any, even the most rudimentary way.

To imagine especially the latter, think, for instance, of a small rock thrown by a baby playing at the playground at some other rock lying on the ground. The thrown rock, while most definitely somehow experienced, sensualised by the baby holding it in its hand and aiming at another rock, of course, cannot see or, in fact, in any other way account for the existence of the lying rock until they collide with each other. Once it happens, in OOO's terms, it means that the thrown rock in the moment of impact sensualised, specifically experienced the lying rock, but, in this very case, also the opposite is true. The lying rock sensualised, experienced the thrown one.

Obviously, both rocks can be said to exist and subsist beyond their encounter enforced by the playing baby, and even beyond that baby or, in fact, any human being or protein-based entity. They can be then said to be basically instances of real objects, with the caveat to make here that Harman appears to propose much more detailed conditions for real objects in his framework. Both rocks as real objects can be interpreted as also creating their highly specific sensual objects. Notice that these are not only based on the real foundation, but are, in fact, so much different from it – there is undeniable difference between the rock as such and the rock as it can be imagined to be experienced by another rock.

Moreover, these sensual rocks came to being as quickly as they ceased to exist soon after the collision that scattered the rocks at some distance to each other. Although this example can be deemed, quite understandably, as highly peculiar for our tastes – rather most usually following, to a varying degree, anthropocentrism – Harman wants to convince us that even such rudimentary cases can illustrate the processes and regularities argued to be common in reality and thus found also among sentients and conscious beings, such as ourselves.

OOO envisages the real – that whose existence is independent of relations (but domestic ones to a smaller degree, as suggested earlier) – capable of sensualising others and being sensualised by others. OOO also envisages the sensual – that which is not in-itself but is somehow experienced (for instance, seen, felt or smelled) and thus exists as long as its experience continues. Of course, even our example above implies that there is much more than such simple differentiation may suggest at first glance. Perhaps most importantly, notice that entities can be both real and sensual (in a sense of being experienced by someone or something). As will become clear later, such instance is especially important for Harmanian way of accounting for interactions. However, the commented framework also allows for what can be named exclusively sensual objects – that what exists on the account of being experienced but without any underlying real object, which may be and remains in its being autonomously. We will return to this later. For now, after bringing to fore the tenet of the real and the sensual, we can say the following.

6.2.5 Pan(?)experientialism

Harman is ready to endow practically (with some caveat that will be revealed soon) everything with the possibility of experiencing other entities and thus rendering sensual objects. Although the ordinary use of words such as "experience" or "sense" presupposes rather much more developed and "higher" beings than the rocks just mentioned, Harman wants to recognise that even the most simple and trivial (from human perspective) entities relate to each other and thus can be said to experience or sensualise each other. However, in the process, they do not experience the other entities just like they really are, but, in fact, grasp their mere images, renditions that are made by the sensing object. Just think once again about the lying rock that is hit by the thrown rock. In the very moment of the collision, the lying rock can be said to have experienced the thrown rock, but such experience is extremely shallow in relation to the actual complexity of the thrown rock. In the end, the latter is so much more than the momentary "pop!" experienced by the lying rock.

In this light, it should be stressed that Harman ultimately does not propose to extend mind or mind-like qualities to everything there is in a panpsychist manner (e.g. Harman 2009: 211–214; 2011: 118–123; 2020b: 94). Instead, as Bogost (2012: 10–11) rightly proposes, OOO is a panexperientialist framework. Practically everything can and actually does experience something. In the process, as soon as the relation of experience is established between the senser and the sensed, the former can be said to create – through its experiencing of the other – a sensual object. That is very often nothing more than a caricature of the underlying real object – the thrown rock, as such, in-itself is much more than its sensualisation by the lying rock.

Although the prefix *pan-* clearly implies that, in OOO, literally everything can experience others, render their sensual objects and caricaturise relevant real objects, this is, in fact, a wrong impression. Namely, the possibility of sensualising others, experiencing them is restricted to the objects that pass the conditions for the real object. Most definitely, the objects that can be deemed as exclusively sensual – actually and exclusively coming from the fact that they are somehow perceived by someone or something – cannot sensualise others themselves. Think, for instance, of what you would consider a monster that does not exist in this or any other universe. My own personal example right now is a transgalactic, sun-sized fluorescent flatworm-like creature that just floats around in the depth of space. As long as we are imagining this or other similar products of our minds, they can be said to exist, but merely as sensual objects, without any underlying real ones. In consequence, if something can be an exclusively sensual object, whose entire existence amounts just to being perceived, then it actually cannot experience anything itself. Just as anticipated earlier, Harmanian panexperientialism is not that universal after all. Nevertheless, it is still a highly important tenet of OOO, which connects well with some other similarly crucial issue.

6.2.6 Withdrawal

Namely, one of the basic principles of the discussed version of OOO is that sensualisation is, in fact, unavoidable in a sense that, for instance, two entities that both realise the conditions of real object just cannot interact with each other as real objects, but each of them creates in their relation a sensual image of the other. Because of this, Harman says that real objects withdraw from relations behind their sensual objects (e.g. Harman 2010c: 127; 2011: 75; 2012c: 256). To put it differently, whenever an object that can be said to be real in Harmanian sense appears to interact with other entity realising the same conditions, there is, in fact, no real object-real object relation between them. As soon as the first object somehow perceives or experiences the other (for instance, a person notices a tree), it can be said to create that other's sensual image, as the underlying real object always withdraws from relations and, to put it in somewhat more imaginative terms, is represented in them by its corresponding sensual object. Moreover, no matter how much time the perceiving real object would devote to the observation and analysis of the other object, it will never reach the real one, but at best "produce" its quite vast sensual account. However, in reference to the underlying real object, it will still be nothing more than perhaps a more elaborate caricature.

The tenet of withdrawal of real objects brings then to mind Kantian distinction between noumena and phenomena (Kant 1998: 354–365). Harman's real objects can be likened to the former, while the sensual ones to the latter, with the following reservation. Namely, while Kant introduced this differentiation in reference to humans only, Harman, in line with anti-anthropocentric sensitivities, common to all flat ontologists, proposes to consider practically the same issue also with respect to relations involving nonhumans exclusively (e.g. Harman 2007: 172). Just as we cannot grasp the real, so there is actually nothing that would be able to do that, because of the tightly interconnected regularities of withdrawing and sensualising. As soon as some real object is approached, somehow related to, it withdraws and all that is left in the established relation is its sensual object. For Harman, this is just the way any relation unfolds, or, to be more precise, any relation where an object realising the conditions of the real object is somehow experienced by another object (which also has to be a real object, because sensual ones cannot experience anything). Obviously, there is an important epistemological consequence of that.

6.2.7 Unknowability of the Real

Namely, the real is unknowable. Any form of trying to know something, for instance, whether practically or theoretically, is also an instance of relating to the object of inquiry (e.g. Harman 2007: 177; 2011: 73). As such, just like any relation, it generates some sensual object on the basis of the real one rather than actually grasping the latter. It should be stressed though here that OOO proposes more than some sort of cognitive scepticism, according to which any cognition is merely of sensual objects, never of real ones.

Namely, when it comes to broadly understood epistemological issues, Harman proposes a highly specific take on approaching the real through aesthetics and knowledge. These two gain original meanings in their reinterpretation through OOO (e.g. Harman 2018: 81–85, 181–185). They both require a dedicated attention to them, but still we allow ourselves to merely mention this particular aspect of OOO. This is justified not only by the fact that Harmanian ontology is definitely more clearly and conveniently distinguishable from his epistemology (than, for instance, in the case of Barad). Moreover, interestingly, even somewhat paradoxically given his realist and anti-anthropocentrist commitments, Harmanian account of aesthetics and knowledge ultimately assume so significant role played by the human observer that the criticism that he slips in this very part of OOO into idealism (e.g. Vaillo 2021: 51) seems compelling. On the other hand, some may respond that such accusation is just redundant when it comes to the broadly understood epistemological matters, human matters after all.

Nevertheless, what seems still worthy to bring to the fore at this stage of tackling Harmanian ontology is basically that, while OOO assumes the largely autonomous and in-itself real, it also states its unknowability. To put it differently, Harman assumes some part of the world to exist, yet it cannot be known.

It finds its perhaps most clear example in Harmanian account of essence. Many entities can be said to have their specific singular essences, but they just cannot be discovered. Needless to say, such a position can be deemed as highly frustrating to some, perhaps especially for those who consider finding some absolute defining trait of some entity as the crucial goal of some investigations or for the firm believers in science and progress of research methods and technologies. However, for Harman, who often comes across as an opponent to scientism (e.g. Harman 2013b: 33, 36), such a consequence is rather perfectly consistent with other fundamental tenets of OOO.

Having provided some basic insights into them, fully aware that not everything has been covered here and that we focused on such tenets that can be said to be the closest to Harman's ontology, which can much easily separate itself from his epistemology, aesthetics and even ethics than in Baradian AGR's case, we may delve into the issue of the basic ontological unit assumed in the discussed framework. On this occasion, next to returning to some of the issues anticipated above, we will also provide some additional information that is relevant to some of the already revealed tenets of OOO. Moreover, only having more detailed insight into Harman's idea on what the world consists of, we may be able to address the extent to which his OOO can be considered an instance of a flat ontology, in its sense proposed in the Introduction, just as we did in previous chapters.

6.3 Focusing on ... Objects

6.3.1 Towards the Current Model

Just as its very name suggests, OOO is focused on object. When engaging in some careful comparative work of Harman's writings throughout the years, it becomes quite easy to track some changes in how he approaches that main concept. In earlier works of Harman, to be an object means basically to be a certain unity, which is inexhaustible by any, even the seemingly fullest, account and which is autonomous and separate from the relations in which it participates and from what it manages to alter (e.g. Harman 2009: 152, 188; 2010c: 199; see also Harman in Latour et al. 2011: 115–116). Additionally, there are arguments according to which general traits, such as the size, complexity, naturalness and durability of some entity are insignificant for its objecthood (Harman 2010c: 147–148). However, there are still some caveats. Namely, with respect to the size issue, Harman (2013a: 252) says that while there can be infinitesimally small objects, the world as an utter whole, entirety is not allowed. Moreover, next to objecthood's already suggested conditions, Harman is clear about requiring an object to have parts, but being ultimately something more than their mere sum (e.g. Harman 2009: 132).

Subsequent publications of Harman, with their much more clearer arguments about the emergence and fundamental distinction between the real and the sensual, can be read as in no way revolutionary, but evolutionary – bringing to fore some details, which are consistent and combinable with the earliest expositions of his idea of object. However, one can also argue that, for instance, the above account wrongly suggests that what later came be known as Harmanian real and sensual objects simply realise all the mentioned basic conditions. In the end, already the previous introductory remarks on the real and sensual distinction clearly state that sensual objects – that which exist on the account of being experienced by someone or something – exist as long as their sensualisation lasts. In consequence, they just cannot be said to be relationally independent, because they are thanks to the relation to the object that somehow experiences them.

Obviously, given the self-confessed incompleteness of Harman's OOO, perhaps even its current non-systematicity (Harman and Roffe 2014: 29, 52), we potentially can engage in comparable nitpicking, especially in the face of the ease with which Harman appears to be writing. However, we can say that such an approach is not necessary for the sake of our investigations here and we can just focus on what seems to be somewhat later and a more theoretically complete vision of Harmanian main unit for ontological inquiries.

6.3.2 Between Undermining and Overmining, and Complete, Exclusively Sensual and Exclusively Real Object

As already suggested, when dealing with its basic tenets, OOO wants to do as much as possible justice to non-relationality or individualism – that entities in the world can still be even beyond various relations, which, in turn, are often treated as indispensable by other thinkers who may be regarded as flat ontologists. In line with such general sentiment and utilising what came to be and to this day (of writing) is a fundamental distinction for OOO – undermining and overmining – there is the following basic condition of objecthood. Basically – this needs to be stressed here because, below, we will somewhat unpack it – an object is an entity that is not exhausted, cannot be adequately grasped by the two main ontological strategies identified by Harman – undermining and overmining (e.g. Harman 2011: 7–13; 2018: 43).

The former amounts to accounting for an entity by what can be considered its components. As a result of grasping something through its relatively smaller elements, the entity in question is practically dissolved without any residue. Namely, undermining is an explicitly reductionist approach that ultimately does not recognise the autonomous, independent existence of the entity subdued to it. Instead of analysing some entity as such, it disassembles it into more or less numerous group of smaller entities. One can then say that undermining renders entities as nothing more than aggregates.

While Harman does not entirely dismiss undermining, in purely ontological terms, he (e.g. Harman 2020b: 124) sees it as in stark conflict with emergence. Most definitely, to say that some entity is an emergent being that came into existence due to the relations established between its components and which has some properties not found among them and even retains certain independence over them, is in opposition to undermining and vice versa. The fact that some entity can be completely disassembled into its smaller elements means that such thing was simply nothing emerging out of them, but, for instance, was just wrongly assumed by some to be a separate being. However, recall that Harman's adherence to emergence – which becomes more explicit with his (Harman 2009: 161) engagement with DeLandaean AST – is strong and clear. An object is supposed to be largely autonomous with respect to its domestic relations between its components and be actually something truly new in comparison to them. As such, it is supposed to be an emergent being, and undermining is just unfit to account for it. While Harman's main accusation regarding undermining not being able to account for emergence is convincing, the more complicated is the case of overmining.

The other main ontological strategy of grasping entities that is supposed to be insufficient to account for Harmanian objects amounts to considering some being not in a downward fashion – through its components (like undermining) – but in an upward one. Namely, for Harman to overmine an entity means to grasp it through its very broadly understood effects on others, for instance, how it appears to some perceiving mind. Notice that just like undermining does not leave any residue of an entity that is reduced to its smaller elements, overmining also denies any separate and autonomous thingness. An entity subdued to it is rendered as its effects or influence on others. As such, an overmined entity ends up being utterly dependent on its foreign relations, relations with others that somehow feel its impact. As long as it happens, the entity in question subsists, but once these relations are severed, the entity ceases to exist.

Interestingly, Harman's main accusation against overmining is that it cannot account for change in entities (e.g. Harman 2020b: 124). Now is a good moment to supplement our previous remarks on Harmanian anti-relationism. It extends into how Harman envisages objects and their dynamism (which is still allowed, despite the general sentiment for stability). Namely, one can say that Harman, in fact, adheres to what can be named nonrelationist account of changeability of things (e.g. Harman 2009: 134, 187; 2013a: 235; 2013b: 157–158, 225, 254, 259; 2018: 49–50; 2020b: 138; but see also Harman 2016b: 49). According to it, the fact that entities undergo various changes is attributed to their inherent features, the rest of their characteristics, which always, to a certain extent, manage to remain unmanifested, despite partaking in various relations. For Harman, some eventual change has its roots in the reserve the entity in question has and no relation or amount of relations can exhaust. Following such a position, Harman argues that overmining cannot account for change, because it renders some entity – mere broadly understood effect on others, without any underlying reserve – as so tightly connected to everything else that being in question can be said to have no possibility to be anyhow different than that at some current moment.

As anticipated above, the sense and critique of overmining in Harman can raise some important doubts. First, Harman appears to make here some, unacknowledged by him, jump in reasoning. In the end, why to assume that accounting for some entity through its effects on others, and thus relations with them, must necessarily mean that the entity in question is somehow engaged in everything? OOO appears here to be based on the opposition to a quite extreme vision of panconnectivism. However, even those who Harman likes to see as utter relationalist ontologists, who consider everything there is in terms of their relations, adopt ultimately a much more nuanced position. Think of Haraway, already mentioned few times a highly important scholar commonly associated with new materialism – which Harman likes to consider as an opposition to his project (e.g. Harman 2016b). The following words of Haraway (2016: 31) are especially in place here: "[n]othing is connected to everything; everything is connected to something". Instead of taking into account this or any other comparable nuance concerning relations and connections between things, Harman criticises accounting for entities on the basis of their relations, on the ground of the most extreme position to take, without some clear argument in favour of such a standpoint. In the end, even if something can be said to be actually nothing more than some specific impact experienced by others, it is still perfectly reasonable to say that there is a plethora of objects that, so far, did not start experiencing the entity in question, but possibly can, and some of them most likely will. In consequence, a fluctuating set of objects feeling the impact of a given entity considered as nothing more than its effects can most definitely be regarded as a mechanism of change for it.

Second, even when one would imagine the actual adoption of the panconnectivist position, it still does not mean that the overmined entity connected to everything else cannot change. Harman appears to imagine relations in the discussed context as taut ropes that leave no room for any movement of the most interconnected element. To put it differently, as Harman (2007: 195) admits himself, he considers being in relation in binary terms – either someone or something is in relations or not. Rather needless to say, but this is another case of adopting an extreme position, instead of allowing some much needed nuance. In the end, one can safely say that some actually established relations are stronger and exert more influence on their participants, while others are weaker. Moreover, the broadly understood strength of relations is not constant but can and often actually fluctuates. Some binds are tightened, while others are loosened. If such is the case, then even the highly interconnected entities can change through fluctuations in relations in which they participate.

Having said that, one can make the following remark. While the mere identification of overmining and the general observation that applying it to some entities may utterly dissolve them, not in their components (like undermining) but in their effects on others so that their entire existence proves to be completely dependent, even merely apparent is highly important, its critique on the account of its opposition to change is based on the adoption of probably the most extreme positions to take in the relevant context.

After this necessary interjection concerning the main reasons for Harmanian critiques against undermining and overmining – with the former case convincing and the latter highly controversial – we may proceed with the reconstructive exposition of OOO's basic unit. An object is that what is not exhausted by undermining and overmining. To put it differently, but in line with some anticipation above, the object is between its components (in relation to Harman adhering to the idea of emergence) and its effects on others (because object can exert its influence on others, but they never experience it as such, but merely project its sensual versions). In terms that are more adequate to some simple visualisation attempt (Figure 6.1), the object is over and above its parts but below its effects (e.g. Harman 2018: 43; 2020b: 124).

However, due to the guiding distinction between the real and sensual, the following question emerges: What kind of object exactly? Although Harman in his writings does not always state it clearly, the answer is as follows. That which passes what can be named the under-/overmining condition for objecthood (proves to have some surplus to itself that cannot be accounted for by

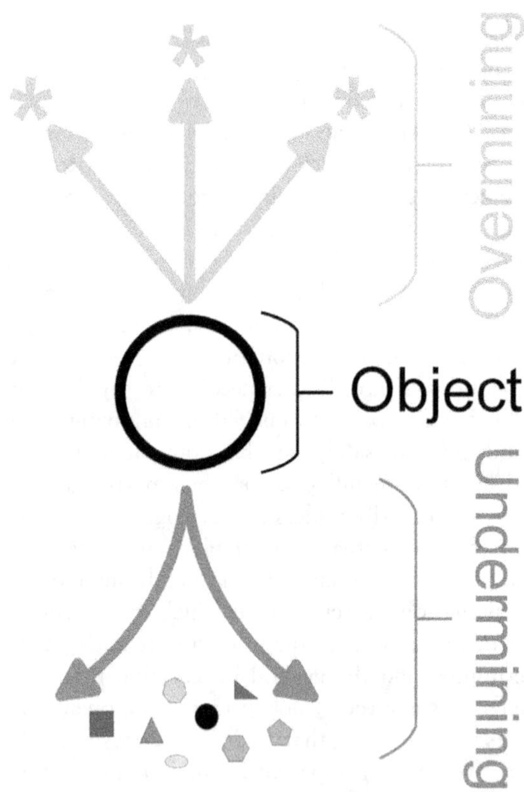

Figure 6.1 Harmanian object (between under- and overmining).

reducing it to its parts and its effects) can be considered a real object (Harman 2009: 215; in Bedford 2020: 18, 104; but see also Harman 2013a: 232). Recall that the real in OOO denotes being in-itself, autonomous, independent of others. This entails both being irreducible to those partaking in domestic relations (in relation to undermining) and to the effects on others (in relation to overmining). However, as said earlier, that what proves to be a real object by being inadequate for under- and overmining, can be sensualised by some other entity (which itself has to be a real object, because only entities that realise its conditions can experience others). In other words, any kind of perception, experience or sense by anyone or anything of that which passes the test is not of the real object but its sensual object.

Consider, for instance, an apple. This fruit most definitely can be said to be something over and above, for example, all chemical components characteristic to its constitution. Moreover, an apple is also something else than a myriad of effects it has or can have on others. In the end, to say that it is nothing else than the way it reflects the light to some perceiver, how it hits the ground beneath when falling ripe from the tree or how it tastes for human or a worm can be confidently dismissed as considerably stripping the apple of what it actually is. Now let us consider for a moment the latter perhaps somewhat odd couple – human and worm. Following Harman, for the quite similar reasons as in the apple case, both can be said to be real objects. In the end, both human beings and worms are neither their components (whatever they are considered to be in the course of some analysis) nor their impact on others. In consequence, as real objects, they can sensualise some other real object, in our case, apple. However, notice that the sensual apple made on its real object basis by human will be significantly different than the one rendered by the worm. Human sensualisation of an apple, for instance, while eating it, biting through it, tasting, chewing and swallowing the bites of it, is different to the worm sensualisation during the analogous ways of relating to the fruit in question.

From this particular example, as well as from the relevant discussions by Harman, one can easily infer that OOO allows for entities that realise the conditions of a real object and are somehow experienced by other real objects and thus also have accompanying sensual renditions of themselves. In the end, one has to remember about real objects withdrawing from contact with each other and, instead, meeting only the sensual objects of the other party in some relations. In fact, given what is to follow – Harmanian quadruple or fourfold model of object – one can say that such objects, which can be named here as complete, because of consisting of both real and sensual aspects, are the main subject of OOO.

However, this is quite far from the entire picture relevant here. Notice that, above, we have already suggested a somewhat different type of entity – exclusively sensual objects. Just think again of some imagined fantastic creature. Due to its utterly mind-dependent character, it cannot be said to be based on some underlying withdrawing real object. Its existence is purely sensual and as soon as someone stops thinking about it, it will cease to exist (e.g. Harman 2009: 215; 2011: 5; in DeLanda and Harman 2017: 50–51, 110).

Following this way of approaching the fundamentals of OOO, but also having a good justification for itself in the words of Harman himself, one can also speak of an exclusively real object – a real object that is, at least at the moment, not sensualised by anyone or anything and thus does not have even a single sensual object corresponding to itself. This category can be likened most easily to the idea of a dormant or sleeping object that appears in some of Harman's writings (e.g. Harman 2009: 214; 2010a: 107; 2010b: 15; 2010c: 207; 2011: 122–123; 2014: 44; 2018: 229; 2020b: 84, 208, 231). Basically, it is meant to denote an utterly relationless (real) object. Obviously, notice that in the light of the already reconstructed basics of OOO, it can be read at least ambivalently – as a real object that does not sensualise anything or that is not sensualised by anything. Without going into the details, the question concerning the empirical plausibility of various analytically possible types of relationlessness and how the distinction between being sensualised and sensualising others can impact Harmanian conceptual apparatus, the following is more important in the current context.

6.3.3 Harmanian Object-Oriented Ontology as Flat Ontology

The crucial differentiation of the real and the sensual can be read as somewhat undermining (in the usual sense of the word) the status of OOO as an instance of a flat ontology (Cogburn and Young 2023). Moreover, such doubts can only be deepened once one starts realising many possible entities due to how the real and the sensual distinction may be relevant to them. Even sticking to what appears to be the most basic differentiation of complete, exclusively real and exclusively sensual objects, one can wonder whether Harman does, in fact, not assume some hierarchisation of being. Especially the latter category provokes that. Namely, an exclusively sensual object, such as some mental content, that can be said to exist as long as being perceived or experienced is something clearly different from a much more autonomous and stable being of that what passes the conditions for a real object.

In consequence, there is the question, postponed until now, whether OOO actually fits our general idea of a flat ontology, as proposed in the Introduction. While it indeed promises the end of anthropocentrism and belittling or ignoring various nonhuman entities and issues and, as such, most definitely adheres to the tenet of pluralism, argued to be crucial for the idea of a flat ontology, the realisation of the other one – that of nonhierarchy – becomes the subject of controversy. Namely, by varying the degree of reality (in Harman's sense) of entities, already given the fact that not everything has to prove itself as inappropriate for under- and overmining, some hierarchisation appears to slip into OOO after all. Instead of one plane, we achieve various strata. These doubts can be even multiplied by provoking to think whether that what can be named exclusively sensual object is not ultimately adequate for overmining. In the end, one can say that some broadly understood mental image without any real object foundation for itself is nothing other than the effect it has on others – in this case, on those who sensualise it.

Sticking to Harman's arguments about flat ontology (e.g. Harman 2018: 54–55), one can address this issue in the following way. Harman most definitely is correct in saying that one should begin some investigations with the assumption of flatness, but it does not necessarily mean that, at their end, they should also realise this idea. Following that, one can say that he does not introduce hierarchisation at the very outset of his project – does not assume it – but rather comes to a conclusion about some inequalities in the course of the analysis. However, if such an argument is actually used to address the controversy considered here, then one can still respond that some inequalities noticeable in Harmanian framework seem not the result of some concrete analyses but rather quite obvious implications of the framework itself, and thus, can be regarded as assumed. This particular ambivalence in assessing the controversy raised here seems rather ultimately unsolvable.

Because of this and the undeniable fact that other sentiments of a flat ontology are realised by OOO, it is still presented here in this book. Nevertheless, bringing to fore some subtle tensions in classifying the commented framework as a flat ontology is in place, especially given the fact that we saw, when dealing with DeLandaean AST, that its mere idea, especially the nonhierarchy tenet, can be problematic in light of some theoretical details.

6.3.4 Not Only Real and Sensual, and Objects, but Also … Qualities

Returning to the main issue addressed in this section, recall that Harman does not only divide the world into the real and the sensual but also objects and qualities. The latter, just like the objects, can be real and sensual. In consequence, we finally reach here the crux of OOO, or, at least, its most explicitly ontological part – the fourfold model of an object.

On the most fundamental level and the one that is actually most often recalled or used by Harman himself, in addition to some other proposals directly connected with that model but rather only provisionally developed and thus rather rarely brought up, we have a structure consisting of real object and qualities and sensual object and qualities, in which considerable attention is devoted to object-quality crossings (e.g. Harman 2011: 124–135; 2012c: 237–243; 2013b: 60–69). As such, it can be read as meant to account for what we allowed ourselves to name a complete object – which passes the under- and overmining objecthood conditions and thus is real, but is also sensualised by some other real object and, as a result, has a corresponding sensual object.

However, such an object is actually not only marked by the duality of being real and sensual but by another duality – of having real and sensual qualities. The former, just like a real object, withdraw from any contact. Nevertheless, they are still considered indispensable as they account for the broadly understood yet fundamental distinguishability of the entity that has them. Namely, following Leibnizian monadology (Leibniz 2014: 15), Harman adopts a position according to which even the withdrawing real objects need to have some real qualities specific to themselves, because, otherwise, they would become indistinguishable from each other (e.g. Harman 2011: 49; 2018: 159). In general, for Harman, qualities always accompany some objects and vice versa – there are no free-floating qualities or quality-less objects.

However, when it comes to sensual qualities, they can be basically understood in the spirit of Husserlian phenomenology – as all very subtle situational and observer-dependent fluctuations in how some experienced (for instance, visually perceived) entity appears. For instance, the touchpad of the laptop used while writing these words can and actually appears differently in dependence on the light source, angle of observation and even when it was last cleaned. However, despite these and other varying and highly changeable sensual qualities, they can still be said to belong to a single concrete sensual object. In the end, no matter how much they may fluctuate, it is still reasonable to say that there is still the same computer part experienced.

With reference to the very last remark here, Harmanian fourfold model of object does not merely distinguish the four of real and sensual object and real and sensual qualities. It also proposes how to understand what can be named the crossings of poles involved. As suggested earlier, Harman appears to devote the majority of attention to crossings between an object and qualities. When it comes to real object and real qualities, Harman names it the essence, in its sense already anticipated above, as a singular core accounting for the object in question and its specificity, which is unknowable.

The second crossing, of real object and sensual qualities, is branded somewhat unintuitively as space. The reason for this is basically the idea of withdrawal. The real object, whenever it is related to by some other real object, withdraws behind its sensual rendering of the relating entity. As such, one can say that the distance and, in fact, space between the real object and its experiential appearance is established.

Taking the opportunity here though and as anticipated earlier, it should be noted that in one of the first expositions of his fourfold model, Harman (2010c: 161–162) appears to understand this highly peculiar take on space differently, namely as crossing between a real object and sensual object. Moreover, such an earlier version not only seems intuitive but also much more in line with one of the principles of OOO – when relating to something, one first experiences the object then its qualities (e.g. Harman 2012b: 6; see also Harman 2009: 198, 225). However, just as said at the beginning of this chapter, given the time of development, there are and perhaps were unavoidable some tensions within the position of Harman, and the somewhat changing idea of space within the fourfold model of object can be regarded as their example, unacknowledged by Harman himself, one might add.

The penultimate crossing, of sensual object and sensual qualities, is named by Harman as time. Before providing some basic exposition of this conceptual decision by Harman, perhaps just another one that might puzzle the readers at first glance, it should be stated clearly that Harman wants here to stop considering time as some already-made framework of reference for various phenomena. Instead, in the fourfold model, time basically denotes its subjectively felt passage, experiencing some changes happening in some period. In consequence, just as space mentioned earlier is rendered in OOO's fourfold model as something that emerges out of some situations, similar is the case with time here. The latter is a crossing involving sensual object and qualities. There is then some object as it is experienced by some sensualising real object and all varying sensual qualities, just like in the touchpad example mentioned above. While the sensual object in question can be said to remain the same, its superficial sensual qualities change, indicating the passage of time. Something is still itself, yet it appears somehow different, just like some interior at the dawn and dusk.

While time in the fourfold model can be said to relate to such dynamism, the last object-qualities crossing concerns stability and durability. Namely, what Harman calls eidos, with the obvious inspiration from Husserl but with ultimately altered meaning, is the crossing between a sensual object and real qualities. Basically, Harman proposes to consider sensual objects as having not only sensual qualities – which can be said to be co-responsible for their "constantly differing, yet still the same" status in some real object's experience – but also way deeper and stable withdrawing real qualities, which account for the fundamental distinctiveness of the object in question.

Obviously, such rudimentary and shorthand exposition of the fourfold model with a focus on its object-qualities crossings – named by Harman as tensions – merely suggests some of its further complexities and often, unfortunately, unclarities, many of which remain to this day unaddressed by Harman himself. Because of this, we allow ourselves not to delve into some analytical avenues provided by the fourfold model, such as possible relations between qualities exclusively and relations between objects exclusively and Harmanian nomenclature proposed for them (e.g. Harman 2011: 131–135; 2012c: 256; 2013b: 66–67). Just in a moment, we will bring to the fore some basic issues connected with relations between objects. However, before that, let us just stress that the fourfold model appears to be, in fact, meant for what we named complete objects.

In the end, consider an exclusively real object. If some real object is not yet sensualised by anything, it also means that as long as such highly specific status is maintained, it is simply devoid of both sensual object and qualities, as these basically come from some experiencing entity. In consequence, there is no complete, fourfold object, but merely twofold – real object and its real qualities, with just one tension – essence.

The actual scope of the full applicability of the fourfold model and all that it implies also becomes debatable when dealing with what was named an exclusively sensual object. Leaving aside the controversy whether overmining is adequate for them, sensual objects without underlying real ones, in accordance with the Harmanian model, are obviously devoid of space – real object-sensual qualities crossing. However, Harman likes to stress that even sensual objects have real qualities (eidos tension). As long as one is talking about sensual objects with underlying real ones, such a position should not raise any doubts. However, when we are addressing exclusively sensual objects, then the idea that they are supposed to still have real qualities without a real object is dubious, to say the least (but see Harman in DeLanda and Harman 2017: 50–51). In consequence, one can venture to say that, with respect to exclusively sensual objects, the fourfold model cannot be applied in its entirety. The above-mentioned category of entities is rather twofold, involving only time crossing, and thus quite far from the map involving four poles, the main issues of which we presented above.

6.3.5 Object-Object Relations and Emergence

Before dealing with OOO from the perspective of law, we should at the end of this section expose clearly some fundamental ideas of Harman concerning relations between entities, some of which we have already hinted at earlier, and their implications for the issue of emergence, in line with our back-to-basics approach. As it should be obvious right now, only real objects can experience or sensualise. Sensual objects – whether having an underlying real objects or not – as, what can be called, contents of experience, cannot experience anything themselves. If they reside next to each other, it just means that some real object sensualises different entities and their sensual objects can never "meet" each other as such, but only thanks to the real object. For instance, the sensual images of real parked cars I see through the window can be said to "meet", but only thanks to my visual experience of them. Moreover, just as two sensual objects cannot encounter each other as such, without the help of real object experiencing them, so two real objects cannot encounter each other as well. To be more precise, they cannot "meet" themselves as real objects, because of withdrawal. Instead, they just "meet" the sensual objects they render on the basis of real ones.

Although it may be thought that this is allowed in OOO, Harman (2009: 209; 2010a: 96), in fact, denies the possibility of any singular interaction involving some mutuality among involved parties. This means that instead of two real objects rendering each other's sensual objects practically at once, Harman argues to consider each sensualisation as a separate interaction. There is some real object A sensualising the real object B into its respective sensual object and separately – there is a real object B sensualising the real object A into its sensual object. While in Baradian AGR, one could find a non-binary account of its main unit for ontological inquiries, in the case of Harmanian OOO, there is very strong attachment to even numbers, ultimately to two. That what can rather most easily be classified as a mutual interaction between two entities, for Harman, should be divided into two practically separate instances.

It is because of his idea and commitment that, using his very own words, can be named the Binary Contact Principle (Harman 2009: 209; see also 2010a: 103). The idea that any contact or interaction has to involve just two parties is a consequence of an even deeper fundamental idea of OOO, the one already shown – that there cannot be a contact between real objects or sensual objects as such, but only between real object which sensualises or renders sensual object, whether the one that has underlying real object or not. For Harman, any interaction is supposed to resemble such dyad of real object and sensual one.

Against such background, let us recall that Harman, in general, adheres to emergence as a defining trait of objects (in relation to undermining). As a result, entities are supposed to come out of relations established among their components (domestic relations). However, sticking to the Binary Contact Principle, Harmanian emergence cannot be a simultaneous and very often mutual interaction of a myriad of components. Instead, if entities are said to have, in general, a compositional character – emerge out of interactions of their components – and interactions cannot involve anything more than the basic Harmanian dyad, then "it follows immediately that any object has only two pieces" (Harman 2010a: 107). Putting it somewhat differently, such binarism ultimately entails a specific monocausality (Harman 2009: 209; 2010a: 107). If something is supposed to involve just two parts connected with each other in a specific way, then one can also say that that something has just one cause for itself – the exact course of interaction between its two parts.

Although such a vision actually flows from the previously presented tenets of OOO and is expressed explicitly by Harman himself, it is a highly unusual idea, especially in light of attachment to emergence. Harman (2010a: 106) appears to address the main controversy here in the following words: "[i]n cases where more than two objects seem to be in relation [...] there will either be a slow accretion of pairs of terms, or a central term that relates independently with each of the others". It appears that the first scenario suggested here – "slow accretion of pairs" – relates to Harmanian intended very broad applicability of the notion of an object, which is also said to be fit for relations (e.g. Harman 2007: 191; 2009: 211; 2011: 117). Nevertheless, even if one would like to stick to the idea of objecthood of relations (between real object and sensual one), many issues remain unaddressed. Leaving aside the issue whether such object out of the real object-sensual object relation actually realises the conditions of (another) real object, it is unclear how such gradual accretion of objectified relations is supposed to account for a new entity. In the end, if while accounting for the emergence one is not supposed to consider some single multielement interaction involving mutuality, but instead divide it into practically a myriad of separate interactions – Harmanian dyads (consisting of real object and sensual one) – then how exactly they can be "added up" and "create" some new being of just two components and one cause? Practically, the same issue is predictable in the second scenario (see also Harman 2009: 209). If some "central" entity is supposed to relate "independently" to others relevant in some situation, then how exactly a number of dyadic interactions treated separately, yet having a "term" common to them all, can be "summed up" to account for something new, of just two parts interacting?

Unfortunately, perhaps given the already mentioned self-confessed incompleteness and that OOO is rather still a project "under construction", the clear answers to these questions, which would also be consistent with the rest of the conceptual apparatus, are not provided (see also Harman 2011: 134–135, where Harman even suggests the necessity of the real object-real object contact to account for compound entities, but does not elaborate). Given the high relevance of raised issues for emergence, they had to be brought up before dealing with OOO from law's perspective. Having dealt just with the fundamentals of OOO – still in a thorough and reflective manner – we may move on to the final section of this chapter.

6.4 Law and ... Harman's Objects

6.4.1 Some Law's Components Are Real Objects, Some Are Not

Practically, the entirety of this book aims at carefully following specific ways of thinking, argued to be universal in their scope and, thus, promising to be also adequate for law. Above, we prepared ourselves to think about law in OOO's terms. As in previous chapters, if we are first interested in the commented framework's adequacy for law, we should address here the question of whether law constitutes an instance of Harmanian object, for which its fourfold model could be used to the fullest. To put it somewhat differently, is law something that cannot be accounted for by undermining and overmining – if so, then it could be said to be a real object – and that is experienced by others – if so, then it would also be a sensual object (on the basis of the real one underlying it). Anticipating what is to follow, we may already say here that OOO poses many, even highly problematic, issues for the adequacy question.

If the idea that law constitutes an instance of Harman's complete object is undermined (in the usual sense of the word), then one cannot fully apply the fourfold model of an object (clearly made assuming such complete object) to law. Of course, some of law's components most definitely fulfil the conditions of such entity, especially the material objects of law. Think of, for instance, speed bumps or even physical documents. As such, they can be said to be real objects that are also variously sensualised by others.

However, when it comes to components of law, it can be said that, among them, there are also meanings or senses, especially normative ones. In the end, it is difficult to come up with a justifiable vision of law that would be devoid of such normative meanings, contained in or expressed through primarily official documents (that passed through various procedures), which are, to a large extent, strictly textual. One can venture to say that law is rather most commonly associated with such senses. But can they be considered real objects that are sensualised? If real objects are supposed to be in-themselves, autonomous and able to exist even beyond relations with others, then any single word, sentence and legal provision or court decision – all as meaning units – will not exist as real objects. This is because they are utterly relational.

To see this, try to consider any legal meaning as we would not be there to actually witness it. We will get, for instance, some ink patterns on paper (if that sense is in printed/written form) or some sound waves (if it is just spoken or played from some record or using a speech synthesiser). Printed/written documents and sound waves as such – as some physical phenomena – will most likely pass the under-/overmining test (prove to be real objects irreducible to their components, and withdrawing from any current perception or experience of them). However, the meaning they carry is something much closer to exclusively sensual object than to complete object in Harmanian sense. Of course, legal meanings are not that private as some utterly subjective imagination products we considered earlier, but still they can be said to be, as long as there is someone who perceives and understands them (see also Ivakhiv 2018: 47–48).

Notice also that their utter relationality should not be considered exclusively in terms of their actual human dependence. Especially, legal meanings are the way they are thanks to the relations that can be found among themselves. Every lawyer, legal academic or even lay person, with some perhaps more than basic grasp of law, will recognise that some particular legal sense is as it is due to other senses, but it also impacts other legal senses. Treating them in some non-relational isolation from each other would either significantly alter them or even render them meaningless. It resembles, to a certain extent, the hypothetical scenario of considering the existence of some chess pawn outside the game of chess and relations that it assumes between different pieces. Interestingly, even Harman (in Latour et al. 2011: 70) himself agrees that, for instance, "a rook in itself is not very interesting, it is a pretty impoverished [object] [...] it has a certain physical structure, and some of them are quite pretty in some of the chess sets". However, outside of the relations with the chess game, its rules and other pieces, it is practically nothing more than some small wooden figure or moulded piece of plastic. Obviously, such mutual dependence of legal senses is an issue that significantly problematised the adequacy of DeLandaean AST due to its attachment to the relations of exteriority as one of the defining conditions of an assemblage.

Continuing the issue of relationality of legal senses, one should obviously take a note that it, in fact, reaches even further beyond the human dependence and mutual dependence of senses on each other. Namely, these issues that significantly problematise a hypothetical attempt to classify legal meanings as cases of Harmanian real objects can be regarded as closely connected to some of the more fundamental ideas from general semiotics. In the end, if one recalls the basic Peircean distinction of indexical, iconic and symbolic signs (Peirce 1960: 4.531), then one can recognise just another proof of relationality relevance in the discussed context. Of course, the indexical sign, where the signifier is "naturally" related to the signified, as "smoke means fire", or the icon, where the signifier simply resembles the signified, as a drawing of a cat meaning "cat", because it is similar to a real animal, are, in most of the cases, not crucial to the legal senses considered at the moment. To these, as predominantly word- or language-based, it is the concept of symbolic sign that is much more relevant. While the relation of the signifier and signified in a symbol is not "natural", nor based on resemblance, but is established by some cultural convention, such as the word "table" means table, it is still a relation that is crucial, even indispensable for the meaning, and, in consequence, for the legal meaning as well.

Such basic remarks already prove that classifying legal meanings as Harmanian real objects is problematic; they are rather a case of exclusively sensual objects. As such, this diagnosis can be regarded as most correct also on the account that, by their very definition, sensual objects are the ones that are experienced by others and cannot themselves sensualise others. In turn, if someone would like to convince that legal meanings are after all real objects, then one would also have to address how exactly they can experience others, as this is one of the basic traits of real objects in OOO. Of course, in reference to the issue of sensualisation or even caricaturisation of that what is experienced and the rather common accusation against law that its grasp of the things it regulates is very superficial and does not do them justice but rather projects their visions only for its own sake, one can say that the classification as real objects would be correct. Law simplifies entities to which it refers – for instance, in its regulations – because everything engages in such simplification in the very moment of relating to something. While Harmanian "normalisation" of such simplification or caricaturisation is as such convincing, in his OOO, it is strictly connected with the status of real object as only it can experience, sensualise others. However, as shown earlier, the idea of legal meanings as real objects is unconvincing and problematic; thus, if one would like to account for the legal simplification of things, one would have to explain it differently than what OOO offers in this respect.

6.4.2 Law, Real-Sensual, Object-Qualities Distinctions and Harmanian Emergence

What is more important here is to say that, so far, we made it probable that law can be seen as consisting of various Harmanian objects – both those that can be deemed as complete ones (real objects sensualised into their sensual objects) and exclusively sensual objects. The exclusively real objects (real but not sensualised by anything) seem irrelevant not only in the discussed context of law but, in general, whenever considering the composition of something. In the end, how anything that is not sensualised by anything else can be said to take part in composing something?

However, what about law as some larger entity that can be said to consist of speed bumps, paper documents, meanings and much more, in line with what we said in the Introduction? For the law so broadly understood, as the mere idea of a flat ontology suggests, to pass the Harmanian objecthood conditions, it cannot be a mere aggregate of its heterogeneous elements. Namely, it cannot be reducible to them (because it would constitute undermining and thus invalidating the real object status, as something over and above its parts), it has to be something largely separate from them (an emergent being) and it cannot be exhaustively grasped through its outside effects (it would be overmining, and the real object hypothesis would be invalidated).

There are at least a few problems with validating the status of the entire law (not only its components) as a real object, some of which are possible to address following Harman's narrative, while others are much more difficult and thus problematise the adequacy issue considered here the most. First, classifying something as a real object does not only entail that it can be sensualised by others – have its sensual object and thus constitute the complete object to which the fourfold model of Harman is dedicated. It also means that such entity has its real and sensual qualities. However, in the case of law, is it actually divisible into its object (real and sensual) and qualities (real and sensual)? In other words, it is very unclear how exactly to use that main object-qualities distinction by Harman, especially its latter part, even if law could be regarded as a real object that is sensualised by some and thus has its sensual objects as well. It is equally puzzling how law's sensualisation of others would look like, because such ability is also one of the defining traits of real objects.

Second, in light of the above remarks on legal meanings, the following question can come to mind. Can there be a real object (in our case, law) that, among parts from which it is supposed to emerge, has exclusively sensual objects (legal meanings)? Does the inherent utter relationality of some part (legal meanings) that is assumed to co-constitute new and separate real object (law) somehow passes on it and, as a result, impairs or even destroys the supposed real object character? Unfortunately, when it comes to such basic issues like being inadequate for under- and overmining or being an emergent entity, Harman tends to assume these traits rather than proving them in accordance with some well-established procedure to follow. Nevertheless, sticking to various examples of social beings he (e.g. Harman 2009: 190, 211) provides in his writings, like the entire intellectual current, corporation or international regional organisation, we can venture to say the following. Given that these and other similar human social entities most likely can be said to be also made from meanings, legal ones included, and that these entities, especially of the organisation kind, appear to have properties not found among their components, there are no clear contraindications to disallow exclusively sensual objects as co-constituting an emergent real object.

Thus, the more pressing problem is rather what exactly is the novelty and distinctiveness of that being of law that is supposed to emerge from many heterogeneous parts, or, to put it simpler, what are law's properties that are not found in its parts? In the end, just as it was suggested in the cases of Tarde and DeLanda, it is more difficult than some seem to consider to prove the emergent status of some social entity. While from the contemporary perspective, Tardean anti-emergentism can be regarded as unfounded if applied to chemistry – recall dihydrogen monoxide case from Chapter 4 – it appears to be still an option to seriously consider in the case of the social human realm. As shown in the final section from the chapter on Tarde, that even when broadly understood auto-creativity would be hypothesised as law's emergent property, not found among its components, it is still possible to account for it without adhering to the idea of emergence. In consequence, while the exclusively sensual objects of Harman can co-constitute emergent real objects, there is still the question whether law actually has properties that are truly emergent – belong to some larger whole and cannot be accounted for by its parts. We may say that this serious problem is unsolvable, at least for now. However, this is still not the end of issues to consider.

Recall the end of previous section and the fundamental problem for OOO and, thus, for its adequacy for law. Namely, while Harman makes emergence a defining feature of an object, due to his attachment to the idea of being inexhausted by undermining, other crucial tenets make it very difficult, if not impossible, to actually account for emergence without deviating from these tenets. Emergence appears very problematic to be explained if one assumes, just like Harman, that any contact or relation takes place between no more than just two beings (real and sensual object). Perhaps most paradoxically for Harman himself, his attachment to the Binary Contact Principle brings him very close to the problems we saw in Barad's binary model of intra-action. Barad is criticised by Harman, but he actually puts himself in a very similar controversy – the idea that any relation can involve only two entities significantly problematises the idea that objects are the way they are due to emerging out of their components. Emergent processes rather involve a simultaneity of often mutual contacts of a myriad of elements. There are rather A, B, C, D, etc. components, which interact with each other as follows. For instance, A, that already relates to B and C (which themselves are in various relations), relates to D (also in relations with some other entities), instead of what Harman appears to suggest. Namely, A interacts with B, C and D, but in a specific separation. There is AB, AC, AD, etc. Although A takes part in all of them, it is unclear how they can "add up" to effectuate the emergence of some new entity without transgressing OOO's principles. Emergence is rather a multifactor process that cannot be reduced to just two elements (real object and sensual one) and, thus, to just one cause – these elements' interaction – but this is what Harman proposes.

In short, then, Harmanian vision of emergence and composition of emergent objects, that, in line with some relevant OOO's principles, should involve just two entities and, as a result, have ultimately just one cause, is so peculiar when one thinks about law that one's potential readiness to announce right here OOO's inadequacy for law may be understandable. Notice, however, that, on more charitable reading, we may say that the final word on emergence in OOO (see also Young 2021) has not been said yet, and perhaps the raised issues will be addressed by some further specification or even convincingly proven as a product of some misreading. However, until then, we may safely say that we most definitely brought to the fore one of the bigger issues when it comes to OOO's adequacy for law.

6.4.3 Around Law and Domestic and Foreign Relations

Another one is Harman's clear attachment to the distinction between the domestic and foreign relations of an object. As said earlier, Harmanian project to do as much justice as possible to certain independence of objects leads him to a concept of object that "lies" over and above its parts (in relation to undermining) but below its effects on others (in relation to overmining). Such a position practically necessitates the idea "that there is an absolute distinction between the domestic relations that a thing needs to some extent in order to exist, and the external alliances that it does not need" (Harman 2009: 135). As stated earlier, perhaps the most puzzling, at first glance, argument about an object's certain degree of autonomy with respect to its elements is, in fact, in line with the assumption of emergence. If something arises out of relations of what can be said to be its components and is supposed to be irreducible to them, then one can say, in principle, that it maintains some independence of what gave rise to it, not to mention relations with completely foreign or outside entities. However, while such a position, in general, holds with respect to such entities, like Heideggerian hammer or Husserlian mailbox – important points of reference for Harman (e.g. Harman 2002, 2009) – the domestic and foreign relations distinction in the case of law is controversial, to say the least. How to separate that what gives rise to the law, which is also supposed to be, to a certain extent, independent of it, and that what law does, what relations with other entities it establishes, when broadly understood law's functioning very often feeds back into what law is?

At the level of concrete legal regulations, one can speak of the already mentioned *desuetudo* principle. According to it, the legal regulation maintains its existence as a valid law as long as it acts, exerts some influence. The circularity of being by doing implied here significantly complicates the clear-cut distinction between the domestic and foreign relations. However, recall that this distinction is dedicated to what passes the conditions for the real object. In turn, as suggested earlier, if one would think of regulations as ultimately legal meanings, then, in accordance with the above arguments about their status of exclusively sensual objects, they cannot be considered in light of the discussed distinction.

Nevertheless, even when we are thinking about law as some much larger entity, the domestic-foreign relations and what they imply in Harmanian framework are also problematic. Of course, at some level of generality of considerations, one can even say that, despite some changes in the component of legal meanings, the law that is co-composed by them is still the way it was prior to those changes. However, adopting a different perspective – for instance, more strictly legal one – one can rather argue that legal meanings are highly susceptible to various changes and fluctuations – of different mechanisms behind them – and with them, the entire law can also change to such an extent that one can ask the following question. Is such changeability of the entire law due to changes in some of its components not too far-reaching to uphold the idea of an object's general stability over its domestic relations? Law is not similar to the hammer or mailbox mentioned earlier. If some of the particles constituting any of the latter are somehow lost, then one can still speak of the hammer and mailbox. Instead, law is an entity marked with much higher chances of significantly changing itself in the aftermath of some changes among its parts, especially legal meanings. Of course, from Harmanian position and its implied and sometimes explicitly expressed attachment to the idea of distinguishing changes that are truly important to some entity and those merely superficial, one can respond that, ultimately, not every fluctuation in legal meanings is that important. At this point, it is difficult to eliminate the impression of having reached a specific moment of inconclusiveness. Some may argue that every change within law is significant for it; thus, law would prove to be unfit for the strong assumption of Harmanian object's stability over what can be named its domestic relations. Others, perhaps Harman himself, can still stick to the idea of crucial and superficial changes and, in consequence, argue that the domestic relations tenet is adequate for law. However, recall once again that domestic relations are relevant in the case of entities that pass the real object conditions. These, as shown above, are entangled in some important controversies when it comes to law, and the idea of domestic relations rather proves here to be just another one.

To address the relevant issue here as much as possible in the space left, let us also consider for a moment foreign relations. At first glance, notice that law appears even highly reactive to what can be said to be happening outside of it. One can obviously think here of geopolitics, internal politics, economy or culture. All of them very often are rendered as something beyond law yet influencing it. In turn, at least since Rudolf von Ihering's *Law as a Means to an End* (1913), thinking about the law in instrumental terms, as made in order to reach some goals with it, has become rather dominating and even default. If so, then notice that law can be regarded as not only a target of some supposed external influences but as an entity meant to specifically deal with that outside. Yes, politics, for instance, influences law, but the opposite is also true – law addresses politics because it was made for this purpose. If that for which law is made to somehow act on it influences law as well, then the commented Harmanian idea of foreign relations is also challenged. Law acts on that which creates it, sustains it and legitimises it. As such, it differs significantly from, for instance, a hammer. That what it does – hammering a nail – can be said not to have a serious impact on it, nor even any impact at all. Different is the case of law. Its regulations tackle various phenomena and processes, which in many cases provoked their original enactment and provoke further amendments.

What law acts on influences it back. For instance, violence among the youth provokes some legal policies against it, which influence the phenomenon in question. Their effects in that specific respect influence, in turn, the very policies, which may undergo various changes depending on how (un)successful they proved to be. In Harmanian terms, it can be read that after all that what can be deemed foreign relations is, in fact, far from being secondary to law. If so, law clearly contradicts Harman's sense of foreign relations, of which the object is supposed to be independent to an even greater extent than that of domestic relations.

However, following the basic idea that objects must be highly autonomous with respect to foreign relations, if law is supposed to actually reach such autonomy and the stability connected with it – so important in Harmanian framework – then one can even consider significantly expanding the catalogue of entities partaking in domestic relations, so that what previously could be thought of as law's outside becomes its inside. At this point, such a potential move should not cause much controversy. In the end, we considered law as ultimately a myriad of heterogeneous things, even up to the point of being all-embracing. However, even such a way of attempting to address the problem of a significant amount of what can be deemed external influences upon law proves problematic for OOO. Most importantly, even when law is considered to be composed of a plethora of diverse beings, even up to the point of embracing that what it is meant to regulate, the problem (for Harman) of law's changeability, and even lability, will remain. Indeed, it will have its source in domestic relations, instead of foreign, but even if the latter are largely, if not completely reduced, because of embracing the entities involved in them by domestic relations, law can be quite far from cherished stability. However, as said earlier, from the position of OOO, one can still generate a response with reference to the idea of crucial and superficial changes.

However, there is another problem with expanding law's domestic relations to include in them that what can be often thought of as foreign relations. Namely, while, in general, Harman's attachment to non-relationality does not seem to disallow in his OOO a prospect of entity of so vast domestic relations that it practically does not and cannot act on others as it is very difficult to localise anything outside to it, recall that Harman also poses some limit when it comes to object size. Namely, he rejects the idea of the world as a whole, some entity that grasps all the others. In light of this and what we considered here, the following question arises. Is the law of such vast domestic relations, so that its foreign relations are minimised if not even inexistent, still allowable in OOO? Unfortunately, rather uncommon Harmanian wanderings into the realm of what can be called social entities cannot help in this issue.

Interestingly, thus far, the most focused analyses of social beings by Harman seem to be rather inadequate for law due to a very specific reason. Namely, when Harman moves from just mentioning in passing some social entities, as was mentioned above, and starts devoting more attention to them, he actually chooses quite peculiar cases for the analyses – the Dutch East India Company (Harman 2016b) and the American Civil War (Harman 2018: 105–146). Notice that both are historical phenomena (in the usual sense of the word), which have some initial moment for themselves, after which they can be said to function, happen throughout a given time period, and then just end. With respect to the broadly understood beings with rather clear birth, life and death moments, one can indeed say that, for instance, some influence that truly and deeply changes some object and is not merely some superficial alteration "will occur relatively early in the life of an object" (Harman 2016b: 118).

However, when it comes to law, even state law, we cannot be entirely sure when it has been born – for instance, just recall Ehrlich's (1922) idea on the sources of legal provisions. Moreover, if we took in this book the law in contemporary Western or Global Northern context as a point of reference, the prospect of death of law in some state also sounds peculiar. Meanwhile, Harman's interventions directly into the realm of the broadly understood social sciences are rather devoted to entities of specified life spans, which already have come to an end. Note also that, while truly far-reaching in their scopes, both Dutch East India Company and American Civil War seem not that vast as law whose foreign relations can be subsumed by domestic ones. This is why Harman's own application and development of OOO for the sake of human social realm cannot address the issue of the allowability of so vast entities, like the law in the considered approach.

6.4.4 A Few Final Thoughts

Slowly reaching the end of the section and the entire chapter, OOO can be said to be the most problematic of the frameworks considered in this book, and, as such, deserves some more extensive commentary at the end, in comparison to previous chapters. OOO proves to be controversial on numerous reasons, and let us just recall some of them. It is very unclear how law is supposed to be fitted into the fourfold model of an object, with all its distinctions (what is real, what is sensual, what is object, what are qualities). Moreover, even if law would be somehow proven to pass the conditions for the real object (which is also sensualised), there is controversy whether the domestic-foreign relations distinction holds with respect to it. Perhaps even more fundamentally, the idea that real objects are emergent entities is in specific tension with other basic tenets of OOO – the Binary Contact Principle, practical exclusion of mutuality of influence within one interaction and monocausality. Obviously, such tension is far from being irrelevant for OOO's adequacy for law.

Leaving aside recalling here in more detail other issues raised above, here let us address the question on the sources of controversies brought to the fore. One cannot help but have the impression that Harman very often orients his analyses keeping in mind rather simple examples of most ordinary, physical objects. In fact, OOO began from the reflection on them. Needless to say, such focus can lead to a theoretical construction that may appear inadequate for other types of entities law most definitely is an instance of. Indeed, Baradian scientific focus and a genesis of AGR drive the binarism emphasis in their framework, which is troublesome for law but also somewhat compensated by the non-binary model of intra-action. In comparison, Harman's thinking, sticking much more strongly to binarism and clearly indebted in and inspired by the mentioned studies of hammer and mailbox, can be controversial with respect to other, somewhat more complex beings.

Moreover, one can say that OOO has been from its very start very peculiar, in fact self-undermining (in general sense), project, especially in the human social domain. In the end, if the phenomenal sphere is the only space where relations take place (Harman 2007: 179), then what is the exact and sound reason to tackle with real objects? Even for those who like to engage in intellectual problems, OOO may be regarded as way too impractical. However, the idea of withdrawal and the utter unknowability of real objects is still highly, though perhaps somewhat perversely, practical. It can be read that any search for the essence of an object is futile. To put it differently, Harman recognises the existence of individual essences, but they cannot be reached in cognitive sense. In turn, important currents in contemporary (and not only contemporary) jurisprudence argue that law does have an essence and that it can be discovered. Harman would most likely want to agree with the former, but not with the latter. However, recall that, in line with OOO, only objects that can be deemed as real have an essence (as tension between the real object and its real qualities). The idea of law realising the condition of a real object and what it entails has been addressed earlier.

However, there is another problem with the law-OOO nexus – law's utter relationality. How something so programmatically anti-relationist can account for an entity highly relational, such as law? Indeed, Harman's sentiment for and attempt to do justice to the broadly understood non-relationality and autonomy connected with it can be deemed as rather understandable and even adequate with respect to various entities. However, when it comes to law, they raise serious doubts. For instance, legal rules acquire their meanings relationally – through connections to other legal rules, ideas of legal academics and practitioners and actual state of affairs, to which they are applied, or for the sake of which they were proposed in the first place. With its rules, law exerts some influence on what often is deemed as nonlaw, but what law actually manages to achieve feeds back into it in a circular manner.

Instead of considering even more basic illustrations of law's relationality, at the very end, we should say that Harman's call to end with overly dynamising accounts of entities and try instead to think of that what is truly crucial to something and what is merely superficial is interesting to consider with respect to law. However, it does not annul all previously considered controversies.

References

Barad, Karen. 2007. *Meeting the Universe Halfway: Quantum Physics and the Entanglement of Matter and Meaning*. Durham: Duke University Press.

Bedford, Joseph (ed.). 2020. *Is There an Object-Oriented Architecture?: Engaging Graham Harman*. London: Bloomsbury Academic.

Bogost, Ian. 2012. *Alien Phenomenology, or What It's Like to Be a Thing*. Minneapolis: University of Minnesota Press.

Brassier, Ray. 2007. *Nihil Unbound: Enlightenment and Extinction*. Basingstoke: Palgrave Macmillan.

Brassier, Ray, Iain Hamilton Grant, Graham Harman, Quentin Meillassoux. 2007. Speculative Realism. *Collapse: Philosophical Research and Development* 3: 307–449.

Bryant, Levi R. 2011. *The Democracy of Objects*. Ann Arbor: Open Humanities Press.

Campbell, Norah, Stephen Dunne and Paul Ennis. 2019. Graham Harman, *Immaterialism: Objects and Social Theory*. *Theory, Culture & Society* 36 (3): 121–137.

Cogburn, Jon, and Niki Young. 2023. Editors' Introduction. In *The Graham Harman Reader*, Jon Cogburn and Niki Young (eds). Winchester: Zero Books.

DeLanda, Manuel. 2006. *A New Philosophy of Society: Assemblage Theory and Social Complexity*. London: Continuum.

DeLanda, Manuel, and Graham Harman. 2017. *The Rise of Realism*. Cambridge: Polity Press.

Ehrlich, Eugen. 1922. The Sociology of Law. Trans.: Nathan Isaacs. *Harvard Law Review* 36 (2): 130–145.

Grant, Iain Hamilton. 2006. *Philosophies of Nature after Schelling*. London: Continuum.

Haraway, Donna J. 2016. *Staying with the Trouble: Making Kin in the Chthulucene*. Durham: Duke University Press.

Harman, Graham. 2002. *Tool-Being: Heidegger and the Metaphysics of Objects*. Chicago: Open Court.

Harman, Graham. 2005. *Guerrilla Metaphysics: Phenomenology and the Carpentry of Things*. Chicago: Open Court.

Harman, Graham. 2007. On Vicarious Causation. *Collapse: Philosophical Research and Development* 2: 171–205.

Harman, Graham. 2009. *Prince of Networks: Bruno Latour and Metaphysics*. Melbourne: re.press.

Harman, Graham. 2010a. Asymmetrical Causation: Influence without Recompense. *Parallax* 16 (1): 96–109.

Harman, Graham. 2010b. Time, Space, Essence, and Eidos: A New Theory of Causation. *Cosmos and History: The Journal of Natural and Social Philosophy* 6 (1): 1–17.

Harman, Graham. 2010c. *Towards Speculative Realism: Essays and Lectures*. Winchester: Zero Books.

Harman, Graham. 2011. *The Quadruple Object*. Winchester: Zero Books.

Harman, Graham. 2012a. On the Supposed Societies of Chemicals, Atoms, and Stars in Gabriel Tarde. In *Savage Objects*, Godofredo Pereira (ed.), 33–43. Lisbon: INCM.

Harman, Graham. 2012b. *Real Qualities*. London: CRiSAP.

Harman, Graham. 2012c. *Weird Realism: Lovecraft and Philosophy*. Winchester: Zero Books.

Harman, Graham. 2013a. Aristotle with a Twist. In *Speculative Medievalisms: Discography*, Eileen Joy, Anna Kłosowska, Nicola Masciandaro and Michael O'Rourke (eds), 227–253. New York: punctum books.

Harman, Graham. 2013b. *Bells and Whistles: More Speculative Realism*. Winchester: Zero Books.

Harman, Graham. 2014. Another Response to Shaviro. In *The Allure of Things: Process and Object in Contemporary Philosophy*, Roland Faber and Andrew Goffey (eds), 36–46. London: Bloomsbury.

Harman, Graham. 2016a. Agential and Speculative Realism: Remarks on Barad's Ontology. *Rhizomes: Cultural Studies in Emerging Knowledge* 30.

Harman, Graham. 2016b. *Immaterialism: Objects and Social Theory*. Cambridge: Polity Press.

Harman, Graham. 2018. *Object-Oriented Ontology: A New Theory of Everything*. London: Penguin Books.

Harman, Graham. 2020a. *Art and Objects*. Cambridge: Polity Press.

Harman, Graham. 2020b. *Skirmishes: With Friends, Enemies, and Neutrals*. Earth: punctum books.

Harman, Graham, and Christopher Witmore. 2023. *Objects Untimely: Object-Oriented Philosophy and Archaeology*. Cambridge: Polity Press.

Harman, Graham, and Jon Roffe. 2014. Propositions, Objects, Questions: Graham Harman, in conversation with Jon Roffe. *Parrhesia* 21: 23–52.

Ihering, Rudolf von. 1913. *Law as a Means to an End*. Trans.: Isaac Husik. Boston: The Boston Book Company.

Ivakhiv, Adrian. 2018. *Shadowing the Anthropocene: Eco-Realism for Turbulent Times*. Earth: punctum books.

Kant, Immanuel. 1998. *Critique of Pure Reason*. Trans. and ed.: Paul Guyer and Allen W. Wood. Cambridge: Cambridge University Press.

Latour, Bruno, Graham Harman and Peter Erdélyi. 2011. *The Prince and the Wolf: Latour and Harman at the LSE*. Winchester: Zero Books.

Leibniz, Gottfried Wilhelm. 2014. The Monadology. In Lloyd Strickland, *Leibniz's Monadology: A New Translation and Guide*, 14–33. Edinburgh: Edinburgh University Press.

Meillassoux, Quentin. 2008. *After Finitude: An Essay on the Necessity of Contingency*. Trans.: Ray Brassier. London: Continuum.

Morton, Timothy. 2013. *Realist Magic: Objects, Ontology, Causality*. Ann Arbor: Open Humanities Press.

Peirce, Charles Sanders. 1960. *Collected Papers of Charles Sanders Peirce. Volume III: Exact Logic and Volume IV: The Simplest Mathematics*. Ed.: Charles Hartshorne and Paul Weiss. Cambridge: Harvard University Press.

Sparrow, Tom. 2014. *The End of Phenomenology: Metaphysics and the New Realism*. Edinburgh: Edinburgh University Press.

Vaillo, Gonzalo. 2021. Superficiality and Representation: Adding Aesthetics to "Knowledge without Truth". *Open Philosophy* 4: 36–57.

Young, Niki. 2021. Object, Reduction, and Emergence: An Object-Oriented View. *Open Philosophy* 4: 83–93.

Chapter 7

Conclusion

Flat Ontologies – With Some Adequacy Problems, Yet Valuable to Law; or, What Comes of It All?

7.1 The Adequacy Question

Having reached the end of our law-focused analyses of the selected representative sample of flat ontologies, we should provide some concluding commentaries. Let us begin with a general summary of answers to the adequacy question: are flat ontologies actually all-encompassing frameworks and therefore adequate for contemporary Western or Global Northern law? Some ideas of specific flat ontologies have actually proved to be at least disputable with respect to law. Let us bring to the fore the most crucial issues from previous chapters, but in as concise form as possible, without recalling here all the subtleties and nuances we have dealt with in detail above.

When it comes to Tardean MON, recall that while some of its tenets can be assessed at least ambivalently from the perspective of adequacy for law, there are also some threads that can be regarded as more clearly problematic. Excluding the idea of law being an emergent entity, with emergent, irreducible properties, not found among its components, may or may not be deemed controversial, especially given the number of doubts Tarde manages to raise with respect to holism. Ultimately, there is some inconclusiveness, at least when it comes to his anti-holism when confronted with law, even when considering law's autocreativity.

Similar is the case of one of the consequences of Tarde's anti-emergentism. Regarding law as nothing over and above its components – nor even their mere sum – but rather as something even less complex than the sum, only an averaging of its components – also entails a practically constant change in law. Again, such dynamism can be assessed both ways – as actually correct in the case of law or as a misguided exaggeration. It appears that the latter position would be adopted by DeLanda and Harman, who both practically adhere to the idea of distinguishing changes among components which do not influence the emergent whole and thus are trivial and superficial and those changes that lead to some actual change of the object in question.

Here, more important is to recall the following. One can say that the idea of far-reaching autonomy of law's parts – which, as all monads in Tardean MON,

DOI: 10.4324/9781003440963-7

are supposed to be free to leave the big they co-create – is the point where the adequacy of MON is more clearly undermined. For the same reason – one can identify some parts of law that will rather simply lose themselves outside or beyond it – the adequacy of DeLandaean assemblage is significantly put into doubt. This idea of moving beyond a larger entity some other being may be co-constituting – the clear common point for Tarde and DeLanda, who, beyond it, propose very different frameworks – also entails the existence of some rather clear boundaries and inside-outside distinction as relevant to various beings. However, as seen most clearly when dealing with Latour, there are considerable doubts about such notions in relation to law.

Speaking of Latourian ANT, that what largely keeps one from proclaiming its adequacy for law is ANT's assumption that actor-networks have an outside (plasma); thus, they are not all-embracing entities and exist by exerting some kind of influence on other beings. Namely, following many diverse criteria – for instance, logical, sociological and psychological – law can be considered as practically boundaryless. If so, let us recall here that it would not only be unfit for ANT, given its attachment to the idea of boundaries and outsides of entities. Following law's plasmaless status, law would also appear not to have any truly other, external beings to itself on which it can act (and thus prove its existence). Given that the assumptions of plasma and acting upon other entities as a criterion of existence practically imply each other in Latour's ANT, one can say that problematising their realisation by law is a truly strong argument undermining ANT's adequacy for law. However, to stick to research integrity as much as possible, recall that we did not confidently confirm law's boundarylessness but openly admitted that this issue (and its consequence for the action-oriented criterion of existence) is rather ultimately inconclusive yet important for the ANT-law nexus.

In turn, when it comes to some much less ambivalent diagnoses on flat ontologies' adequacy for law, let us return for a moment to the already recalled issue – how much law's parts are in/dependent of/on the law they create (issue common for Tarde and DeLanda). In relation to our analyses of DeLandaean AST, its commitment to emergence as such should not raise any doubts in the context of law, but recall also that engagement in Tarde can lead to some scepticism about emergence and that illustrations of emergent properties in the social domain by DeLanda himself are not entirely convincing. However, even in connection with the following noticeable issue in AST – how to even imagine properties and dispositions of law (quite close to one of the doubts in the case of Harmanian OOO – how to distinguish object and qualities in the case of law), DeLandaean emergentism and its controversies are not the core of the problem addressed here.

As already suggested, relations of exteriority – one of the defining features of assemblages and perhaps the most specific element of the commented framework – prove to be the most significant issue for DeLanda's AST in connection with law. Most definitely, many of law's components can be separated from the whole they co-constitute, but others – like specific legal institutions, which undoubtedly are parts of law – are hard to imagine outside of law, which is simply foundational to their identity. Such influence of the whole upon its parts, which contradicts the idea of exteriority, is even clearer in the case of legal provisions. Contemporary law is made from various linguistic entities, such as provisions in legal acts. If a specific provision would be removed from its original act (and law in general in given time and space), then it would be significantly altered, even up to a point of losing its identity (meaning), which was constituted by being a part of a much larger system (not to mention it would most surely stop being anything legal).

In the case of Baradian AGR, the issue of its adequacy for law looks quite different in comparison to the previous three flat ontologies considered. When it comes to the binary model of intra-action – which ultimately seems to be the focus of Barad – it is at least troublesome for the sake of accounting for law. Given some controversies on how exactly such binary intra-action could account for the contemporary law considered a multipart entity, and, even in the first place, why one should utilise such dyadic concept, its adequacy for law can be put into doubt.

Even though the non-binary model of intra-action, identifiable in Barad's relevant writings, does not cause similar controversies, there is a different doubt – whether Baradian take on law using non-binary intra-action actually offers something not offered by other, often older approaches, also in a flat ontology. In the end, let us recall that a non-binary intra-action, though avoids the downsides of a binary model, ultimately does not say much about an entity analysed with its help, other than that it is the way it is due to a plethora of mutual relations. Nevertheless, Baradian AGR still proves to be valuable when dealing not so much with law as such, its ontology, but more with its actions, as will be recalled in the next section.

Now is a proper moment for some reminiscences concerning Harmanian OOO. His fourfold model of object suggests clear attachment to, even specific prioritisation of what we allowed to name complete objects, entities that prove to be inadequate for both under- and overmining (thus are real objects) but are also sensualised by others (thus are also sensual objects, with underlying real ones). While some entities that can be argued to be law's components can be said to be instances of Harman's complete objects, others can be rather regarded as exclusively sensual objects (entities existing on the account of being sensualised by others, yet without any underlying real objects).

Even when assuming that exclusively sensual objects can actually take part in the emergence of an entity that realises the real object conditions and can be and really is sensualised by others, the idea of law as some larger, emergent entity, a real object is dubious on few accounts. It is unclear how to use the distinction between object and qualities, as well as between real and sensual, with respect to such entire law. In the end, law as a potential real object can be also sensualised by others and thus become a complete object, to which the entire fourfold model is dedicated. In addition to such issue and the question concerning law (as a hypothetical real object) also sensualising other entities, there are even more pressing problems for OOO's adequacy for law.

Harman's commitment to the Binary Contact Principle leads to quite peculiar ideas of entities made from just two components and having just one cause for themselves, which are problematic not only in the case of law but, even more generally, in relation to emergence as such. In turn, Harmanian ideas of domestic relations (among the components of some emergent entity, thus necessary for the object in question, yet it is still supposed to be relatively autonomous with respect to its parts) and foreign relations (between some particular object and entities said to be external to it, of which the object in question is to remain far-reaching independence, as these relations are ultimately unnecessary for it), tightly connected with the very fundamentals of his ontological project, are very difficult to convincingly maintain when dealing with law, especially given the fact that what law does feeds back into what law is. Moreover, some potential avenues for avoiding some issues with the domestic-foreign relations distinction appear to cause tensions with other important assumptions of OOO. In summary, it seems that while Harman's ontological sentiments and assumptions are understandable themselves, they appear not to fit when dealing with law, which is perhaps due to law's practically inherent relationality.

Having reached the end of the concise recapitulation of the most important points on the adequacy of the analysed flat ontologies, and before moving on to the findings concerning the value question, let us just say the following. In addition to each of the discussed flat ontologies having very specific problems with adequacy for law and specific underlying reasons for these identified controversies, one can venture to say that there are some flaws common to all. That what is the strength and the source of certain attractiveness of flat ontologies – proposing practically a single set of various principles and regularities that are supposed to address the utter myriad of actual concrete beings – can also be said to be the deep, underlying source of their adequacy problems. Namely, notice that all discussed flat ontologies seem to commit fallacy, which can be named over-X-fication. They focus so much on the assumed basic unit of ontological inquiry ("X" in "over-X-fication" is a symbol for those specific units, like monads, actor-networks, assemblages, intra-actions or objects) that they, in consequence, omit addressing entities, which do not fit the properties of the category that is fundamental for them. It is, of course, closely connected with two guiding motifs of the mere idea of a flat ontology, pluralism and, especially, nonhierarchy.

However, in the discussed cases, over-X-fication also appears as a consequence of merely assuming in the commented flat ontologies that various entities are instances of their own basic units for ontological inquiry, and not actually proving that some concrete beings fall under the proposed categories. Against such background, our investigations, focused on the specific entity of law, can be read as a clear proof that, in order to come up with a flat ontology that meets its promise of far-reaching applicability, one should actually test one's assumptions by confronting them with very specific beings, especially the ones that appear as quite distant from those that directly inspire the tested framework.

7.2 The Value Question

Even though our representative sample of flat ontologies proves to be at least questionable in terms of its adequacy for law, it still offers some valuable insights, which can be utilised when engaging, both theoretically and practically, law. Notice that our analyses show many reasons why flat ontologies should be of interest to the representatives of legal sciences and others interested in law. Interestingly, when it comes to the latter, flat ontologies can be said to be both destructive and constructive. Basically, they, often quite explicitly, undermine many rather usually held beliefs about law and its functioning. However, it would be unfounded to regard them as an instance of critique for the sake of critique. Flat ontologies actually propose many ideas, also of practical worth, in place of what should be ultimately left behind in thinking about and practically dealing with law, at least from their perspective. Let us then compile here what can be regarded as the main arguments illustrating the value of flat ontologies for the law mentioned in previous chapters – in a similarly concise form as in the previous section – first with the focus on specific analysed frameworks, and then proposing an even more generalised account.

In relation to Tardean MON, notice that even despite some adequacy problems, it is still very inspiring. For instance, if one accepts, even tentatively, Tarde's thesis that anything, the big and easily noticeable included, comes from the infinitely small and everything in this scheme wants to possess everything else, but also avoid being possessed by others – in line with replacing the question of being with that of having and in accordance with avidity – then one can start to wonder whether law is an example of a relatively stable average of influences of all of its parts or maybe a product of some dominant monad.

Speaking of Tardean possessivism and avidity, notice that Tarde's MON invites us to consider law's broadly understood functioning in quite original terms. Namely, law can be said to specifically possess a myriad of entities but also to control the avidity of others – keeping it in a certain balance.

While when one thinks about it more carefully, there are, in fact, some crucial differences between Tarde's commented project and Latourian ANT – for instance, there are some interesting implications of the former's preference of having and the latter's focus on acting as specific criteria of existence – but there are also some common points, also intriguing for law. Namely, for Tarde, the properties of beings, also their broadly understood strength, come from the other entities they can be said to possess. Obviously, it is quite similar to Latourian idea of action and strength coming from others, not from within of some analysed entity. As a result, from both, one can infer the idea, perhaps iconoclastic for some, that law itself does not have any strength of its own.

Notice also that its implication – in order to do more, to be stronger, one has to have more, make more allies and thus become more multiple and heterogeneous – does not only contradict some ideas of law's ontological purity. It also leads to an interesting take on the problem of scope of law's regulations, even overregulation and juridification. While contemporary undeniable spread of law is often presented critically or, at best, ambivalently, from Tarde and Latour one can actually infer the idea that it is just a perfectly understandable strategy for law to maintain itself in its existence, perhaps even a strategy with no good and comparable alternative. However, in addition to these specific similarities, highly interesting for law, there are actually many valuable ideas that can be found in Latour only, without some anticipations in Tarde that would be similarly clear as those considered above.

In the end, let us just recall the number of Latourian ANT's ideas, concepts and distinctions that are valuable, both theoretically and practically, for law. First, though still in line with some issues recalled earlier, notice that Latourian universal necessity of making broadly understood allies can account not only for the strength of law, its spread and functioning, but also, in a dialectical manner, for its weakness. Indeed, that what has multiple allies is powerful but also proves to be weak, because of its utter dependence on others, which may or may not remain allied. Not only this fundamental thought in ANT can, in fact, be used to account for law.

Just recall that the idea of translation corresponds well with how much law's grasp of things to which it relates can be deemed as merely superficial and that law can actually be conceptualised as an entire chain of heterogeneous delegates and mediators. Moreover, in relation to the latter concept, its opposition, intermediaries, while in accordance with Latour, should be kept at minimum when accounting for various entities, law included, they still are specifically useful as a tool while assessing some competitive positions. In the end, some more usual ontologies of law can be accused of treating many objects relevant to law as mere intermediaries, while they actually are and should be treated as mediators. This is especially the case of broadly understood nonhuman, even the most trivial materiality, whose increasingly common recognition is to a significant extent thanks to Latour.

Obviously, as shown repeatedly above, materiality also proves to be crucial to law and, thus, ANT as a framework that pays so much attention to tangible nonhumans is also highly valuable when dealing with law. On a side note, this far-reaching appreciation of materiality and the trivial in ANT can be seen as a specific consequence of more general methodological advice of Latour to be as thorough, as detailed and as patient while researching some object as possible and thus avoid any shortcuts in reasoning about it – a lesson to take also when addressing law.

While in DeLandaean AST, one can also find some very general ideas and methodological principles that are, at least, inspiring in the context of law – just think of the possibilities, yet also problems with which his idea of contents-of-mind independence is connected and the analysis scheme for accounting for a given entity that advises to start from the very bottom of its emergence – what caught our attention earlier were mostly more substantive ideas. Namely, the axes of territorialisation-deterritorialisation and coding-decoding are quite interesting and perfectly useable tools to diagnose law.

Moreover, even that part of AST that turned out to be the most significant in critically assessing DeLandaean framework's adequacy for law – relations of exteriority – is still valuable. In the end, it provokes us to think carefully about the impact law has on its supposed parts, and how much some of the latter are dependent on staying within law or, to put it differently, to look more closely at the strength of relations between the law considered as a whole and the plethora of its parts. Such a provocation should be considered even more seriously given the already mentioned fact that somewhat similar issues are clearly noticeable in Tardean MON, though, of course, in a completely different, anti-holistic context.

Despite some reservations with respect to Baradian AGR in terms of its adequacy for law, even the non-binary model of intra-action, it offers much valuable food for thought, especially on that what can be considered law's actions. AGR's anti-representationalism and rejection of pre-relational existence of things can be of significant value for stressing that what law somehow addresses is co-constituted through such relation with law. In consequence, one can, say that law always relates, for instance, in its regulations, to that what is already legal and that there is nothing truly extralegal that law somehow addresses. It can also be read as an invitation to specifically expand the usual threads in law's effectiveness and legal policy discussions. Namely, the idea that any relation constitutes its elements provokes not only to think how to regulate some issues but also to analyse how the mere legal definition of some issue, even the slightest legal formatting of it, influences that issue, even before going into detail about the possible regulatory measures to utilise and their consequences.

Given the constituting influence of intra-actions is mutual – all involved in some intra-action are said to emerge out of it – it also means that the distinction between the input of law (that what creates law) and the output of law (that what the law does) becomes significantly blurred. Of course, it can be further discussed whether such a consequence of AGR is an exaggeration, largely counterfactual or a perfectly correct, even obvious, point about law. Recall, however, that the somewhat parallel distinction of domestic and foreign relations, understood in OOO in very strict terms, is one of the reasons we ultimately undermined (in usual sense of the word) the adequacy of the Harmanian framework for law. Since some specific Barad–Harman comparison came up, notice also that some controversies concerning the exact number of entities taking part in the broadly understood relations – identifiable most explicitly just in AGR and OOO – can be read somewhat more constructively, as an invitation to carefully think through how the relations in some chosen objects, law included, unfold.

In turn, speaking of OOO beyond similar comparisons, while it proved to be the most problematic in terms of adequacy for law, one can still find in it interesting and attention-worthy ideas. Recall Harmanian emphasis on the unknowability of the real, especially essences of objects. The latter are considered most definitely possible in OOO, yet they are and will remain unknowable. This tenet of Harman's thought is especially interesting when considering various positions in legal theory and philosophy that state their aim at revealing the essence of the law as if it could actually be done, while perhaps, using Harmanian terms, they ultimately do nothing more than separating the sensual object of law from its sensual qualities (under the condition of actually being able to separate object and qualities in the case of law).

Moreover, Harmanian caution against ontologies that emphasise dynamism, even lack of stability, makes one wonder (once again) what is (and under what conditions) stable in law. In the end, as already shown on many occasions earlier, many flat ontologies basically stress constant changes, and perhaps in the case of law, it is an exaggeration that should be remedied with some appreciation of durability.

Having recalled the most important specific insights on the value of each considered flat ontology, following the summary on the adequacy question, now we can also provide some more general remarks on their worth, yet of course not without some possible doubts, for dealing with law. Perhaps most crucially, flat ontologies can provide a very general, holistic way to think about the structure of an entity called law, its parts, relations among parts and between them and the whole of law, irrespective of the exact character of such whole, to name just a few most basic issues. To put it differently, notice that ultimately flat ontologies offer rather only rudimentary conceptual resources and, as such, cannot account in a very detailed, meticulous and in-depth manner for very specific aspects or components of law, like, for instance, its linguistic parts. However, flat ontologies can be regarded as frameworks at the higher level of generality that can account for law, its components and relations between them, regardless of whether they are, for instance, human, nonhuman, artificial or natural. In the end, flat ontologies in line with their universal ambition propose a highly general, even abstract, way of thinking about very diverse beings. Accordingly, one can say that, for instance, law is a heterogeneous multipart being and some of its distinguishable aspects can be addressed by more specialised studies, but still a particular flat ontology can give account of relations between law's components, their basic structure and effects on the whole (understood in holistic way or some other possible) and, in consequence, address law in its entirety.

As already suggested, such a standpoint on flat ontologies and law also entails, even necessitates, dealing with more concrete issues such as whether there is some essence of law (if talking about it is admissible); is law holistic, emergent with respect to its components (and what are these), or perhaps their mere sum, or something even less complex than sum (in the spirit of Tardean average); what are the necessary and unnecessary components for law's existence or is it possible that the lack of or poor condition of some component will be compensated by other component. In short, a flat ontology's value for law is the prospect of being a wide, bird's-eye-view ontology of law that embraces, though generally, its entirety. The word "prospect" is used here deliberately because, as proven earlier, one still has to come up with a flat ontology that would be actually adequate for law – not raise similar doubts as those considered earlier.

We will return to the issue of possible ways of obtaining a flat ontology, both valuable and adequate for law, in the last section. Now, let us recall that, in light of flat ontologies, law is, in practice, so much more than what it is usually assumed to be. This is a consequence of at least few motifs that are present in the analysed frameworks with varying explicitness. Namely, the provocation by flat ontologies to appreciate nonhuman materiality is also an incentive to finally stop being silent about the very often neglected parts, which also constitute law, like buildings of legal institutions; tools used by officials, lawyers and judges; outfits or symbols worn by different legal professionals and a plethora of inventions to improve law enforcement. These and many other similar examples also illustrate the extent to which law alone, especially when considered mostly in terms of some mental or linguistic content, cannot do much, and all the talk about law as such doing or achieving something is, at best, too far-reaching shortcut in reasoning.

Obviously, this undermining of the idea of completely independent actions also corresponds well with the idea of test of removal. What very often and easily may be ignored in more usual standpoints about law as ultimately only secondary and insignificant to some core of law, if actually were missing, then that law would also not remain unaltered. In the aftermath of some element missing, law may be somehow harmed or malfunction – which, in turn, can necessitate some compensation by other, still present element, or in the most extreme scenarios, law may even cease to exist.

Notice now that expanding the range of what law is in the mentioned interconnected ways is not without consequences of how to practically deal with law, deliberately influence and make it better. Interestingly, thinking through once again law and its effectiveness from the perspective of flat ontologies can lead to at least few different takes on that issue. For instance, on the basis of flat ontologies, it can be quite clearly shown how many things are nearly completely outside of the influence of legislators, officials, lawyers and ordinary law's addressees but still co-determine law and its functioning that impacts these people as well.

On a somewhat different reading, many flat ontologies seem to imply that in order to make a successful deliberate socio-legal change (for instance, make society better in some respect through legal intervention), one can try to initiate this change quite far from the referent of the more classically understood law (rather usually considered in terms of text or discourse with particular institutions). In the end, if one acknowledges that law is also many different, even seemingly completely non-legal entities, then the number of possibilities for those wanting to change something is even larger than some functionalist approaches can enlist (in the spirit of, for instance, Bronisław Malinowski, Parsons or Robert K. Merton; e.g. Malinowski 1944; Merton 1968). Just to be clear, it does not mean ignoring what is in the valid, text-based law, yet simply seeing many more opportunities. Recognising law also in the trivial, in the things and processes most usually seen as rather far from law, multiplies our possibilities of attempting some changes in law in order to reach some intended goals. Flat ontologies' practical constructiveness lies, then, in the extent to which they can broaden our intellectual horizon, make us think out the box and expand our catalogue of regulatory tools.

When it comes to just another possible flat ontological take on law and its effectiveness, paying attention to and, in fact, taking often tiny details of law seriously can, in the end, incapacitate any intervention. Namely, if these details are composites themselves, then the amount of details ultimately taking part in law and its actions can be just enormous, if not infinite, which significantly complicates any regulatory agenda. There can be at least two approaches to that, corresponding to flat ontologies' take on hierarchy. Either one can argue in favour of equality of law's co-determining factors and components, according to which ultimately "everything counts", or one can try to distinguish those (not only human-dependent) that are somehow more significant to law than others, for instance, because without them, the very emergence (if this idea's adequacy with respect to law is proven), maintenance of law and, in consequence, its actions would not be possible.

Naturally, whatever path one will take, there is also at least one very serious issue to keep in mind – transgressing classical dichotomies, such as nature–culture or is–ought. The anti-dichotomy approach is rather common for the analysed flat ontologies, yet of course differently presented in each of them, for instance, more explicitly (like in Latour or Barad) or more implicitly (like in Tarde). What is more important here is that flat ontologies can also undermine the law–society or even the law–nonlaw distinctions. Indeed, we considered that the idea of law as something all-embracing – debatable as such – for some specific flat ontologies may be difficult to reconcile with some of their explicitly stated assumptions. However, let us also recall that some of the investigated flat ontologies can also be read as actually suggesting to see law as something practically boundaryless or as a specific confirmation of such characteristic of law (in dependence on one's own take on the issue of law's reach).

Either way, the boundarylessness of law and flat ontologies, in general, force to significantly reorient many usually held assumptions in discussions about law. Just consider the issue of functions of law (e.g. Wróblewski 1973; Raz 2009: 163–179; Ehrenberg 2016). The discussions on them are most usually based on a clear distinction between what law is and what it does, or that law is but also does something beyond itself in the surrounding environment. Such differentiation stops being clear from the perspective of flat ontologies that, as recalled earlier, expand the range of what law is, and in light of the limitlessness of law, stops making any sense. As a result, the concept of functions of law needs to be reworked, at the very least.

Even beyond the more specific question of law's boundaries, notice that similar is the case of other classical threads for a broadly understood reflection on law. If law is also out of various material nonhumans, which, among other roles they play, are highly important in keeping law in existence – in reference to materiality appreciation so typical of flat ontologies – then it appears that we should also think through the issues of validity of law, as well as its derogation. In the end, the material infrastructure meant to enforce some rule may prove itself to be much more durable than that very rule, which may be quite swiftly amended in the whirlwind of parliamentary work unlike this infrastructure (Dudek 2017: 18).

7.3 Doing Justice

Even though the above generalising take on the value of flat ontologies is obviously based on some identifiable similarities between the analysed frameworks, notice that our investigations revealed and still allow to see many significant differences between them, even incommensurabilities. In the face of the still quite frequent practice of way too easily putting various ultimately different flat ontologies next to each other in various discussions (e.g. Lemke 2021: 13; Boysen and Rasmussen 2023), we may bring to the fore some contrast between the analysed frameworks and thus stress even more one of the sentiments guiding this book – doing justice to the chosen flat ontologies and thus not obscuring their specificities. Of course, any comparison of some theoretical frameworks can be even quite easily extended for a considerable length. The following remarks are in no way a comprehensive comparison, but they still can be regarded as just another argument in favour of what also guided the proposed analyses.

First, think about some important, relating directly to the fundamental tenets of respective positions, examples of differences between Tarde and Latour – as mentioned above, conceptualising being either by having or by acting; Latour and DeLanda – the rejection of potentiality by the former is in tension with acknowledging the virtuality by the latter; DeLanda and Barad – if the former is critical of the relations of interiority – remaining in which is said to be crucial for the identity of their participants – then his position is in tension with the latter's idea of intra-action and priority of relations over relata; Barad and Harman – the former clearly fights with representationalism that the latter practically allows due to his foundational distinction between the real and the sensual; and Harman and Tarde – while the former puts an emphasis on certain, even far-reaching autonomy of objects, for the latter, independence and self-sufficiency will rather result in death.

Second, in addition to these and other highly specific differences between concrete pairs of analysed flat ontologies, one can also recognise the contrast among all of them by using broader criteria. In certain cases, such more general comparison can be made rather quite easily. Consider, for instance, comparing selected flat ontologies in line with assuming in them stability or dynamism as a default feature of the world and, yet in connection with that first criterion, transformativity of contact – whether any contact is said to have an impact on the entities involved. In the end, it should be by now rather obvious to see frameworks of Tarde, Latour and Barad as those which treat dynamism as something ordinary and stability as a state to explain, largely due to the assumption of transformativity of contact (in relations of possession, alliance-making and intra-actions). In turn, DeLanda and Harman are much closer to the assumption of stability, especially Harman, which also connects well with the idea that not every relation between entities causes some far-reaching change in them. Of course, such sentiments can be associated with emergentism – entities being over and above their parts – present in both AST and OOO, though still differently realised in detail. In the end, just recall DeLandaean sense of properties, also in the context of virtual dispositions, to see some aspect of that difference in comparison to Harman.

However, in addition to such rather easy comparisons, we should also recognise that some criteria, even the ones that may come to mind immediately after considering the presented flat ontologies, prove to be insufficient. In other words, while some criteria allow to contrast the discussed frameworks on a single scale, others are unable to do so. Of course, this can be interpreted as a proof that some criterion is still poorly specified. However, some criterion's insufficiency can also be read as an indication due to what aspect these theories are incommensurable.

Perhaps the most telling example of this is to consider how difficult it is to classify the analysed frameworks in line with holism-anti-holism. Indeed, Tarde is anti-holistic, but notice also that he significantly complicates even the basic sense of anti-holism, because, after all he has in mind entities that are less complex than mere sums of their components, and are only their averaging. In turn, when it comes to Latour, recall his Irreduction Principle which makes it very difficult to ascribe his ANT to holism or anti-holism. DeLanda does not pose any problem here, due to his explicit commitment to emergence. In comparison, it is very unclear, perhaps even more than in the case of Latour, how to situate Barad somewhere on the holism-anti-holism axis. Finally, although Harman explicitly announces his adherence to emergence, similarly to DeLanda, one can have serious doubts whether his OOO can account for emergence because of controversies in which its Binary Contact Principle is entangled.

Moreover, when one already knows relevant details and subtleties, it is also actually quite ungrateful to try to classify the analysed flat ontologies in line with essentialism-anti-essentialism. Namely, even flat ontologies that seem quite easy to present as anti-essentialist – Tarde's, Latour's and DeLanda's – can be read as proposing very specific forms of essentialism, because of commitments to avidity, some inherent strength to make allies and what we allowed to name *a posteriori* relational essentialism and the idea of properties. Even though Barad also likes to present their AGR in anti-essentialist terms, notice that ultimately intra-active, relational specification of entities may be interpreted as a position somewhat similar to Latourian *a posteriori* relational essentialism. In turn, while Harman is most clearly the closest to essentialism most usually understood, in comparison to previously considered frameworks, one still has to remember that he actually adheres to the vision of singular or individual essences.

As said earlier, we could easily carry on such comparisons, both more straightforward ones and the ones that rather reveal some incommensurabilities or the need to utilise differently formulated comparison criteria. Now, we will take the liberty of leaving such enterprise to another occasion and just reiterate one point. Indeed, there are some similarities, even overlaps, among the analysed frameworks, but there are also some serious differences, even so fundamental that flat ontologies can be regarded as incommensurable in certain important aspects, important also from the perspective of being used for law.

7.4. What to Do Next?

Finally, there is the following issue to address, the one already announced above. If flat ontologies, or at least their chosen representative sample, prove their value for dealing with law, but they all appear to have some problems, often serious, with adequacy for law, then what about a flat ontology as valuable for law as the discussed instances, at the very least, but with minimised, as much as possible, adequacy problems? How to come up with such a framework? It appears there are at least four possibilities to consider.

First, recall that we did not check all flat ontologies out there. In consequence, there is still a lot to verify. For instance, in reference to ANT, we may investigate some proposals other than Latour's; in relation to new materialisms other than Baradian AGR, we can deal with the already mentioned vital materialism of Bennett, and in connection with the Harmanian framework, we can discuss some of the propositions of the second wave of OOO. With respect to the latter, given the fact that out of its representatives, it is Bryant who appears to most clearly take up the issue of social entities (e.g. Bryant 2011a, 2011b), one can begin with his framework. Perhaps some of these and other already developed flat ontologies combine value with adequacy to a satisfactory level.

The second option is similar to the first possibility. Namely, we may simply turn our attention to what we called in the Introduction flat ontology-inspired ontologies of law and subject them to a thorough assessment.

Third, there is a potentially realisable idea of generating in a considerably structured way other possible flat ontologies, which can avoid problems with the adequacy for law of more well-known flat ontologies, such as those analysed in the book. Recall that the mere idea of a flat ontology can be differently realised, and we considered above just few, though representative and highly influential in current debates, concrete flat ontologies. We can bring out some crucial features of these analysed flat ontologies, which are most usually built in opposition to some idea that is basically rejected in them. Think, for instance, about Tarde and his disagreement with holism, Latourian preference of mediators over intermediaries, DeLandaean rejection of totalities, Baradian anti-representationalism and Harmanian scepticism, at least, with respect to constant dynamism.

Following such a potential scenario, we can then classify once again the analysed flat ontologies in accordance with the identified, brought to the fore, oppositions. This would give us a map that even more conveniently displays crucial differences between known flat ontologies than in the previous section. It would also show us what kind of combinations of features and commitments remain unrealised and, perhaps, some of them may prove to be much less problematic when it comes to their adequacy for law. In the end, if relations of exteriority, some quite far-reaching independence of parts of the whole prove to be a very significant obstacle for DeLandaean AST's and Tardean MON's adequacy for law, then what about a framework that assumes relations of interiority or some gradual position on the issue in question? Of course, to assess thoroughly its adequacy, one would also have to take into account other potential features, for instance, in line with opposition essentialism-anti-essentialism, priority of relations over relata or relata over relations.

Although the idea of a very structured generation of other flat ontologies on the basis of clear comparison criteria used for the sake of known flat ontologies and showing what combinations of commitments have not been proposed so far is very interesting, the previous section showed that this scenario is actually dubious. Indeed, our investigations show that the analysed frameworks fall under the mere idea of a flat ontology and have some other similarities and differences. While some of the latter can be compared in line with some criteria, other differences seem to be about fundamentals so specific to a particular flat ontology that they make sense only with respect to it. As a result, some proposed comparison criterion needs to be significantly reworked in order to account for all compared frameworks, or it simply means that, in some respect, they are actually incommensurable. Needless to say, if the latter situation relates to some tenet of a given flat ontology that is also highly significant to the rest of its specifics, then the realisability of the considered idea for generating other flat ontologies becomes even more questionable. On a more positive note, however, one cannot be sure unless one takes up this challenge.

Fourth, we can also try a completely different approach. Instead of testing some already developed flat ontologies, the ontologies of law inspired by them or trying to generate new flat ontologies on the basis of a structured comparison of the existing ones, we can build what can be called a flat ontology of law, an ontology that is meant for and dedicated from its very inception to account for law, but does this in the spirit of flat ontology, beginning with the basic tenets of its mere idea – pluralism and nonhierarchy. In reference to these, we can start building such framework by mapping all elements empirically involved in law, of course, without any ontological hierarchising prejudices. Then, we may further our investigations and try to uncover some logic among them, find that which may be said to run through all these elements and somehow connects and groups them. On this occasion, we not only can or even have to return to the issue of hierarchy – whether some of the identified objects relevant to law are actually somehow more important than others, or perhaps arguing about some inequalities between them is ultimately unjustified. Moreover, we may and, in fact, should refer to the issues revealed during our investigations above, or, at the very least, explain why we do not follow some ideas or propositions.

For instance, we may conclude that we should locate law somewhere on the holism-anti-holism axis – highly complicated itself, because of involving, at the very least, being a mere sum of components, and something more but also something less complex than the sum. Additionally, we may develop the issue of the influence being a component of law has on components themselves – in reference to both DeLandaean and Tardean threads of in/dependence of parts of/on the whole. At the same time, we might as well come to a convincing conclusion that thinking in categories of essentialism-anti-essentialism is not necessary in dealing with law.

Of course, this is still not even the tip of the iceberg of the considered scenario. Already the focused investigations on particular distinguishable entities somehow partaking in law will reveal even more specific problems to address, as suggested by the mentioned issues of law's functions, validity and derogation.

What is much more certain even right now is that building practically from scratch an ontology of law in the spirit of flat ontologies will not only be a very difficult task to finalise. Some, perhaps even many concepts, propositions and conclusions it will ultimately propose will rather not be received at first well as often going quite strongly against the many usually assumed ideas in relevant discussions in humanities, philosophy, social sciences and theory and, most importantly, the broadly understood reflection on the law. In fact, such reactions must also be taken into account when choosing one of the three paths outlined earlier.

However, let us here return to the figure with which we began our journey through flat ontologies and law, Tarde. In *Monadology and Sociology*, he says that "the fear of ridicule is the most antiphilosophical of sentiments" (Tarde 2012: 34). Well, it seems our journey thus far proves we are not afraid. We might add that we should remain so, in the promising yet demanding prospect of coming up with a better framework to grasp law in its entirety.

References

Boysen, Benjamin, and Jesper Lundsfryd Rasmussen (eds). 2023. *Against New Materialisms*. London: Bloomsbury.

Bryant, Levi R. 2011a. On the Reality and Construction of Hyperobjects with Reference to Class. *Speculations* 2: 86–103.

Bryant, Levi R. 2011b. Of Parts and Politics: Onticology and Queer Politics. *Identities: Journal for Politics, Gender and Culture* 8 (1): 13–28.

Dudek, Michał. 2017. What Legal Rules are Suitable for Protruding Media of Law and Why? Contribution to the Concept of Locality/Non-Locality of Legal Rules. In *Synesthetic Legalities: Sensory Dimensions of Law and Jurisprudence*, Sarah Marusek (ed.), 9–26. Abingdon: Routledge.

Ehrenberg, Kenneth M. 2016. *The Functions of Law*. Oxford: Oxford University Press.

Lemke, Thomas. 2021. *The Government of Things: Foucault and the New Materialisms*. New York: New York University Press.

Malinowski, Bronislaw (Bronisław). 1944. *A Scientific Theory of Culture and Other Essays*. Chapel Hill: The University of North Carolina Press.

Merton, Robert K. 1968. *Social Theory and Social Structure*. Enlarged Edition. New York: The Free Press.

Raz, Joseph. 2009. *The Authority of Law: Essays on Law and Morality*. Second Edition. Oxford: Oxford University Press.

Tarde, Gabriel. 2012. *Monadology and Sociology*. Ed. and trans.: Theo Lorenc. Melbourne: re.press.

Wróblewski, Jerzy. 1973. Functions of Law and Legal Certainty. *Anuario de Filosofía del Derecho* [*Philosophy of Law Yearbook*] 17: 313–321.

Index

actor-network theory (ANT): action in 77, 80–84, 87, 89, 91–95, 100–101, 108–109, 168, 216–217; actor-network in 30, 72–73, 75, 77–78, 82–84, 87–88, 90–91, 93–98, 100–102, 104–106, 109, 113, 213, 215; alliance-making in 77–78, 82–85, 87–89, 93–97, 105, 108, 110, 217, 223–224; collective in 91, 100, 107; criterion for existence in 9, 76–78, 80, 82–84, 89, 91–95, 100, 105, 107–109, 113, 151, 162, 213, 216, 222; and critical theory 78–79; delegation in 81–83, 87, 98–101, 112–113, 174, 217; descriptivism in 78–79, 82, 217; and emergence 86–87, 223; and essence 77, 83–86, 88–90, 95, 178, 183, 223–226; and hierarchy 32, 78–80, 82, 88–91; humans in 80, 82–84, 88–89, 111; interaction in 94–95, 98; Irreduction Principle in 86–87, 95, 223; materiality relevance in 20–21, 26, 29, 80–84, 87–89, 91, 112–113, 217; mediator-intermediary in 73–74, 81–82, 87, 90, 95, 97–101, 111–113, 167–168, 174, 178, 217, 225; and modernity 70–71, 91, 110; plasma in 72–73, 76, 100–102, 104–108, 113, 151, 168, 213; and pluralism 78, 84, 87–89, 110; and potentiality 79, 92–93, 96, 104–105, 107, 110, 222; programme-antiprogramme of action in 99, 112; risky-risk-free object in 90–91; strenght in 77–78, 82–85, 87–89, 93–97, 105, 108–111, 216–217, 224; strenght-weakness dialectics in 77–78, 95, 97, 109–110, 217; symmetry in 78–80, 91, 221; translation in 73, 85–86, 95–101, 106, 111, 167, 174, 183, 217; and transcendence 79
the adequacy question 1, 9, 11–12, 32–37, 47, 58, 61, 64, 66, 71, 74, 76, 102–108, 113, 119, 120–121, 126, 135, 137–141, 144, 146, 172–174, 178, 200–201, 203–209, 212–216, 218–221, 224–225
agential realism (AGR): agential cut in 160–161, 163–166; binary model in 159–168, 172–173, 204, 209, 214; and domains of reality 154, 156, 171–172, 221; and emergence 223; and essence 153–154, 157–158, 224–226; ethico-onto-epistemology in 14, 47, 152, 169, 187–188; fragility in 153–154; and hierarchy 154; intra-action in 34, 153–155, 157–174, 183, 215, 218, 222–224; and metaphysical individualism 153–155, 157–158, 169, 218; non-binary model in 162, 166–167, 172–173, 198, 209, 214, 218; phenomenon in 158–166, 168–169, 172–173; and pluralism 154, 161, 163; priority of relations over relata in 11–12, 153–155, 157–159, 161, 168–169, 183, 218, 222, 225; and realism 156; and representationalism 154–157, 171, 218, 222, 225; and social constructivism 156
Akrich, M. 72
Alldred, P. 8
Alliez, É. 45
Allott, A. 2–3
an inquiry into modes of existence (AIME) 71–72, 74–76, 106, 111
artifact theory of law 20–21
Ash, J. 8
assemblage theory (AST): assemblage in 30, 34, 119–121, 124, 127–142, 145–146, 154, 201, 213, 215; capacities in 124–126, 128–129, 134, 138, 141–143, 146, 213,

223; contents-of-mind independence in 122–123, 217–218; contingency in 123–124, 126; (de)coding and (de)territorialisation in 132–135, 138–140, 145, 147, 174, 218; diagram in 120–121, 125, 129, 138; downward causation in 129–131, 133–134, 136, 141–144, 146; emergence in 10–11, 118–119, 121, 123–131, 133–138, 140, 142–144, 147, 203, 212–213, 218, 223; and essence 121, 123, 126, 223, 225–226; expressivity in 128, 131–132, 134–135, 138–139, 147; and hierarchy 121–122, 125–126, 134–135, 142, 195; historicity in 123–125; immanence in 121–123, 125, 127–128; and macroreductionism-micro-reductionism 127–128, 136; and materialism 122; materiality in 128, 131–132, 134–135, 138–139, 147; multiscalarity in 121, 134, 142; and pluralism 134; properties in 124–126, 128–130, 133–138, 140–144, 146, 213, 223–224; and realism 122, 126; relations of exteriority in 127–128, 130–131, 134–135, 140–147, 151, 201, 213–214, 218, 225–226; and relations of interiority 127–128, 130, 144–145, 222, 225; tendencies in 124–126, 128–129, 134, 138, 142–143, 146, 213, 223; and totality 127–128, 130, 134, 140, 145, 225; virtuality in 118, 120–121, 124–126, 128–129, 134, 138, 142, 147, 162, 222–223

Barad, K. *see* agential realism (AGR)
Benjamin, W. 112, 151, 162
Bennet, J. 5, 151, 180, 224
Berger, P. L. 22
Bergson, H. 45–46
Bhaskar, R. 7–8
Bogost, I. 180, 185
Bohr, N. 12, 151, 156–161, 166, 171
Bourdieu, P. 119
Braidotti, R. 149, 151
Brassier, R. 180
Braudel, F. 119
Bryant, L. R. 9, 180, 224
Buchanan, I. 119
Burazin, L. 21
Butler, J. 151

Callon, M. 72, 97
Cielemęcka, O. 150
Critical Legal Studies 102, 169
Critical Race Theory 169
Crusoe, R. 78

Davies, M. 26, 31, 33
DeLanda, M. *see* assemblage theory (AST), flat ontology (in general)
Delaney, D. 26, 32
Deleuze, G. 8, 44–45, 69, 117–120
derogation 62, 136, 141, 143, 222, 226
Derrida, J. 151, 162
desuetudo 4, 109, 205
distinction: of human-nonhuman 7, 10, 14–16, 45, 47, 52, 78, 80, 94, 118, 124, 149, 154, 219; of is-ought 30, 152, 168, 171–172, 221; of natural-artificial 7, 13, 124, 219; of organic-nonorganic 7, 14, 52, 94, 124; of social-natural 7, 15, 30, 64, 70, 78, 88, 118, 132, 149, 154, 156, 221; of symbolic-physical 9, 52, 88
distributed cognition theory 89
Durkheim, É. 22–23, 45, 47–49, 63, 69, 86, 119, 127

Ehrlich, E. 4, 20, 208
Elder-Vass, D. 23–24
extended mind theory 89

fact: brute 21; institutional 12, 21, 30; social 12, 21, 30, 48, 63
Finnis, J. 20
Fittipaldi, E. 20
flat ontology (in general): adopted sense of 2, 7–17, 28, 31–32, 34, 45, 47, 76, 128, 134–135, 154, 188, 194–195, 202, 215, 224–225; basic units in specific instances of 10, 12, 14, 30, 34–35, 150, 215; Bhaskar's definition of 7–8; claim to universality of 1, 11–12, 30, 32–34, 37, 215–216, 219; DeLanda's definition of 8, 117; and determinism 14–15; and domains of reality 7, 10–12, 14–16, 28, 30; epistemological character of 47; humans in 10–11, 14–16, 30; narrow definitions of 8–10; nonhierarchy in the adopted sense of 10, 13–14, 16, 24–26, 28, 30–32, 215, 221, 225–226; pluralism in the adopted sense of 10, 13, 16, 24–26, 28, 31, 215, 225–226; possibility of differentiations in 13–14, 32; practicality of 10, 12–16, 34, 216, 220–221

flat ontology (specific) *see* actor-network theory (ANT), agential realism (AGR), assemblage theory (AST), monadology (MON), object-oriented ontology (OOO)
Foucault, M. 13, 44, 151
Fox, N. J. 8
Frydman, S. 143
functionalism 48, 61, 76, 135, 221

Gerlach, W. 161
Gilbert, M. 23
Grant, I. H. 180
Grosz, E. 150
Guattari, F. 118–119

Habermas, J. 102
Hacking, I. 36
Haraway, D. J. 3, 12, 151, 154, 191
Harman, G. *see* object-oriented ontology (OOO)
Hartmann, N. 11
Haslanger, S. 24–25
Hauriou, M. 21
Hegel, G. W. F. 127
Heidegger, M. 177–179, 205
Husserl, E. 177–178, 196–197, 205
Hume, D. 119

Ihering, R. v. 206
institutional legal theory 21

James, W. 103
Jones, E. 32

Kant, I. 157–158, 181, 187
Kaufmann, A. 168
Käll, J. 32
Kelsen, H. 26

Lagerspetz, E. 21
La Torre, M. 21
Latour, B. *see* actor-network theory (ANT), an inquiry into modes of existence (AIME)
law: adopted sense of 1–3, 6–7, 17, 29–30, 32, 34, 75, 102–103, 106, 111, 136, 138, 172, 202, 208, 212; autopoietic properties of 59–61, 136–138, 204, 212; boundaries of 61–65, 102–108, 110, 113, 207–208, 213–215, 218, 221–222; effectiveness of 6, 65, 169–171, 174, 218, 220–221; and emergence 59–61, 63–64, 66, 135–136, 203–204, 212–214, 219, 221, 226; functions of 34, 65, 75–76, 110, 169–171, 216, 218, 221–222, 226; geneses of 4–5, 208; input and output of 170–171, 205–209, 215, 218; materiality of 3–7, 17–22, 25–30, 62, 109, 112, 139, 141, 200, 202, 217, 220–222; meanings of texts of 3, 5–6, 25, 30, 63, 111, 136, 139, 143–145, 200–203, 205–206, 209, 214; media for texts of 3–6, 17–18, 20–21, 25, 28, 30, 109, 111–112, 139, 143–144, 200–202; and nonlaw distinction 170–171, 209, 218, 221; proliferation of 65–66, 102, 110–111, 217; relationality of 62–63, 141–146, 168–169, 201–203, 207, 209, 213–215, 218; and society distinction 64, 171, 221; stability-fragility of 60–61, 64–65, 109–110, 205–207, 212, 217, 219; superficiality of 105–107, 202, 217; texts of 3–6, 21, 25, 30, 62–63, 65, 102–103, 109, 111–112, 136, 139, 143–146, 169, 171–172, 200–202, 214, 220–221; validity of 4, 25–26, 62, 109, 143–144, 205, 221–222, 226
Law, J. 13, 72, 97
Lawson, T. 24
legal consciousness 102
legal deontic modalities 102–103, 105, 107, 110
legal institutions 4–6, 51, 62, 65, 75, 107, 109–112, 122–123, 137, 141–144, 214, 220–221
legal officials 4–7, 20, 75, 99, 109–110, 112–113, 140–141, 143, 220
legal policy 169, 171, 218
legal positivism 20
Leibniz, G. W. 48–49, 53, 56, 195
Levinas, E. 178
Lorenc, T. 56
Luckmann, T. 22
Luhmann, N. 18–19, 45, 59, 136
Lukács, G. 11, 22

MacCormick, N. 21
Malinowski, B. 221
McGee, K. 34
Meillassoux, Q. 180
Merleau-Ponty, M. 178
Merton, R. K. 221
monadology (MON): avidity in 52–53, 55–57, 65–66, 216, 224; the big and the

small in 48–52, 54–64, 66, 135, 145, 213, 216; boundaries in 58, 61–64, 66, 103, 213, 218; cognitive scepticism in 47; criterion for existence in 46, 51–56, 61, 65, 216, 222; death in 52–53, 60, 222; definition of society in 46, 54, 57, 62–63; and emergence 10–11, 45, 47–52, 54–55, 57–64, 86–87, 127, 135–138, 151, 203–204, 212–213, 218–220, 223, 225; and essence 52, 57, 223, 225–226; fragility of the big 49–50, 52, 57–58, 60–61, 66, 152, 212; and hierarchy 32, 45, 54–55; infinitesimality in 49, 54–57, 65, 216; monad in 34, 48–49, 53, 55–58, 60–65, 215–216; and panpsychism 53; and pluralism 45, 53–55; possession in 51–57, 63–65, 183, 216–217, 223; properties in 50–54, 57, 63–65, 135, 183, 216–217; the small's independence of the big in 49–50, 52, 57–58, 61–64, 66, 145, 152, 212–213, 218, 225–226; and transcendence 54
Morton, T. 180

natural law theories 19–20
Nail, T. 119
new materialism 3, 5, 149–151, 153, 180, 191, 224
Norman, J. 32

object-oriented ontology (OOO): Binary Contact Principle in 198–199, 204, 208–209, 215, 223; causality in 14, 199, 204, 208, 215; cognitive scepticism in 187, 209, 219; complete object in 185, 193–195, 197, 200–203, 214; domestic relations in 182–183, 185, 190, 193, 199, 205–208, 215, 218; dormant object in 194; dynamics-stability in 8, 182–183, 190–191, 197, 206–207, 209, 212, 219, 223, 225; eidos in 197; emergence in 182, 188–190, 192, 198–200, 203–205, 208, 212, 214–215, 223; essence in 8, 183–184, 188, 196–197, 209, 219, 224–226; exclusively real object in 194, 197, 202; exclusively sensual object in 183, 185–186, 193–194, 197–198, 201–205, 214; foreign relations in 182, 190, 205–208, 215, 218; fourfold model in 193, 195–198, 200, 203, 208, 214–215; and hierarchy 181, 194–195; object in 30, 34, 181–183, 186, 188–190, 192, 195–197, 200, 202, 204–206, 208, 213–215, 219, 222; and onto-taxonomy 181–182; and overmining 189–195, 197, 200–201, 203, 205, 214; and panpsychism 185–186; and pluralism 194; quality in 184, 195–196, 208, 213–214, 219; the real in 184–185, 187–189, 192–195, 208, 214, 222; real object in 183–187, 189, 193–206, 208–209, 214–215; real quality in 195–198, 203, 209; and relationality 8, 182–183, 189–191, 201–203, 207, 209; sensualisation in 184–187, 189, 192–195, 197–198, 200, 202–203, 208, 214–215; the sensual in 184–185, 188–189, 192, 194–195, 208–209, 214, 222; sensual object in 182–187, 189, 192–200, 202–203, 214, 219; sensual quality in 182, 195–197, 203, 219; space in 178, 196–197; time in 196–198; and undermining 189–193, 195, 199–201, 203–205, 214; withdrawal in 186–187, 193, 195–196, 198, 201, 209
Olivecrona, K. 26–27
ontology of law: dimensions in 28; extrapersonal 19–20, 28; flat ontology-inspired 18, 26, 31–33, 224–225; immodest materiality equalisation in 26, 31, 89; intrapersonal 19–20, 27; interpersonal 20, 30; materiality belittling in 18, 21–22, 24–25, 27–30, 98; materiality ignorance in 18–22, 24, 26–29, 98; modest materiality equalisation in 18, 22, 25–26, 28, 30

Parsons, T. 22, 45, 221
Pasteur, L. 70
Peczenik, A. 25, 30
Peirce, C. S. 201
Petrażycki, L. 19–20, 27, 169
Philippopoulos-Mihalopoulos, A. 26, 31–32
Pickering, A. 14
Pinch, T. 174

Rogowska-Stangret, M. 150
Romano, S. 21
Ruiter, D. W. P. 21
Rumsfeld, D. 36

Sartre, J.-P. 85
science and technology studies 70, 72–73, 151

Searle, J. R. 12, 21–25, 89
semiotics 172, 201–202
social ontology 12, 21–25, 84
Sparrow, T. 180
speculative realism 180–181
Spinoza, B. 71
Stern, O. 161
Summers, R. S. 27

Tarde, G *see* monadology (MON)
Tamanaha, B. Z. 76
test of removal 15–16, 29–30, 120, 220
Toews, D. 36
Tonkonoff, S. 32
Tournier, M. 78
Tuomela, R. 22–23

the value question 1, 9, 32–37, 58, 64, 66, 108, 138, 140, 147, 172, 174, 178, 209, 214–222, 224

Weber, M. 22–23, 119
Weinberger, O. 21
Whitehead, A. N. 69, 117
Wittgenstein, L. 71

Znamierowski, C. 25–26, 30

For Product Safety Concerns and Information please contact our EU
representative GPSR@taylorandfrancis.com
Taylor & Francis Verlag GmbH, Kaufingerstraße 24, 80331 München, Germany

www.ingramcontent.com/pod-product-compliance
Lightning Source LLC
LaVergne TN
LVHW021124300926
849160LV00010B/853